Alfred L. Kroeber and the Arapaho

Decorative Symbolism of the Arapaho

The Arapaho

and

Arapaho Dialects

Alfred L. Kroeber

Primary Sources in Native North America

DECORATIVE SYMBOLISM OF THE ARAPAHO

BY

A. L. KROEBER

DECORATIVE SYMBOLISM OF THE ARAPAHO [1]

By A. L. KROEBER

The Arapaho, a tribe of Plains Indians belonging to the Algonquian stock, practise a form of art very similar in material,
technique, and appearance to that of the other Plains tribes, of
whom the Sioux are the best known. This art is in appearance
almost altogether unrealistic, unpictorial, purely decorative. For
the greater part it consists now of beadwork, which has nearly sup-
planted the older style of embroidery in porcupine quills, plant
fibers, and perhaps beads of aboriginal manufacture. The other
products of this art are objects of skin or hide which are painted
with geometrical designs. On the whole the decorative, geometric character of Arapaho art is very marked. Almost all the
lines are straight. The figures in embroidery are lines, bands,
rectangles, rhombi, isosceles and rectangular triangles, figures
composed of combinations of these, and circles. The designs
painted on hide are composed of triangles and rectangles in different forms and combinations.

On questioning the Indians it is found that many of these decorative figures have a meaning. An equilateral triangle with the
point downward may represent a heart; with its point upward, a
mountain. A figure consisting of five squares or rectangles in
quincunx, the four outer ones touching the central one at the
corners, is a representation of a turtle. A long stripe crossed by
two short ones is a dragon-fly. A row of small squares at intervals represents tracks. Crosses and diamonds often signify stars.
All this is in beadwork. In painted designs a flat isosceles triangle

[1] Published by permission of the Trustees of the American Museum of Natural
History.

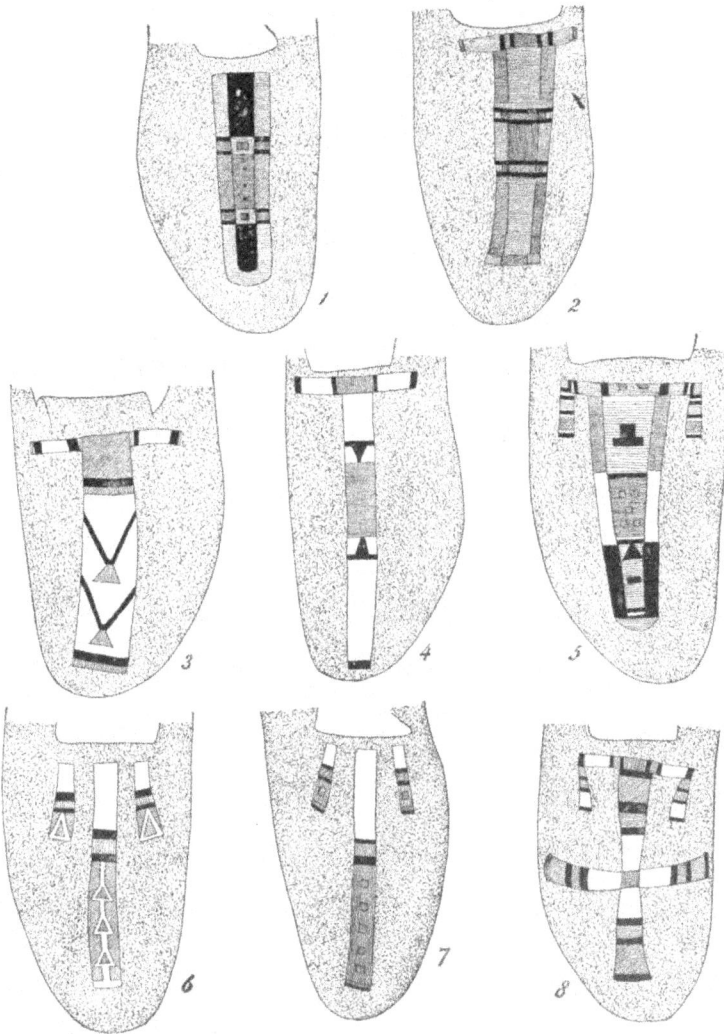

ORNAMENTATION ON ARAPAHO MOCCASINS

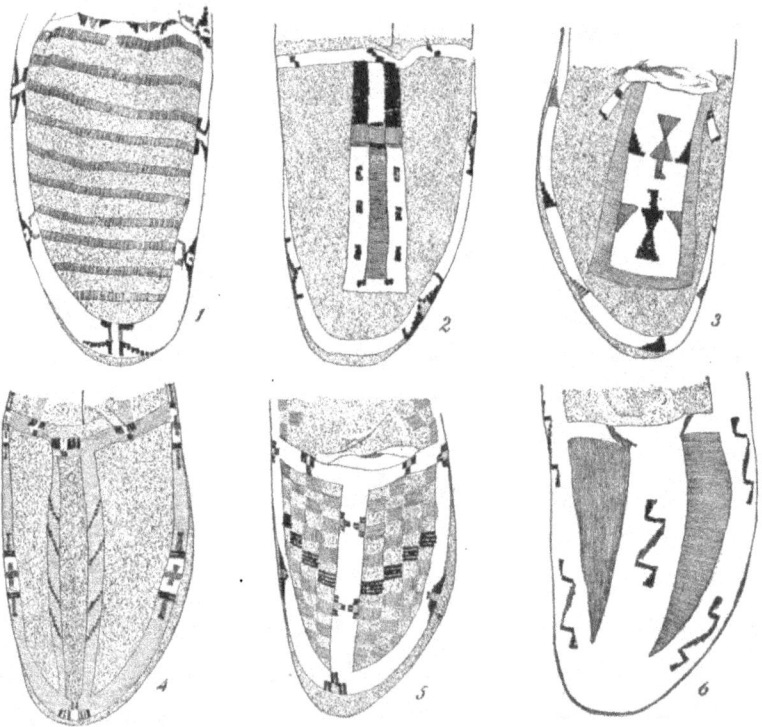

ORNAMENTATION ON ARAPAHO MOCCASINS

often represents a hill ; an acute isosceles triangle, a tent. Many other objects are similarly represented.

An ornamental feature is the symmetrical duplication of most designs. Bags, pouches, skins, moccasins, cases, and other objects are ornamented by being treated as a decorative field within which the designs are symmetrically doubled, or even more numerously repeated. Thus a moccasin, if decorated with the symbol of a mountain on the outer side of the heel, has the same symbol also on the opposite inner side of the heel. Another purely ornamental feature of this art is repetition of a single figure to form a pattern. A stripe is often the representation of a path. This symbol is sometimes used singly, standing alone ; sometimes it occurs double, owing to the tendency just mentioned, toward symmetry ; and sometimes it is found in a pattern that may be described as a many-colored, drawn-out (i.e., rectangular, not square) checker-board, in which each rectangle or short stripe, whatever its color, still represents a path.

This strongly-marked decorative character of Arapaho art, however, is accompanied by a realistic tendency of such development as at first acquaintance would not be suspected by a civilized person. Several figures connected in meaning may be put upon one object and thus produce something approximating a picture containing composition. When as many as ten or a dozen symbols having reference to each other are combined, a story can almost be told by them. In this way the stiff embroideries on a moccasin or the geometric paintings on a bag may represent the hunting of buffalo, the acquisition of supernatural power by a shaman, a landscape or map, a dream, personal experiences, or a myth.

Arapaho art thus is at the same time imitative or significant, and decorative. Can the origin of this art be determined ?

Since Arapaho art consists of the intimate fusion of symbolism and decoration, two theories as to its origin are possible. Either of its two elements may be the original. The Indians may have begun with realism, drawing or working lifelike forms in their art; then, however, the obstacles inherent in the material asserted themselves, or the well-established tendency toward symmetry and repetition into a pattern came out, or perhaps other causes were influential, until the early imitative representations became abbreviated into the conventional decorations that have been described. Or it is possible that the Indians began with mere ornaments. Perhaps even these were not originally ornaments but peculiarities of construction of purely useful articles, which technical peculiarities were later considered beautifying and developed into pure ornaments. At any rate, whatever their own origin, decorations may in the past have existed *per se ;* later, some conventional ornament may have accidentally suggested a natural object, whereupon it was modified to resemble this object more closely; the same process occurred with other ornaments; until finally a whole system of symbolism was added to the older system of decoration. The first of these theories is that original pictures were conventionalized into decorative symbolism; the other theory is that original ornament was expanded into symbolic decoration. These are the logically possible explanations of the origin of Arapaho art because we recognize in it two factors, the realistic-symbolic and the decorative-technical.

Let us see if either of these theories can be rendered through the evidence of fact actually certain or at least probable.

One of the most frequent embroidered designs on Arapaho moccasins consists, in its simplest form, of a stripe or band which runs from the instep to the toe. This decorative motive takes varied forms, of more or less elaborateness. The following are a number of moccasins with this type of ornament.

One moccasin [1] (Pl. V, fig. 1, catalogue number $\frac{1}{5709}$) is embroidered merely with a stripe from the instep to the toe. This stripe of beadwork consists of a number of bars or lengthened

---

[1] The Arapaho objects described in the course of this article are in the American Museum of Natural History. Their catalogue numbers are given in parentheses.

rectangles of different colors. No information was obtained as to the meaning of the design on this specimen.

Another specimen (Pl. v, fig. 2, cat. no. $\frac{50}{883}$) has a similar stripe, about an inch in width, running from instep to toe, and composed of bars or small stripes of six different colors. The distribution of these colors is not like that in the last described specimen, but the pattern and the idea of color arrangement are identical. On this moccasin, however, there is one additional piece of embroidery, a narrow stripe across the instep, that is, transverse to the main stripe and touching it at its upper end. The large stripe as a whole, the smaller bars separately, and the transverse stripe all represent buffalo paths.

A third specimen (Pl. v, fig. 3, cat. no. $\frac{50}{883}$) also has a stripe from instep to toe. This is white, except for a rectangular green portion in the middle. At the two ends of this green part of the stripe are two dark-blue (=black) marks, which are approximately triangular. Across the instep we again find a narrow transverse stripe. This represents a bow. The main longitudinal stripe represents a buffalo path. Its green rectangular portion is a buffalo. The black marks are arrowpoints shot into it. Small projections on these marks, which render them not really quite triangular, represent the barbs of the arrowheads.

Another moccasin (Pl. v, fig. 4, cat. no. $\frac{50}{1021}$) again has the longitudinal stripe. This represents a path, probably with implication of the path traveled by the wearer of the moccasin. The major part of this stripe is white, but portions are beaded in dark-blue (=black), red, and grayish-blue. These colors denote respectively night, day, and hazy atmosphere. On the white stripe are also two curious symbols, which are said to signify sunrise or going over a mountain. A narrow transverse stripe is found in this specimen also ; but instead of being contiguous to the end of the main stripe, as on the last two moccasins, it is cut in two by it, so that it exists only in two fragments, one on each side of the large stripe. These two small bars represent insects that are desired to be out of the path, beside it, instead of being where the moccasin will travel in the path.

Another specimen (Pl. V, fig. 5, cat. no. $\frac{50}{410}$) has the main stripe down the foot slightly modified in that it tapers a little toward the toe. In arrangement of colors, this moccasin resembles closely the second one described. In all the specimens just discussed, except the last, the bars of which the main stripe consists are arranged in three groups. In this moccasin this triple division of the stripe also exists. Moreover, in the middle section of this stripe there is a green rectangle, and in contact with this a small dark-blue mark approximately triangular in shape. These two symbols are very like the representations of the buffalo and arrowpoints on the moccasin above described as symbolic of the buffalo hunt. Unfortunately it is not known whether the design on the present specimen had any meaning. So far, accordingly, this moccasin agrees closely with those previously examined. It is further like them in possessing a narrow, transverse stripe of beadwork at the instep. But a totally new feature is found in two small bars that start from the ends of the transverse stripe. They are parallel to the main central longitudinal stripe, but very much smaller.

In all the preceding specimens but one (fig. 4), the large stripe consists of three sections. In the exceptional specimen the upper third or fourth of the stripe is of one ground color, the remainder all of another ground color. Such an arrangement is also found in another specimen (Pl. V, fig. 6, cat. no. $\frac{1}{5707}$). The smaller portion of the stripe is white, the longer part is blue with a pattern imposed upon it. Nothing is known of the significance of any part of this design. The two small bars are present, as in the last specimen, and repeat the markings of the large stripe in simplified form. But the transverse stripe at the instep is missing.

Still another moccasin has its stripe divided into a short upper and a long lower portion of different colors (Pl. V, fig. 7, cat. no. $\frac{50}{582}$). As in the last specimen, there are two small bars parallel to the central stripe and repeating its design, and the transverse stripe is again absent.   The stripes and bars all represent buffalo paths.   In certain parts of the stripes are small squares colored light blue ; these represent buffalo tracks.

The last specimen of this series (Pl. v, fig. 8, cat. no. $\frac{50}{184}$) has the main central stripe, the transverse stripe at the instep, and the small bars repeating the markings of the large stripe.   In addition to these three decorative devices that are found in previous specimens, it possesses a fourth one that is new.   The central longitudinal stripe (slightly constricted toward its middle) is bisected by a duplicate of itself running transversely.   These two stripes thus form a cross.   This cross represents the morning star, the variety of colors upon it denoting the variety of colors the star appears to assume.   The transverse stripe at the instep represents the sky or horizon.   The two small bars are said to be the twinkling of the star as it rises, in other words its rays.[1]

The symbolism of some of these designs is elaborate.   The representation of the buffalo in his path shot by arrows from the hunter's bow is coherent and neatly compact.   We do not know whether it is a commemoration of a particular event or the expression of a wish for plenty of food, but in either case it has pictographic function.   In fact, it is a pictograph, except for the fact that its geometric form renders it illegible for any one but its writer.   The star-moccasin is also a pictograph in an ornamental dress.[2]

The conventionality of the decoration seems to have reached an equally strong development.   It is apparent that the large stripe from instep to toe is the fundamental motive of this style

---

[1] Some of these moccasins, it will have been noticed, are without known symbolism. This is due merely to their having been collected without inquiry being made as to the significance of their designs.   Consequently, to judge from analogy, it is more probable that they do have meaning than that they really lack it.

[2] Even in true pictographs free from decorative limitations and therefore drawn with the greatest realistic fidelity of which the Indian is capable, the symbols for the morning-star, the horizon, and rays of light are the same as those on this moccasin—a cross, a horizontal line, and vertical or sloping lines.

of ornamentation. All the other motives are also stripes, and even of these there are only two (the transverse stripe and the two short bars), except in the one morning-star moccasin where the basal element is introduced in a new position as a fourth decorative motive.

In short, in these moccasins the tendency to realistic symbolism and the tendency to decorative conventionalism are clearly about in equilibrium. Hence we cannot fairly say that either of these tendencies is the older and original. If one concentrates his attention on the symbolism, or happens to be temperamentally more interested in it, he is very likely to see it more abundantly than the decoration, to be more impressed by it, to consider the entire present art as merely corrupted or abbreviated symbolism, and to advance as an explanation of the origin and development of these designs the theory of conventionalized realism. But if one thinks more of the decoration as such, or if one's mind runs naturally toward the ornamental and technical, he will probably notice mostly this side, regard the significations of markings as trivial and irrelevant additions that may be ignored, and finally champion the theory of expanded decoration. With the one bias we are so overwhelmingly aware of the almost pictographic coherence in the buffalo-hunt moccasin, that we believe that pictures of such topics must have given rise to the present form. With the other bias the conventionality of the pattern that possesses this buffalo-hunt significance is so impressive that we come to think that decorative motives of just such persistence as this must have been the origin of the present form. A first investigator is so struck with the enormous difference of meaning between the ordinary path-stripe moccasins and the morning-star-cross moccasin that he cannot believe they had a common source ; each must have sprung from a picture, which was as different from the other as the objects represented are different. A second observer is so impressed by the fact that the morning-star moccasin with four decorative elements differs less from some of the buffalo-path moccasins than many of these with from one to three decorative elements differ from each other, that he thinks that all these designs, however variable their superficial meanings, must have originated in one typical ornamental form.

Both these explanations are thus, in the case of these moccasin-designs, not only logically possible, but they are very naturally believed and advanced as the result of certain mental predispositions. But if we try to remain free from any such inclinations of mind, and if we remember how strongly developed and intimately fused are both the tendencies, we must come to the conclusion that, because symbolism and decoration balance each other, the two theories of conventionalized realism and expanded ornament, though logically admissible, are actually untenable. Rather it seems likely, since the two tendencies are vigorous, and combined, that they are both well established, old, and long in close union; so that formerly designs on Arapaho moccasins, though perhaps ruder than now, were of the same general character, both symbolically and decoratively, as those we know.

Let us consider a second style of moccasin. Whereas in those just discussed the fundamental element of the embroidery was the longitudinal stripe, it now is a border running all around the foot just above the sole. In one particular specimen illustrated (Pl. VI, fig. 1, cat. no. $\frac{1}{5708}$) there is besides this border of beadwork a series of lines of quillwork filling the large space on the front of the moccasin, but as this is embroidery of a different material and appearance, we can disregard it in the present consideration and confine our attention to the ornamentation consisting of the border. It should be added that in addition to the border there is the narrow stripe across the instep.

In a second specimen (Pl. VI, fig. 2, cat. no. $\frac{50}{983}$) there is besides the border and the transverse stripe, the large longitudinal stripe with which we have become familiar. As previously, this signifies paths.

A third specimen (Pl. VI, fig. 3, cat. no. $\frac{1}{5720}$) has the border, the large longitudinal stripe, and the two small bars at its upper end, but lacks the transverse instep-stripe. On the central stripe are two representations of birds, but there is no information as to the meaning of the design.

It is evident that in these last two moccasins there is a combination of the stripe motive with the border motive.

In another specimen (Pl. VI, fig. 4, cat. no. $\frac{50}{658}$), of whose symbolism we are ignorant, the longitudinal stripe is continued farther than previously, so that it meets the border. The stripe is not solidly embroidered : its edges are beadwork, but its interior is left open and merely painted red.

In any moccasin of this design there is left a blank space on each side of the foot. This is the area enclosed by the stripe, the border, and the transverse instep-stripe. It has the shape of a pointed right-angle triangle whose hypothenuse instead of being straight is convex. These two triangular or horn-shaped areas occur in another moccasin (Pl. VI, fig. 5, cat. no. $\frac{50}{327}$). The border, stripe, and transverse stripe are all white. The two enclosed areas are half covered with a checker-board design in several colors, which is said to represent buffalo-gut. This checker-board embroidery also extends around the heel.

If, now, this half-open checker-board work were replaced by solid beading, we should have a moccasin completely covered with beadwork. Such specimens occur in abundance. In one (Pl. VI, fig. 6, cat. no. $\frac{50}{1028}$), whose groundwork is white, the two triangular areas taken together represent buffalo horns. The buffalo trample the ground ; this is represented by the coloring of the two areas. One is red, which denotes the soil, or bare earth ; the other is green, which denotes vegetation or grass-covered earth.

A child's moccasin, also solidly beaded (cat. no. $\frac{50}{1032}$), has as usual a groundwork of white. The two triangular areas are green, and represent horse ears—a symbol of good fortune and future wealth. Between them, the central stripe, slightly modified, represents a lizard.

A last moccasin (cat. no. $\frac{50}{1075}$) is solidly beaded in white. The two triangular marks are banded dark-blue and white, and represent fish.

In these last cases, in fact in most fully beaded moccasins, the decorative elements of border, stripe, transverse stripe, and triangular area are still visible in the embroidery; even though they often become identical in color and are not distinguished in the design, they are used technically.

If we follow the transition from the merely bordered moccasin to the solidly beaded one, and see the same technical or decorative features persisting in all parts of the series from the simplest to the most highly developed form, the ornamental nature of these productions is striking and their decorative origin seems probable. If we consider the realistic representation of, for instance, the buffalo horn, and the pretty symbolism of its coloring, the realistic origin of these decorations seems very hard to disbelieve. Of course there is no reason for leaping at either of these conclusions. Neither phase of this art must be ignored, but both recognized. It is necessary to be aware both of the strong ornamental tendency influenced by symbolism and the symbolic tendency modified by ornamental system.

So far as these moccasins are concerned, it accordingly seems impossible to determine with certainty how the symbolic decoration originated.

Parfleches and bags of rawhide made by the Arapaho are painted on the front with designs that cover most of the surface. The back or bottom is sometimes left blank, or may have from six to ten straight lines (or narrow stripes) painted transversely across (fig. 49). These lines on the bottom usually represent roads or rivers. All parfleches are perforated in front to allow of being fastened with thongs. Occasionally, however, a cautious person winds a rope a number of times around his bag, in order to tie it up more securely. On one parfleche seen by the writer such transverse lines were painted across the bottom. The owner and

maker declared that they represented a rope passing over the surface of the back several times for fastening the bag. She showed
another parfleche in her possession which was actually thus tied.

In this case the markings may appear to be an instance of the
survival, as a decoration, of an atrophied useful feature: first
ropes were regularly wound around the parfleche to fasten it,
then these were left off but were represented by painting. This
technical-ornamental theory seems at first glance to offer the true
explanation of the origin of these lines on the back of all rawhide bags. But a moment's consideration shows that it is also
within reason to believe the oppo-
site: we can de-

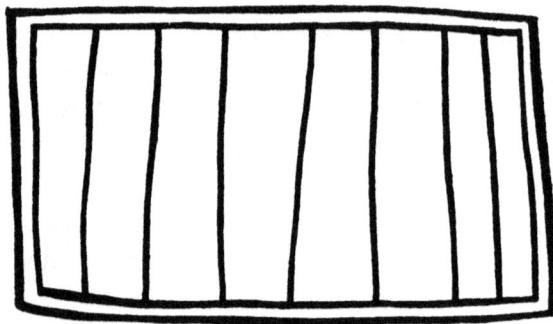

FIG. 49—Marking on Arapaho bag.

clare that the lines originated from attempts at representing
rivers or roads, but that in this case the maker of the bag was
struck by the resemblance of the lines to a rope as it was occasionally used, and then gave the new signification of rope to
what really were conventionalized representations of rivers or
roads.

So here again we have two explanations (there may be still
more) that are plausible, while neither can be proved conclusively.
As soon as we go beyond the description of existing circumstances
into the inquiry of origin, we enter the realm of uncertainty, of
irrefutable doubts.

A peculiar Arapaho medicine-case shows unusual symbolism.
The design painted on this is shown, spread out flat, in fig. 50
(cat. no. $\frac{50}{889}$). The ornamentation, which is less geometric than in
most specimens of painting, represents the acquisition of super-

natural power.   Below, on the right side, is the sweat-house into which the owner and maker of the case went before beginning his fast to acquire supernatural power.   This ornament also represents a small mound in front of the sweat-house, on which a buffalo skull is lying.   The fish-tail ornament just above this is the mountain on which the man fasted, and hence also represents himself.   To the right of this, the crescent-topped design is "the over-seer" (the sun), also called "the one that lights."   The pedestal or stalk of this figure

FIG. 50—Design on Arapaho medicine-case.

represents "information" (supernatural power) flowing down from this being to the earth (the horizontal line).   At the extreme left, the same design is a representation of himself after he had acquired information and power ; and to the right of this, the fish-tail ornament now represents this very medicine-case.   But the case is made of buffalo-hide, and his supernatural power consisted largely in control of the buffalo ; therefore this same symbol also denotes buffalo. Below, on the left, is the sweat-house into which he went after his fast.

We have here an example of highly-developed symbolism.   It might seem that when so long a story is told and so much abstract information is conveyed, the ideographic design must have arisen directly from the attempt of the artist to express his meaning, i. e., that the design is quasi-realistic in origin.   But there is another medicine-case (fig. 51a, cat. no. $\frac{50}{401}$) with similar ornamentation (about whose signification we unfortunately have no information). The resemblance of the two designs is great.   One consists of an alternating arrangement of two symbols, both forked, the other of an alternating arrangement of these two symbols with a third, the semicircle, added.   Some Arapaho say that this style of case was used by a powerful medicine-man and his followers or scholars ; but it is uncertain whether this man invented the design or used an already existing one. It is doubtful whether even the symbolism was originated by this man or was similar to an earlier current of symbolism. The most usual ornamentation on Arapaho medicine-cases is a pattern of tents (fig. 51 *b*, cat. no. $\frac{50}{688}$) or a combination of triangles and

FIG. 51—Arapaho medicine-cases.

diamonds similar to that painted on parfleches.

So here again there is pictographic symbolism fused with a more or less conventional decoration, and it is impossible to say whether the symbolism or the decoration is the older and original.

Small paint-bags—buckskin pouches to hold body-paint—are in general use among the Arapaho. Some of these represent half of a double-ended fringed saddle-bag. The rest all represent small animals, such as the beaver, lizard, rat, fish, mussel, horned toad, and frog. The opening represents the animal's mouth, two strings that serve to tie up the opening are its forelegs, a loose flap at the end may be the tail, the pouch itself is the body, and other parts are indicated, as there is need, by beadwork, strings, or attached ornaments. The resemblance to the animal represented is often detailed, but never accurate, being ideographic rather than visual, in keeping with all the symbolism of this art. It is generally impossible to recognize what species of animal is meant, and only the maker knows this.

One pouch represents both a beaver and a fish (fig. 52a, cat. no. $\frac{50}{361}$), according to information given by its owner. When it

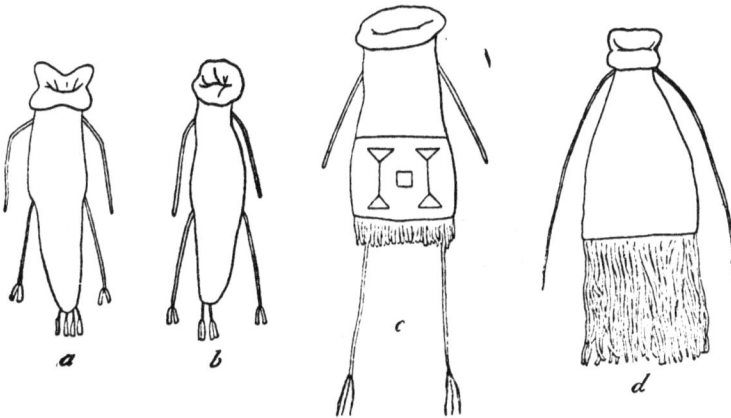

FIG. 52—Arapaho paint pouches.

is regarded as a beaver, both pairs of strings are legs, and the scallops or notches at the opening are the prominent teeth. A design in beadwork on the pouch, which represents a stream with a dam and beaver-huts, also refers to this signification. When a fish is meant to be represented, the upper pair of strings are the barbels, the lower pair the pectoral fins. The fish-signification is strengthened by a rough line of beads at the edge of the pouch, which are interpreted as fish-scales.

A very similar pouch represents a lizard (fig. 52b, cat. no. $\frac{50}{862}$). Mouth, body, legs, and tail are represented in the conventional manner by opening, pouch, strings, and attached flap.

A pouch that lacks the long flap represents a frog (fig. 52*c*, cat. no. $\frac{50}{344}$). Two long strings indicate the frog's hind legs. A fringe at the bottom represents the grass in which it is sitting. A design in beadwork on this pouch denotes the shoulder and hip joints of the frog, and the food in its stomach.

Another pouch (fig. 52*d*, cat. no. $\frac{50}{801}$) differs in shape from this one only in lacking the two longer strings. It represents half a saddle-bag.

The realistic tendency manifested in the animal symbolism of these pouches is undeniable. A conventional, formal, decorative tendency is evident in the close similarity between the frog-pouch and the saddle-bag pouch, and between the beaver-pouch and the lizard-pouch. Both the tendencies come to light in the pouch with the curious double signification.

Some of the Arapaho say that at the beginning of the world, when the first men, their ancestors, obtained paint, they had only the skins of small animals to use for paint-bags, and that this is the origin of the animal symbolism of the present-day paint-pouches.

It is necessary not to be misled into a belief of this origin and development on the authority of the Indians. Their authority on such a point is absolutely valueless. They believe that the time when the first men obtained paint-bags was four hundred years ago, just after the formation of the world by a solitary mythic being floating on the water, and after a female whirlwind enlarged the minute earth by circling about it. Like all American savages they are almost completely without historical sense or knowledge. Occasionally a striking event may be remembered in a distorted form for a century or two, but on the whole, whatever of actual occurrence is retained in their tales is inextricably blended with mythic and supernatural elements. We have no right to reject the greatest part of their creation myth as so absurdly impossible that it would enter no one's mind to accept it as true, and at the same time to select here and there a point that is within the limits of possibility and proclaim it as historical and reliable.

The mythic and historical elements in primitive legends are not simply mixed together so that they can be distinguished and separated, but they are both equally wonderful and equally true for the savage. No myth can be intrepreted into history by mere elimination of its supernatural portions: it must be rejected in toto. Even though it may be founded on a basis of actuality— and this must often be the case—it is altogether myth. In law, and exact science, and wherever evidence is judged, an account that is in great part manifestly absurd or palpably impossible is not accepted as true after the impossibilities have been subtracted, but is disregarded as a whole. So, too, it is necessary to attach no importance to the statement of the Arapaho as to the origin of these paint-bags.

We have considered several forms of Arapaho art—various objects, various styles, and various materials and techniques. In all cases we have found a well-developed symbolism and a conventional decoration. The symbolism and the decoration exist not side by side but in each other. It has been easy to manufacture explanations of the origin of this art that are plausible theories. But as soon as we are open to recognize all possibilities, such theories are seen to arise from our opinions and methods of interpretation, and to be unsubstantiable by fact. Therefore we can describe Arapaho art, we can characterize it, and distinguish its various coexisting tendencies. We can even, to a certain extent, enter into the spirit of the people who practise it, and understand (i. e., feel) their mental workings. We cannot in fairness lay claim to knowing the cause or origin of this art, nor can we hope to ascertain its cause and origin by studying its products.

In the art of other primitive races conditions very much resemble those just discussed. Everywhere art is conventionalized, under the influence of a definite style. Practically everywhere also it is decorative. This is obviously true of such high arts as those of the Japanese and Chinese. It is true also of Greek sculpture and of Renaissance paintings: though in our modern civilization we are in the habit of regarding the products of these arts detachedly, and enjoy them as if they were complete in themselves, yet every one is aware that the intent to decorate always accompanied the conception and execution of the classic and Italian masterpieces. Even so strenuously realistic an art as modern impressionism is unable to free itself totally from the reproach of being ornamental ; for whatever the purpose of the artist, the owner of such a picture has almost certainly secured it for the purpose, ostensible at least, of decorating a vacant wall. In primitive civilizations, the combination of the imitative and decorative tendencies is of course much greater. With very few exceptions, such as in some Eskimo tribes, the realistic, representative impulse is thoroughly impressed and influenced by the highly conventional style ; and in all cases this conventional style is decorative. Correspondingly, most primitive decoration, no matter how geometric or simple, has significance and thus is, visually or ideographically, realistic. This is a fact that has not become known until recently, because until lately savages were rarely questioned thoroughly.[1] Accordingly the main characteristic of Arapaho art, its fusion (which is more truly an undifferentiation) of the realistic and decorative tendencies, is also the characteristic of all primitive art.

In Brazil we know of tribes whose painted and incised designs, which are exceedingly simple and geometrical and usually in patterns, are all significant. Diamonds whose corners are slightly filled in are rhomboidally shaped fishes ; a pattern of flat isosceles triangles stood up on end is hanging bats, and so on. There are also other representations of the same animals that are slightly more realistic. The same tribes use pots of oval shape with half a dozen variously shaped projections at the rim. The

[1] The scarcely suspected inherence of realistic significance in primitive ornament has been independently demonstrated from California, British Columbia, Central America, Brazil, Mississippi valley, Siberia, Indo China, Borneo, New Guinea, Australia, and Polynesia, in arts as diverse as pottery, weaving, carving, basketry, drawing, and painting.

whole vessel represents an animal, the projections being roughly modeled into head, tail, and limbs. Birds, bats, mammals, reptiles, and invertebrates are indicated by very slight modifications. A civilized person unacquainted with the mode of sight and thought of the Brazilian aborigines might very readily mistake a bird-pot for a mammal-pot, and so on.

In Central Australia bullroarers and other objects are decorated with incised lines. These consist of concentric circles, bands of parallel lines, concentric arcs or curves, and rows of dots or small marks. The ornamentation is not symmetrical, nor even regular; it appears random and rude. Yet in general character these decorated bullroarers resemble each other closely. It has been found that the designs are all ideographic, though the total range of significance is apparently not very wide. Similar marks may on different objects mean things as different as trees, frogs, eggs, or intestines. It is interesting to note that while this art is remarkably crude and unformed both as regular ornamentation and as an attempt to represent objects accurately, it contains a system of realistic expression as well as a system of decoration, both of which are conventionalized—or rather, the union of which is a convention.

The remarkable art of the North Pacific coast of America is certainly one of the most stylistic and conventionalized in the world, while its realistic character is sufficiently marked to give no one room to doubt its presence. Its decorative tendency is so strong that, in obedience to its demands, an animal that is being represented may be cut into parts which are then arranged as suits the requirements of the decoration and not as they are in nature. The chest of an animal may be put over its head, and the tail below ; two opposite sides of an animal, which are of course invisible at the same time, will be represented, in order to meet the strong demand for symmetry. The chief decorative motive of all this art is an oblong figure whose corners are rounded and whose sides are very slightly convex, the upper long edge generally curving the most. Almost everything that is represented is brought into this shape or some modification of it. Heads, eyes, mouths, ears, joints, tails, fins, are usually of this shape; the whole decorative field itself often is the same; and in such cases the remaining portions occupied by unenumerated parts, such as back, belly, and wings, are almost necessarily of the same shape. Eyes and faces appear everywhere—on representations of joints, of the chest, of dorsal fins, of hands, in vacant spaces—and their shape is regularly the ornamental one described. Yet with this remarkably strong decorative tendency pervading and deeply influencing every representation, all examples of decorative art from this region are recognizably realistic in intent and often in execution. There is no geometrical ornament that one might take to be meaningless. In short, on the North Pacific coast of America all decoration is realistic and all realism is decorative.

It is of course impossible to prove by selected examples such as these that all primitive art consists of the combination of representative realism and ornamental conventionalism. But that such is the fact, that this undifferentiation continues often into a higher civilization, must be obvious to any one familiar with primitive art. This fusion of two differing tendencies is not merely a frequent or widely distributed occurrence, as are a great many special ethnic phenomena, such as circumcision or doctoring by sucking or angularity of ornament, but this fusion is a rule practically without exceptions. It is universal because it is necessary. Both the representative tendency and the decorative tendency are deep rooted in the human mind, so that it must be virtually impossible to suppress them for any length of time or among any considerable number of men. At times, indeed, as in European civilization, the two tendencies become more separated: our wall-papers are chiefly ornamental, our oil paintings chiefly realistic. But a glance at the past and present races of the world shows that this condition is exceptional, just as a civilization of the extremity of ours is exceptional. The more primitive a people is, we may say, the more intimately fused in its art will these two tendencies be, though, as there is no absolute or fixable scale of primitiveness and civilization, this rule cannot be applied to special cases but merely tends to be true. Other tendencies also are still combined with these two in a sufficiently early and rude condition of society. The symbolism of the Arapaho is as ideographic as it is realistic, and is as much a primitive method of writing as it is of artistic representation. The Australian bull-roarers referred to are, in addition to other things, very primitive maps or charts; so that they are the products of diagrammatic, graphic, visually artistic, and decorative tendencies or activities still undifferentiated—all this in addition to their still more marked religious functions. Of course it is possible for a race to over-develop one of several related tendencies at the expense of others. To a certain degree this does happen in all races, and is what makes the difference between them. But every culture must contain among its motive forces more or less of every tendency, because the tendencies are in the human mind and hence ineradicable. These many tendencies are on the whole less differentiated in more primitive conditions of society. Hence all art, and especially primitive art, contains the combination at least of representative and decorative tendencies, perhaps of others.[1]

---

[1] The differentiation here and previously spoken of as accompanying or constituting evolution in civilization is at once too important and universal a matter to be proved here in a few incidental words, and too obvious to require it. A striking example of this differentiation is found in the mythology of our more primitive forefathers, in place of which, and more or less developed from which, we have products as different as romantic novels, fundamental scientific theories, and the doctrinary beliefs of our religions. There is no intention, however, of implying here by differentiation a continuing separation. Where in a savage tribe every man, though in somewhat varying degree, is hunter, warrior, participant in government, shaman, artist, and myth-maker, a higher nation has its separate politicians, soldiers, food-producers, physicians, poets, and so on ; but though the tendencies have in this transition differentiated, and have far more than formerly become specialized in individuals, yet they exist only in the culture as a whole : in this, the only true unit, i. e., the only organic entity, they are all combined. For instance, our

The invariable method of explaining the origin of an art has been to select that one of its tendencies which was the most marked or appeared so to the investigator, to imagine the products of this tendency in its most isolated and pure form, and to pronounce these the original state of the art. An observer is struck by the fact that in a certain primitive art many ornamental features coincide with technical ones that are present for practical reasons. He concludes that the technical-practical tendency which he has discovered among the decoration, is the original unmixed impulse that caused the art. Or he may become aware through inquiry or study of the fact that geometric ornament in an art has realistic significance. The realism impresses him; true, it is now modified and corrupt, but that only proves to him that originally it was pure. Ergo, this art began with representative pictures. Such has been the only method of explanation, however much the actual results in different cases differed. No other method of ascertaining or explaining the origin of a primitive art whose history we lack, is even possible.

This method has the fundamental fault that it presupposes tendencies to have existed more unmixedly and separately at some former time than at present. In reality they must in all cases have been in the near past very much as now and in the very remote past more mixed or mutually undifferentiated. Thus we have seen that Arapaho art must some time ago have been very much as now. What it was still earlier we know even less definitely, but we cannot doubt that its spirit must have been similar. Different objects may then have been represented, other

---

present-day science could not have arisen nor could it exist without modern industrialism, and this is equally dependent on science. Our literature is absolutely and intimately interwoven with our social conditions, not so much in that poets and novelists actually describe these, but in that the emotions and ideas which form the content of their writing are the typical emotions and ideas accompanying our social circumstances. In proportion with the differentiation of tendencies in evolution proceed their combination and recombination. Very analogously, a mammal is far more highly differentiated than a jellyfish, but none the less are its various organs interdependent and itself a distinct organic unity.

ornamental motives employed in other materials, but even then there certainly was the combination of ideographic symbolism with crude, heavy decoration.   As we go farther backward in time, we can be sure that the details of the art were more and more different from those of its present condition.   Now perhaps one of its component tendencies was relatively stronger, then another.   But whatever these temporary slight fluctuations, it is certain that if we only go back far enough we must arrive at a stage where the tendencies were even more numerously and more intimately combined than now.   But if one should believe that Arapaho art can be explained, for instance, by the coventionalized realism theory, the realism being original and the conventionalization subsequent, he holds the view that at some time past this Arapaho art consisted of pictorial representations.   This view is logically possible, but in reality it is absurd.   This art could not have had so ideally simple a development that we could still trace its original condition, if it were very old.   But if it, therefore, were comparatively recent in origin, there must until a certain time have been no art among the Arapaho, while at that moment it sprang up full-blown, not as a crude undifferentiated thing, but a highly-specialized pictorial art.   Such an event would be extremely remarkable, not to say marvelous, and more in need of an explanation than the phenomenon it explained.   By isolating any tendency that we find in any art, we are led to imagine a purely ideal condition which not only could not have been the original state of the art, but is probably even more different from its original state than from its present known state.

In short, it is impossible to determine the origin of any art whose history we do not know.

Let us briefly consider the field of mythology.   There have been numerous explanations of myths and several theories of the origin of all mythology.   The principal of these theories are the following.

What may be called the physical or science theory accounts

for myths by making them the outcome of a desire to explain natural phenomena. The shapes or colors of animals, the motion of sun and moon, the existence of the stars, strange geologic formations, such phenomena are supposed to have stimulated the wonder of primitive man so much that he made myths to explain them.

The personification theory supposes that deities and other mythic characters, together with their actions,—in a word, mythology—are personifications of natural phenomena. Phœbus, Indra, Agni, are said to have originated in personifications of the sun, heaven, and fire. The solar myth theories, and others of an analogous kind, belong here.

The animistic theory says that there was originally a belief in soul, out of which arose the various systems of spirits and deities. It believes that myths originated from a state of the human mind to which all objects seemed equally endowed with human personality.

These three theories are at bottom the same.

What has been called the allegorical or ethical theory supposes myths to be allegorical inventions with a moral import. Miraculous stories of gods, men, and animals are thought to have been composed in order to teach, by illustration, ethical precepts. This view is not so much in favor now as formerly.

The historical theory makes myths the distortion of actual events. A powerful king of Crete gave rise to the mythic character of Zeus.

The etymological theory calls mythology a disease of language. Misinterpreted metaphors or false etymologies gave rise to myths. To use a familiar example, Zeus is thought to have been originally called Kronion, with the meaning " existing through all time." Later this epithet was misunderstood to mean son of Kronos, and thus gave rise to the conception of a god Kronos.[1]

As explanations, all these theories are untrue. But the tendencies which they recognize exist.

---

[1] This does not necessarily exhaust the number of theories.

There is undoubtedly a tendency to explain natural phenomena in myths. The Indians of British Columbia have this story: The bear and the chipmunk disputed whether there was to be darkness or light. The chipmunk triumphed, and for the first time it became light. The angry bear attacked the chipmunk and pursued it. The chipmunk escaped by tearing itself from under the claws of the bear. From this it is striped down its back. This little story, whatever its origin, clearly reflects the tendency to mythologize about such natural phenomena as day and night and the color-markings of animals. Hundreds of similar myths concerned with the spots on the moon, or the blackness of the crow, or a certain peculiar stone, or a similar fact, are known from all parts of the world.

There is also a tendency to identify mythic personages with parts of nature; Thor with thunder, for instance. And the tendency toward animism is so widespread and so deep-seated that it will be recognized without an example.

It must also be admitted that there is something of an ethical tendency in mythologies. Among primitive races ceremonial and ritual partly take the place of our later morality. And very frequently myths deal with ceremonial. The American Indians, the Jews, the Australians, and the Greeks have such myths.

The existence of a historical tendency in myths is demonstrated by the introduction of Attila into the Sigurd saga.

The etymological tendency, finally, is revealed in the following extract from a Dakota myth [1]: An old couple have adopted a foundling. When he grows up he is so successful in killing buffalo that he makes his parents very rich in dried meat. "Then the old man said: 'Old woman, I am glad we are well off. I will proclaim it abroad.' And so when the morning came he went up to the top of the house and sat, and said, ' I, I have abundance laid up. The fat of the big guts (*tashiyaka*) I chew.' And they say that was the origin of the meadow-lark (*tashiyakapopo*)

---

[1] Riggs, *Dakota Grammar, Texts, and Ethnography*, 1893.

It has a yellow breast, and black in the middle, which is the yellow of the morning, and they say the black stripe is made by a smooth buffalo horn worn for a necklace."—From this point the myth deals with the adventures of the boy.

It is thus clear that for every one of these theories there really exists a tendency in primitive man which influences his myths.

This multiplicity of tendencies or causative forces necessarily refutes any explanation that uses and allows only one of them. Such have been all explanations of myths. Such they must be, for when more than one tendency or cause is admitted, we can have several tentative suggestions but no longer one positive explanation. The case is analogous to that in art, and does not require detailed restatement. It may be said, in short, that all explanations of myths consist of the ignoring of all the eternal and indestructible tendencies in man with the exception of one which is isolated and elevated as the sole cause of the myth. That such explanations, however clear and impressive they are, cannot be true, is obvious.

Thus we come to the conclusion that all search for origins in anthropology can lead to nothing but false results. The tendencies of which we have spoken are at the root of all anthropological phenomena. Therefore it is these general tendencies more properly than the supposed causes of detached phenomena that should be the aim of investigation.

These tendencies, being inherent in mind,[1] are everlasting. On

---

[1] The tendencies spoken of throughout this essay must be understood to be the tendencies of social man. They are those tendencies which exist in individuals being parts of a culture, not in isolated individuals as such. There are psychological causes or mental conditions—generally considered physiological—which might also be called tendencies. Such are the tendency to fatigue, the tendency to form habits, the tendency toward imitation by suggestion, and others. These exist nearly identically in all men, whatever their degree of civilization ; they seem even to occur with little modification in animals. It is evident that these physiological tendencies are totally independent of cultures. Our knowledge concerning them is due to a psychological study of individual men. On the other hand those tendencies which alone are referred to above are determinable only from a historical study of social groups. The manifestations of these tendencies are activities such as mythology, writing, ceremonials decorative art, castes, commerce, and language.

the other hand they are constantly changing and developing, and varying in their differentiations and combinations. The phenomena of activity have changed as these tendencies and their relations to one another have become modified. Therefore the products of mind (the phenomena studied by anthropologists) are, like mind itself, beginningless (for us). They have no origin. All arts and all institutions are as old as man. Every word is as old as speech. The history of every myth is at least as long as the history of mankind. Of course no myth was ever alike from one generation to the next; no decorative style has ever remained unaltered. But no myth, no artistic convention, nor any other thing human, ever sprang up from nothing. It always grew from something previous that was similar. These principles are obvious, but they are ignored and implicitly denied in every search for an origin.

Every explanation of an origin in anthropology is based on three processes of thought which are unobjectionable logically but are contrary to evolutionary principles and the countless body of facts that support these principles. First is the assumption, implied in the word *origin*, that before the beginning of the phenomenon explained, itself and its cause were absent; second is the belief that a suddenly arising cause singly produced the phenomenon; and the third is the idea that this cause as suddenly and completely ceased as it had before sprung up, and that its product has remained, unaffected by other causes, unaltered but for wear and tear, to the present day. These three thought-processes are present in every explanation of the cause or origin of a human phenomenon, whether the explainer himself be conscious or unconscious of them. Generally, indeed, the origin is not stated unhesitatingly and clearly enough for these three steps of thought to be visible in all their baldness. Often, perhaps, the investigator advancing a theory of origin would himself deny these processes to exist in his reasoning. Nevertheless, every determination of an origin, whether origin means the beginning of a phenomenon or its cause, must imply the existence of, first, a previous different state, secondly, a change produced by an external (non-inherent) cause, and, thirdly, the state that is being investigated.

This three-step process of reasoning is not in itself wrong. When it is declared either that steam in a particular case was, or in general can be, produced from water by heat, this method of thought is employed. The early state is the water, the altering cause the heat, and the present state the steam. In all the physical sciences thinking in this manner is not only permissible but necessary and is constantly done. It is when these thought-processes are used in anthropology[1] that their results become absurd. When we say that the origin of decoration is technique, or that the origin of marriage is promiscuity, or that the origin of the Polynesian Maui is personification of the sun, or that the origin of an alphabet is pictorial art, or that the beginning or cause of anything in human culture is a certain other thing—we assert or imply a distinct and separate antecedent condition and an isolated, definitely limited efficient cause. That such a condition and such a cause really existed we have shown in the consideration of primitive art to be so highly improbable as to make the belief in their reality absurd ; and it must be obvious that in all other cases within the scope of anthropology the three suppositions made in every explanation of origin where direct historical knowledge is lacking, possess the same degree of improbability.[2]

If, then, the specific causes or beginnings of specific phenomena

---

[1] By the term anthropology there are meant here not those portions of the science which are clearly anatomical and physiological (i. e., resting upon mechanical science and included in it), but those domains generally covered by the titles ethnology, archeology, and history.

[2] If it is true that origins cannot be determined, the supposed origins of words, namely roots, must be imaginary. Whoever gives adherence to the currently accepted theory that language began with roots, deliberately or unconsciously commits himself to these beliefs: That previous to the making of roots, language in the proper sense, as something articulate and definite, was wanting. That with the roots, language began to be, essentially as it is now. That after the formation of the roots no new ones ever arose, but language remained unchanged except for mod-

are a delusion in anthropology and may not be sought, what can be the subject of investigation? The tendencies that have been referred to so much? Like words and styles and myths and ideas and industrial processes and institutions, all of which are their products, tendencies are both eternally living and everlastingly changing. They flow into one another; they transform themselves; they are indistinguishably combined where they coëxist. So, if our view is wide enough, we cannot properly determine and separate and name and classify tendencies. They really exist only in the whole unity of living activity as parts in the endless organism. This great unity is the true study for the student of man. In it, as parts of it, cultures and civilization-movements, tendencies and individual phenomena, are comprehensible. In it we know their interrelations. Only by understanding its totality can we really understand its smaller parts, those productions that have always a predecessor but never a beginning.

The fundamental error of the common anthropological method of investigating origins is that it isolates phenomena and seeks isolated specific causes for them. In reality, ethnic phenomena do not exist separately: they have their being only in a culture. Much less can the causative forces of the human mind, the activities or tendencies, be truly isolated. Every distinction of them is not only arbitrary but untrue. Both phenomena and

---

ifications of its roots or their combinations into new words and inflectional forms. The improbability of such a process having ever taken place must be clear to any one who believes that never-dying, ever-changing, interrelated tendencies have unceasingly and unitedly been operative in man. The belief in roots as the sources of languages is totally unevolutionary: it is contrary to the axiom that nothing living ever comes but from what is similar and that all change is gradual development and not a process of finished creation. The weakness of the theory of roots is most palpable in the absurdity of the various explanations that are frequently given of the origin of the primary roots. It is true that there is something that may be called roots. In every language there are groups of words similar in sound and related in meaning. The ideal, non-existent centers of these groups of words can well be named roots, and they must be recognized and used in philology. But roots that once existed as such, and gave rise to languages of words in which they can still be seen,—such there never were

causes can be properly apperceived only in the degree that we know their relations to the rest of the great unity that is called life. The more this is known and understood as a whole, the more do we comprehend its parts. This, the whole of life, is the only profitable subject of study for anthropology.

The Mrs. Morris K. Jesup Expedition.

The Arapaho.

By Alfred L. Kroeber.

I. GENERAL DESCRIPTION.

II. DECORATIVE ART AND SYMBOLISM.

BULLETIN

OF THE

American Museum of Natural History,

Vol. XVIII, Part I, pp. 1–150.

New York, Sept. 3, 1902.

BULLETIN

OF THE

AMERICAN MUSEUM OF NATURAL HISTORY.

VOLUME XVIII, 1902.

THE ARAPAHO.

By ALFRED L. KROEBER.

PLATES I–XXXI.

INTRODUCTORY.

IN 1899 Mrs. Morris K. Jesup generously provided the means for a study of the Arapaho Indians, and the writer was entrusted with the work. He visited that portion of the tribe located in Oklahoma in 1899, the Wyoming branch and a number of neighboring tribes in 1900, and the Gros Ventres and Assiniboines in 1901. The principal results of his studies are contained in the present volume, in which the general culture, decorative art, mythology, and religion of the Arapaho will be described. Two preliminary articles on the decorative symbolism of the Arapaho have been published by the writer, —

Symbolism of the Arapaho Indians (Bulletin of the American Museum of Natural History, Vol. XIII, 1900, pp. 69–86).
Decorative Symbolism of the Arapaho (American Anthropologist, N. S., Vol. III, 1901, pp. 308–336).

The former is a preliminary general account of Arapaho symbolism and art, stress being laid particularly on the symbolism. Both decorative art and the more or less pictographic symbolism connected with religion are included in the scope of this paper. The second paper deals with the question of the origin of symbolic decoration.

A. L. K.

NEW YORK, July, 1901.

EXPLANATIONS.

The following alphabet has been used in rendering Arapaho words: —

a, e, i, o, u	have their continental sounds.
ā	as in *that*.
ā̆	as in *mad*.
â	as in *law*.
ô	nearly as in *hot*.
û	somewhat as in *hut*, but nearer *u*.
ê	between *a* and *e*.
A, E, I, O, U	obscure vowels.
ᵃ, ᵉ, ⁱ, ᵒ, ᵘ	scarcely spoken vowels.
aⁿ, äⁿ	nasalized *a*, *ä*.
b, k, n, t, w, y	as in English.
c, s	English *sh* and *s*, but similar
ç	English *th* as in *think*.
h	as in English, but fainter.
tc	English *ch* as in *church*.
x	aspirate *k*.

Owing to the changed conditions under which the Arapaho now live, and to the comparatively short time that the writer was among them, the information presented in this paper could not be obtained to any extent from direct observation, but only by questioning. Unless the opposite is stated or is obviously the case, all statements in this paper are therefore given on the authority of the Indians, not of the writer. In some cases explanatory remarks by the writer have been distinguished by being enclosed in parentheses.

I.— GENERAL DESCRIPTION.

The Arapaho Indians first became known at the beginning of the last century. Since that time they have inhabited the country about the head waters of the Arkansas and the Platte Rivers. This territory, which they held together with the Cheyenne, covers approximately the eastern half of Colorado and the southeastern quarter of Wyoming. The language of the Arapaho, as well as that of the Cheyenne, belongs to the widely spread Algonkin family, of which they form the most southwesterly extension. These two tribes were completely separated from the Blackfoot, Ojibway, and other tribes speaking related languages, by the Dakota and other tribes inhabiting the intervening territories. In physical type and in culture, the Arapaho belong to the Plains Indians.

The Arapaho have generally been at peace with the Kiowa and Comanche, and at war with their other neighbors. They had no permanent settlements, nor any fixed dwellings. They lived exclusively in tents made of buffalo-skins. For food they were dependent on the herds of buffalo that roamed through their country; and much of their clothing and many of their implements were derived from the same animal. Agriculture was not practised. They had the sun-dance that existed among most of the Plains Indians, and possessed a ceremonial organization of warrior companies similar to that of several other tribes.

The Arapaho men have generally been described as more reserved, treacherous, and fierce, and the women as more unchaste, than those of other tribes. Those acquainted with their psychic nature have characterized them as tractable, sensuous, and imaginative.

The fullest and most accurate account of the Arapaho has been given by James Mooney.[1] On several points, however, Mr. Mooney's information does not agree with that obtained

---

[1] Ghost-Dance Religion (Fourteenth Annual Report, Bureau of Ethnology, pp. 653 et seq.)

by the present writer.   Other accounts of the Arapaho, as by Hayden and Clark, are brief and sometimes vague.

One portion of the Arapaho is now settled in Oklahoma; the other part, on a reservation in Wyoming.   The Gros Ventres, who form an independent tribal community, but are so closely akin in language and customs that they may be regarded as a subtribe of the Arapaho, are in northern Montana.

Nothing is known of the origin, history, or migrations of the Arapaho.   A little light is thrown on their past by their linguistic relations.

Apart from the Cree, the western Algonkin languages belong to four groups,— the Ojibway, Cheyenne, Arapaho, and Blackfoot.

Of these, the Blackfoot is the most isolated, and the most differentiated from the typical Algonkin.   Grammatically it is normal: the methods of inflection and the forms of pronominal affixes resemble those of Ojibway, Cree, and more eastern dialects; but etymologically it seems to differ considerably more from all other Algonkin languages than these vary from each other.

Cheyenne and Arapaho are quite distinct, in spite of the identity of habitation of the two tribes.   Cheyenne, Arapaho, and Ojibway are all about equally different one from another. Arapaho and Ojibway seem to differ a little more from each other than each varies from Cheyenne; but Cheyenne is by no means a connecting link between them.

Superficially, Arapaho appears to be very much changed from the average Algonkin, etymologically as well as grammatically; but its words vary from those of Ojibway, Cheyenne, and eastern languages largely on account of regular and consistent phonetic changes.   When once the rules governing these changes are known, and the phonetic substitutions are made, the vocabulary of the Arapaho is seen to correspond closely to those of kindred languages.   This does not seem to be the case with the Blackfoot, which gives the impression of being corrupted, or irregularly modified lexically.

Grammatically, Arapaho is more specialized.   It possesses

three features that are peculiar to it. First, it makes no distinction between animate and inanimate nouns in their plural forms, — a distinction which is made in the other Algonkin languages. It recognizes this category only in the verb. Secondly, all the pronominal particles which are used to conjugate the verb are suffixed. In all other Algonkin languages, when there are two such particles (in the objective conjugation), one is generally prefixed and one suffixed; when there is only one such particle (intransitive conjugation) it is prefixed. Except in one form of the negative, Arapaho suffixes its pronominal elements throughout. This gives a very different appearance to its conjugation. Lastly, its pronominal particle for the second person, which elsewhere in Algonkin is k-, is $-n$ in the verb, and a vowel-sound in the noun. In this last feature Arapaho is approximated by Cheyenne, which uses n- to indicate the second person.

Blackfoot and Arapaho, the two most western Algonkin languages, thus appear to be the most specialized from the common type, — one etymologically, the other grammatically. They have so little in common, however, that they probably differ more from each other than from any other languages of the stock. On the other hand, the Arapaho declare that one of their extinct dialects resembled the Blackfoot. Cheyenne and Arapaho are so different that the recent association of the tribes must have been preceded by a long separation. The Cheyenne appear to have been more lately in connection with the Ojibway or kindred tribes, as is also indicated by several resemblances in culture.

The Arapaho call themselves "Hinanaē′inaⁿ," the meaning of which term they cannot give. They declare that they formerly comprised five subtribes. These were —

1. Nāⁿwaçinähā′änaⁿ.
2. Hāⁿanaxawūune′naⁿ.
3. Hinanaē′inaⁿ (Arapaho proper).
4. Bāäsaⁿwūune′naⁿ.
5. Hitōune′naⁿ (Gros Ventres).

They extended from south to north in the order given.

The term Nāⁿwaçinähā′änaⁿ has some reference to the south,

the windward direction. The other elements in the word are not clear. The sign for this subtribe is said to have been the index-finger placed against the nose. This may mean "smelling towards the south." This sign is now the usual one for Arapaho in the sign-language of the Plains.

Hāⁿanaxawūune'naⁿ means "rock-men." It is said to have reference to stone-chipping or the working of flint. The sign for this subtribe is the sign for rock or rough flint.

Hinanaē'inaⁿ (the Arapaho proper) were indicated by the sign for "father."

Bāäsaⁿwūune'naⁿ means "shelter-men," "brush-hut-men." The sign for this tribe is that indicating a round camp-shelter.

Hitōune'naⁿ (the Gros Ventres) are indicated by the gesture for a large or swelling belly. The word means "begging men," or "greedy men," or "gluttons."

These five tribes were separate, though allied. Occasionally they came together. Later, most of them grew less in number, and were absorbed by the Hinanaē'inaⁿ. There is more Bāäsaⁿwūune'naⁿ blood among the present Arapaho than there is of that of the other tribes. The Hitōune'naⁿ, however, maintained a separate existence. Known as Gros Ventres, they are an independent tribe considerably north of the Arapaho. The Gros Ventres have a mythical story, analogues of which are found among other Western Plains tribes, about their detachment from a previous larger tribe; but there appears to be no reference in their traditions to any common origin with the Arapaho. The Gros Ventres call themselves "Haä'ninin."

Each of these five tribes had a dialect of its own. The Bāäsaⁿwūune'naⁿ speech is very similar to the Arapaho, and is easily understood. There are several individuals among both the northern and the southern portions of the Arapaho tribe that still habitually speak this dialect.

Next in degree of similarity is the Gros Ventre. There are several regular substitutions of sounds between the Arapaho and Gros Ventre dialects, but they are not numerous enough to prevent mutual intelligibility.

The Nāⁿwaçinähā'änaⁿ is considerably different from the

Arapaho. It alone, of all the dialects, has the sound *m*. In the form of its words, it diverges from Arapaho in the direction of Cheyenne. Grammatically, however, it is clearly Arapaho. This dialect is still remembered by some old people, but it is doubtful whether it is still spoken habitually by any one.

The Hāⁿanaxawūune'naⁿ is said to have differed most from the Arapaho and to have been the most difficult to understand. No one who knew this dialect could be found.

It is said that there was once a fight between two of the tribes. This quarrel was between the Hinanaē'inaⁿ and the Bāäsaⁿwūune'naⁿ, over the sacred tribal pipe and a similar sacred lance, and occurred on account of a woman. The Bāäsaⁿwūune'naⁿ were the first to have the pipe and the lance. The Bāäsaⁿwūune'n keeper of them married an Arapaho woman, and lived with her people. Since then the other tribes have all lived together and helped each other in war. The present condition of alliance, and of possession of the pipe by the Arapaho, has come about through intermarriage.

Both the northern and southern Arapaho recognize these five tribes or dialects as composing their people. There seem to be no historical references to the three absorbed tribes, except that Hayden, in 1862, called the southern half of the Arapaho tribe Nāⁿwaçināhā'änaⁿ (Nawuthinihaⁿ). Mooney gives these five tribes somewhat differently.

The northern Arapaho in Wyoming are called Nāⁿk'hāaⁿ-sēine'naⁿ ("sagebrush men"), Bāaⁿtcīine'naⁿ ("red-willow men"), Bāäkūune'naⁿ ("blood-soup men"), or Nănăbine'naⁿ ("northern men"). They call the southern Arapaho in Oklahoma Naⁿwuine'naⁿ ("southern men"). These two divisions of the Hinanaē'inaⁿ appear to have existed before the tribe was confined to reservations. The two halves of the tribe speak alike, except that the northern people talk more rapidly, according to their own and their tribesmen's account. The author has not been able to perceive any difference between the speech of the two portions of the tribe.

There are also said to have been four bands in the tribe. Three of these were the Wāⁿxuē'içi ("ugly people"), who are now about Cantonment in Oklahoma; the Haxāaⁿçine′naⁿ ("ridiculous men"), on the South Canadian, in Oklahoma; and the Bāaⁿtcῑine′naⁿ ("red-willow men"), in Wyoming. The fourth the informant had forgotten. Apparently corresponding to these were the four head chiefs that the Arapaho formerly had. These bands were properly subdivisions of the Hinanaē′inaⁿ subtribe, and appear to have been local divisions. A man belonged to the band in which he was born or with which he lived; sometimes he would change at marriage. When the bands were separate, the people in each camped promiscuously and without order. When the whole tribe was together, it camped in a circle that had an opening to the east. The members of each band then camped in one place in the circle. All dances were held inside the camp-circle.

There are no clans, gentes, or totemic divisions among the Arapaho. The local bands of the Gros Ventres seem, however, to partake also of the nature of gentes.

All informants agree that the tribe against which the Arapaho fought most were the Utes, the bravest (after themselves). An old man said that the Arapaho fought most with the Utes because they were the strongest, and next with the Pawnees because they were the fiercest, and that the Osages and Pawnees were the first Indians that wished to establish friendly ties with the Arapaho. His son has a model of the pipe with which friendship was made with these tribes. A younger man said that his ears had been pierced by visiting Osages, because his father had formerly fought chiefly with them.

The first whites with whom the Arapaho came into contact were Mexicans. The word for "white man" is nih′ā′ⁿçaⁿ, which is also the name of the mythic character that corresponds to the Ojibway Manabozho. This word also means "spider."

The Arapaho had four chiefs, as against five of the Cheyennes. They also had no official principal chief, while the Cheyennes did have one. When one of the four head chiefs died, another was chosen from among the dog-company, — men about fifty years old, who have performed the fourth of

the tribal series of six ceremonials. If a chief was unsatis-
factory, he was not respected or obeyed, and so gradually lost
his position. Another informant stated that chiefs were not
formally elected: the bravest and kindest-hearted men became chiefs naturally, but there were no recognized or regular
chiefs.

The following are the terms of relationship and affinity in
Arapaho and Gros Ventre. All the words given have the
prefix denoting "my."

English.	Arapaho.	Gros Ventre.
father	neisa'naⁿ	niiçinaⁿ
mother	ne'inaⁿ	neinaⁿ
elder brother	nääsä'hää	nääçähää
elder sister	nä'biᵉ	nibyᵉ
younger brother or sister	nähäbä'hää	näⁿhäbyⁱ
son	ne'ih'äⁿ	neih'ä
daughter	nata'ne	natan
grandfather	näbä'cibä	näbeseip
grandmother	neibä'häⁿ	niip'
grandchild	neicI'	niisä
father's brother	(?)	niiçinaⁿ
mother's brother	nä'ci	nis'
father's sister	nähe'i	nähei
mother's sister	(?)	neinaⁿ
son of brother of a man } son of sister of a woman }	(?)	neih'ä
daughter of brother of a man } daughter of sister of a woman }	(?)	natan
son of sister of a man } son of brother of a woman }	näçää'çä	nêt'êt
daughter of sister of a man } daughter of brother of a woman }	nääsä'biᵉ	nääçibyⁱ
father-in-law	näci'çä	nêsit
mother-in-law	nähe'ihäⁿ	näheihä
son-in-law	näçä'Ox	nataos
daughter-in-law	nääsä'biᵉ	nääçibyⁱ
brother-in-law of a man	näyaⁿ'	näyaaⁿ
sister-in-law of a woman	nato'u	natou
brother-in-law of a woman } sister-in-law of a man }	neiçä'biᵉ	niitibyⁱ
husband	nä'ac	(?)
wife	nätä'ceäⁿ	näticää

The terms for "niece" and for "daughter-in-law" seem to be identical. There is another word for "younger sister" or perhaps "sister,"— nātä'se.

The total number of Arapaho kinship terms is thus twenty-three. Four of these —"father-in-law," "mother-in-law," "son-in-law," and "daughter-in-law"— are clearly related to four others, —"uncle," "aunt," "nephew," and "niece." Several others appear to have common elements: -äbie occurs in the words for "elder sister," "niece," and "sister-in-law of a man."

In this series of terms the distinction between elder and younger is confined to the brother and sister relationships. The terms for the consanguinities of a man and for those of a woman are alike, except in the case of brother-in-law and sister-in-law. Here the category according to which terms are differentiated is not so much absolute sex as identity or contrariety of sex. Thus, a man calls his sister-in-law neiçäbie, and she calls him the same; brothers-in-law call each other nāyan; sisters-in-law, natou.

Cousins, even of remote degrees of kinship, are called "brothers and sisters." Among the Gros Ventres, the father's brother is called "father;" the mother's sister, "mother;" so that the terms for "uncle" and "aunt" are used only for mother's brother and father's sister. The same is true of "nephew" and "niece;" a man calls his brother's children "son and daughter," but his sister's children "nephew and niece;" conversely with a woman. Even a cousin's or a second cousin's children are called "son and daughter" instead of "nephew and niece," if the cousin is of the same sex as the speaker. The same may be true among the Arapaho.

The restrictions as to intercourse between certain relations, which are so widespread in North America, exist also among the Arapaho. A man and his mother-in-law may not look at or speak to each other. If, however, he gives her a horse, he may speak to her and see her. The same restrictions exist between father and daughter-in-law as between mother and son-in-law, say the Arapaho (though perhaps they are less rigid). A brother and sister must not speak to each other more than is necessary. A sister is supposed to sit at some distance from her brother. A woman does not speak of child-birth or sexual matters in the presence of her brother, nor he in hers, but in other company no such delicacy is observed. Obscene myths are freely told, even in the presence of children of either sex, except that a man would not relate them before his mother-in-law, daughter-in-law, sister, or female cousin, nor a woman before her corresponding male relatives. Brothers-in-law joke with each other frequently; often they abuse each other good-naturedly; but they may not talk obscenely to each other. If one does so, he is struck by the other. A brother-in-law and sister-in-law also often joke each other. They act toward each other with considerable freedom: a woman may pour water on her brother-in-law while he is asleep, or tease him otherwise, and he retaliates in similar ways.

When a man died, his brothers took from their sister-in-law as many horses as they pleased. Sometimes they were generous and allowed a grown-up daughter or son of the dead man to keep some. Another informant stated that after a man's death, his brothers took all the property they could, especially horses. The family tried to prevent them.

There are no fixed rules as to inheritance. When a wealthy man dies, there is generally some jealousy as to who is to take his property and his family. Those who are not satisfied sometimes kill horses or destroy property of those who took the belongings of the dead man. Each one tries to get as much as he can. There is little generosity or charity towards the wife and children. Adult sons of the deceased may be anxious to secure some of the property; but, as they are in mourning, they cannot resist. It is generally brothers and sisters of the deceased who go to take his property.

In the absence of any gentile or other organization regulating marriage, the only bar was that of known relationship. Cousins could not marry. As to distant relations the rule was not so strict. If relationship was discovered after a marriage, the marriage was not annulled.

The following are statements by the Arapaho on the subject of marriage.

When a young man wants to marry, he sends a female relative to the tent of his desired father-in-law with several horses (from one to ten), which may be his own or his friends'. She ties the horses in front of the tent, enters, and proposes the marriage. The father has nothing to say, and refers the matter to his son. The son decides upon the proposal, unless he wishes to refer it to an uncle or other relative. The woman goes back and reports her success. If the proposal of marriage has been refused, she takes the horses back. If the suitor has been accepted, he waits until called, which is done as soon as the girl's mother and relatives have put up a new tent which is given her, and have got property together. This may be the same day or the same night that the proposal was made. The girl's brothers and father's brothers' sons all give horses and other presents. They bring the things inside the new tent, the horses in front of it. Then the girl's relatives notify the young man's father to come; sometimes they send the bride herself. Then the young man's relatives come over with him to the new tent, and enter it. His entering this tent signifies that he and the girl are married. He sits down at the head of the bed, which is on the left as one enters the tent (the entrance to Arapaho tents is always at the east; the owner's bed, along the southern side, with the head toward the west). The girl sits next to him at the foot of the bed, the other people all around the tent. The girl's father, or, if he is still young, an old man, stands before the door and cries out the names of those invited, calling to them to come and feast. Then they eat and smoke. Sometimes an old person that wants to, prays. Any one of the girl's male relatives makes a speech to her. He says to her that she is a woman now, and tells her to be true to her husband. The visitors leave whenever they please. The friends of the young man each take away as many horses as they gave (to the girl's relatives). Sometimes he gives his friends other presents besides. Now he is married. He pitches his tent by his father-in-law's. The young wife at first does not know how to cook, and goes to her mother's tent for food.   The young man, however, does not enter this tent, because he and his mother-in-law may not look at or speak to each other.

Sometimes a young man and a girl run off without the knowledge of their parents.   They remain some time in the tent of the young man's father or of some friend.   Then his friends contribute horses and other property.   The girl mounts a horse and leads the rest.   Accompanied by her sister-in-law or mother-in-law, she brings the horses and other gifts to the tent of her parents.   Then her parents are not angry any longer, and send her back with horses and presents of property, sometimes with a tent.   They also give her food, with which a feast is held in the young man's tent.   Then his friends take the horses and goods which he has received. Sometimes a young man, after taking a girl away, abandons her on the prairie.

Relatives know nothing about the courtship of a young man and a girl.   This is kept secret by them until she is formally asked for by his relatives.

When a man wishes to run off with another's wife, the two make plans.   They go off together a long distance.   At first the husband, perhaps, does not know what has happened. When he becomes aware of it, he is angry.   He may follow his wife; but he is not allowed to enter the tent where she and her lover are, because he might do them injury.   If he finds them and speaks to them, they do not answer him, in order not to enrage him more, because they may not make any resistance to him.   The lover tries to find the (ceremonial) grandfather of the husband.   He gives him a pipe and two or three horses.   The old man takes the pipe, the horses, and the wife to the husband.   When the man sees his grandfather, he must do no violence nor may he become angry. The grandfather hands him the pipe.   If he takes it, his wife is safe from harm.   Sometimes he keeps her, sometimes he sends her back to her lover to keep.   Often the husband cuts off the tip of her nose, slashes her cheek, or cuts her hair. Both men and women are jealous.   A man will hit his wife for looking at a young man too much.

If a man treats his wife badly, her brothers may take her back to her father, tear his tent down, and take away his household property. Sometimes the man and woman live together again, sometimes she marries some one else. But the man still has a claim on her; and if another takes her, he must pay her first husband one or two horses to relinquish his claim.

Sometimes a husband, to show his love for his wife, gives away several horses to her relatives.

A wife's next younger sister, if of marriageable age, is sometimes given to her husband if his brother-in-law likes him. Sometimes the husband asks and pays for his wife's younger sister. This may be done several times if she has several sisters. If his wife has no sister, a cousin (also called "sister") is sometimes given to him. When a woman dies, her husband marries her sister. When a man dies, his brother sometimes marries his wife. He is expected to do so. Sometimes she marries another man.

In courting women, men cover themselves completely with a blanket except the eyes. Often they exchange blankets, so as not to be known. They wait on sand-hills, or similar places, until the women leave the camp for water or wood. Sometimes at night they turn the upper flaps of the tent, so that the smoke of the fire remains in the tent; when the woman goes outside to open the top of the tent, the man meets her. At night men catch women outdoors and hold them, trying to persuade them to yield to their wishes. (The Arapaho affirm this of the Cheyenne, but have the practice themselves.) Courting is much easier and more open now than formerly. In making advances to a woman, a man often begins by asking for a drink of the water she is carrying.

It is said, that, on account of fear of unchastity, women are married at an earlier age now than formerly. The Omaha, according to Dorsey, make a similar statement. This seems to be an Indian opinion which is not founded on facts.

A man with two wives generally has a tent for each. An Arapaho in Wyoming lived with his two wives, who were sisters, in one tent. His wives' relatives wanted to give him a third sister. The girl objected, and he did not get her.

Once a young man was said to have sat with the women too frequently, and to have teased them too much. A number of them seized him, stripped him, and then buffeted and maltreated him without delicacy. Young men were ashamed to be alone with a number of women too long. There were a few bachelors, who were half-witted, or considered so.

At the sun-dance an old man, crying out to the entire camp-circle, told the young people to amuse themselves; he told the women to consent if they were approached by a young man, for this was their opportunity; and he called to the young men not to beat or anger their wives, or be jealous during the dance: they might make a woman cry, but meanwhile she would surely be thinking of some other young man. At such dances the old women say to the girls: "We are old, and our skin is not smooth; we are of no use. But you are young and plump; therefore find enjoyment. We have to take care of the children, and the time will come when you will do the same."

Women do not spend several days in solitude during menstruation, as is the case among the Sioux, the Utes, and many other neighboring tribes. They sit quietly, keeping away from other people, especially from women and young men. But they eat with other people, and cook for them. They wrap their clothes tightly about the waist. They change their clothes every day, and wash themselves. There is no practice or ceremony connected with a girl's first menstruation. A menstruating woman is not allowed to enter the mescal (peyote) tent; and if a man who has had intercourse with a menstruating woman takes part in this ceremony, he is found out by the smell. Sickly people and menstruating women are not allowed to enter a tent in which there is a sick person. The smell of the discharge would enter the body of the patient and make him worse. A woman just delivered also refrains from going into the tent of a sick person. Medicine-women, after delivery, go into the sweat-house (steam-bath) to cleanse themselves. Menses were called bäätä′äna^n ("medicine," "supernatural," "mysterious"), or näniiçe′hina^n (näniiçext, bäätäät, "she menstruates").

A woman nursing a child does not drink coffee because it burns or cooks the milk. She may not go into the heat of the sun, or work near the fire. She covers her breast and sometimes her back as thickly as she can from the heat. If a mother dies, an old woman takes the infant to another woman who is already nursing a child. This is advantageous to the woman, as it prevents her surplus milk from becoming bad. For this reason pups are sometimes applied to the breast. Early in the morning a man sometimes drains a woman's breast, spitting the milk on the ground; or a child some years weaned drinks from her. This is done that her infant may have the newly formed milk.

If a man is married, his sister may want to make a cradle for his child. She provides food for a number of old people, shows them her materials, and asks how she is to make the cradle. The old people tell her how to make it, and show her the designs with which it is to be decorated. Then they all pray in turn that the child's cradle may be made perfectly, and that it may be for the good of the child. After the woman has finished the cradle, she repeats her invitation to the old people. Then the child is put into the cradle and taken to its father. He receives it, and makes a gift to the maker.

Cradles are embroidered with porcupine-quills or beads. They are used for carrying the child. Some can also be suspended on ropes from two tent-poles, and swung. Several are described on p. 66.

When a person dies, his relatives cry and unbraid their hair. Sometimes they cut their hair. The greater their love for him, the more hair they cut off. Women tear off a sleeve; they gash themselves (lightly) across the lower and upper arm and below the knee. The dead body is allowed to lie so that all the dead person's friends can see it. It is dressed in the best clothing, some perhaps being contributed by friends. Those who thus contribute toward dressing a dead man receive one of his horses or other property. A horse is also given for digging the grave and for similar assistance. The body is buried on the hills, being taken there on horseback.

The grave is made deep enough to prevent coyotes from digging out the corpse; with this object in view, thorny brush is also put on the grave. The relatives go out to the grave for several days. They mourn there, crying while sitting in one place. Hair that has been cut off by friends and relatives is wrapped up with the body and buried. The dead man's best or favorite horse is shot next to his grave, and left lying there. The tail and mane of the horse on which the body was taken to burial are cut off and strewn over the grave. Before the body is taken away to be interred, an old man speaks encouragingly to the relatives. The dead man's family move to another place. They give away the tent in which he died. If he happened to die in a brush shelter, it is burned. Clothing, beds, and other articles that were where he died, are burned, in order that his shadow (spirit) will not come back. Sticks that may have touched him while he was dying are buried with him or laid on the grave. Immediately after the burial the relatives bathe because they have touched the corpse. For several nights they burn cedar-leaves; the smoke or smell of this keeps away the spirit. For some time they wear old clothing and do not paint. They seek no amusements. At first they eat little. As long as they wear old clothes and keep their hair unbound, they are in mourning. This period is not fixed. When they have finished mourning, they provide food and invite in old men and women. An old man paints their entire faces and their hair red. This is called cleaning; it is done in the morning, so that they may be under the care of the sun all day. Now they braid their hair again, and go about as before.

For a murder or accidental killing, horses were given to the relatives of the dead. The murderer had no influence or position, and was shunned. He was not, however, excluded from tribal affairs. He could camp in the camp-circle, and enter dances. Everything that he ate was supposed to taste bad to him.

The name of the dead was apparently as freely mentioned as that of the living. Old men sometimes gave their own name to young men. Red-Wolf (haaxăbaani) gave his name to his son, and was then called "One-Crow" (houniisi). Names are not infrequently changed.

The giving of presents is a very extensive practice among the Arapaho, as among all the Plains Indians. Horses are given to visitors from other tribes, especially by chiefs, in order to show their position and rank. A horse given to a stranger counts for more in public estimation than one given to an Arapaho. When a party of Utes came on a visit in 1898, the Arapaho decorated their best horses, charged upon the Utes, struck them lightly with switches (symbolically counting coup upon them), and then gave them the horses that they had ridden in the charge. Within the tribe, gifts are also very frequent, especially on ceremonial occasions.

When a woman, especially a young girl, wishes a present, she cooks a puppy and takes it to her brother or some other male relative or friend. If he wishes to distinguish himself before those who are present, he gives her a horse or a tent. Sometimes he gives her less. If he gives a tent, it is left standing when the camp-circle breaks up; then, in the sight of all, the new owners take it down. This custom is practised when the whole tribe is encamped together (the especial time for ceremonials). When no pup is available, the woman makes a gift of other food.

Young men sometimes fill a bucket made of bladder with water, and go about the camp, giving drink to the oldest men and women.

Three semi-ceremonial practices bringing honor and reward to the agent, and supposed to be for the good of the child upon whom they are performed, are piercing the ears (tceita^n'hätiit), cutting the hair over the forehead (tawana'axawa^{n}t), and cutting the hair on one side (nakaçä'äciit). Ear-piercing counts for more than the other two. Children's ears are pierced when they are small. It is done during the sun-dance or some other dance. It makes the children grow up well and become men and women. The more they cry during the operation, the better it is thought to be, for the crying signifies that hardship and pain have already been endured, and that therefore they will grow up. A horse and other presents are given by the father to the man who is summoned, through an old man who cries out in public, to pierce the child's ears. Generally he receives the father's best horse. If the man who is summoned has never killed or scalped any one, he keeps the horse, but gives away his other presents to a man who has thus distinguished himself in war, and who actually does the piercing. If the man who pierces the child's ears belongs to another tribe, the honor is so much the greater. One man, when a child, had his ears pierced by an Osage, because before peace was concluded his father had fought chiefly against the Osages. The piercing is performed with a sewing-awl; but, if the piercer has ever cut or slashed an enemy or cut a scalp, he uses a knife instead of an awl. The awl symbolizes a spear; the hole pierced, a wound; the dripping blood, ear-ornaments; the cutting of the child's hair, scalping. The wound is kept open by means of a little stick.

Berdaches (men living as women) were found among the Arapaho, as among the Cheyenne, Sioux, Omaha, Ute, and many other tribes. They are called haxu'xan, which is thought to mean "rotten bone." The following accounts concerning them were obtained.

The haxuxana^n become so as the result of a (supernatural) gift from animals or birds. Similarly, in the beginning of the world, animals appeared as women (in certain myths, such as that of Elk-Woman and Buffalo-Woman). Nih'a^n'ça^n (the character corresponding to Manabozho and Ictinike) was the first one. This is told in a myth. (He pretended to be a woman, married the Mountain-Lion, and deceived him by giving birth to a false child.) These people had the natural desire to become women, and as they grew up gradually became women. They gave up the desires of men. They were married to men. They had miraculous power and could do (supernatural) things. For instance, it was one of them that first made an intoxicant from rain-water.

Apud Indianos quos Cheyenne vocant, femina vixit cui viri vox genitaliaque fuerunt. Vestibus mulierum usa est, et ut femina cum feminis vixit. Hospitum oculos attraxit moribus magis liberis. Viro connexum petente, consensum præbuit;

dorso recumbens et penem ventri deponens, permisit acces-
sum in anum.

The Arapaho declare that they never had any women that
dressed and lived as men, but they have a story of such a
woman among the Sioux.

Insanity, when it occurs, seems mostly to be acute and
violent delusion. One man became insane from excitement
in making a charge in battle. He thought himself a wolf, and
ran about like one. He did not, however, attack men or
animals; and later he recovered. Another man, who subsequently also recovered, ran about with a knife, and gashed
or pierced trees; deinde intromisit penem. A Gros Ventre,
an elderly man, recently began to see crowds of spirits close
about him; he swung his arms and shouted in order to drive
them away. Soon after being taken to an asylum, he was
said to be recovering. Among the Oklahoma Arapaho a man
named Big-Belly imagined himself a deer, and in consequence
of his actions received the name "Deer" (bihii). He had
several attacks of his delusion. The following is a translation
of an account by an eye-witness.

"*Deer* went hunting. Accidentally he came to a pretty
woman. She was completely dressed in deer-skin. Straightway he wanted to court her, when he saw the woman. She
motioned to him to approach. 'Well, I will have you for
sweetheart,' *Deer* said to her. 'And yourself do so' (please
yourself), she said to him. Then he went to her. He was
just going to touch her — to his surprise, she gave the cry of a
deer, suddenly jumped, and ran off, looking backwards. Then
he saw her to be a deer. Then *Deer* was ashamed at being
deceived from desire to make love. Then he went back because he was ashamed. Some time afterwards *Deer* became
like a deer. In the middle of the camp-circle *Deer* was chased
like a deer; like a deer he cried, like a deer he leaped, like a
deer he fled on the open prairie; all pursued him. When
they caught him, his eyes looked different. *Deer* had his
mouth open; all held him. At last he ceased being a deer.
For this he is named *Deer*."

Intoxicants seem to have been lacking formerly; but it is

said that when there was a thunderstorm, some people set
out buckets and vessels, and drank the water caught
in them. This water was powerful, and made them
foolish. Of late years the mescal (peyote) worship
has spread among some of the Arapaho. The effects
of this plant are, however, not strictly intoxicating.
It is eaten only in connection with the religious cult,
and occasionally as medicine.

Smoking the pipe plays as large a part in the life
of the Arapaho as among other Prairie tribes. Their
most sacred tribal object is a pipe, that, according
to their cosmology, was one of the first things that
existed in the world. The Gros Ventres had several
such sacred pipes. A man who had eloped
with a woman, and wished to become
reconciled with her husband, sent him
hounaçaniitcaa^n ("a pipe of settlement")
by an old man, together with presents.
When the Arapaho made peace and friendship with the Pawnees and Osages, a pipe
was used in the peace ceremonial.

Pipes are generally of red catlinite and
of the forms usual among the Plains
tribes. Sometimes black stone is used,
especially for small pipes. The wooden
stem is more frequently round than of
the flat shape usual among the Sioux. A
small straight or tubular pipe is shown in
Fig. 1. This is made of the leg-bone of an
antelope. The tobacco is pressed into the
larger end. In one place the bone is
wrapped with a tendon. This was said
to have been put there in order to prevent
the heat from going to the mouth. The
sacred pipe of the tribe is also tubular,
seeming to be made of a piece of black and
a piece of white stone; but it is called
"flat pipe" (säeitcaa^n).

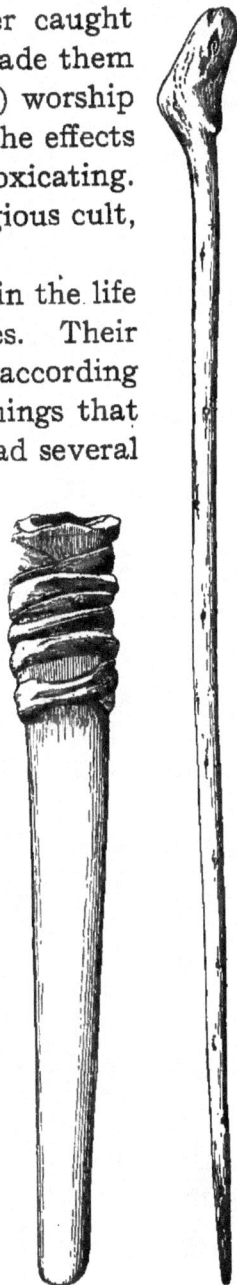

Fig. 1.   Fig. 2.

Fig 1 ($\frac{12}{100}$). Tubular Pipe. Length, 19 cm.

Fig. 2 ($\frac{12}{100}$). Pipe-stoker. Length, 51 cm.

A stick for stoking pipes is shown in Fig. 2. Its end is flat, and is said to represent a duck's bill.

The following is told about the origin of tobacco. Before the fifth (or present) life (generation, or period of the world), cottonwood-bark, buffalo-dung, and dried meat were used as tobacco. Then an old man obtained tobacco supernaturally. He cut it up fine, put it into a pouch, and threw it behind him. Thus he gave it to others.

Fans made of an eagle-wing are used by old men very frequently. Younger men sometimes have fans made of the tail-feathers of hawks or eagles. Such fans are also used in the peyote worship.

Old men use their eagle-wing fans for the good of all (the tribe). They use them as shades for the eyes when they cannot see very well. With them they also drive away flies, brush off dust, fan themselves when sweating, and pat themselves when they have had enough to eat. They have been used since Clotted-Blood (a mythical character) gave one to his father.

Eagles were caught, as among the Blackfoot and other tribes, by a man concealed in a pit covered with brush, on which meat was placed. Only certain men could hunt the eagle. For four days they abstained from food and water. They put medicine on their hands. In four days they might get fifty or a hundred eagles. A stuffed coyote-skin was sometimes set near the bait.

In hunting deer, calls are used. These are made either of wood or of a bone whistle like those used in ceremonials.

The following account of buffalo-hunting was given by an old man.

Bows and arrows were made by the man who was the father of the mythical twins (boyish monster-destroyers, who are the heroes of a myth called "Tangled-Hair"). This was the first bow and arrow. Hāⁿxäbi'nää (one of the twins), when blown away by the whirlwind, was found in the rushes and called Biaxuyā'n ("found in the grass"). He caused the buffalo to come out of a hole in the ground. When he was about to do this, the people made a strong corral of timber; into this he called the buffalo. The last one of the herd he shot with an arrow just at the opening of the corral, and gave it to his father-in-law. It was the ambition of a young man to make presents of this kind to his father-in-law. The people killed the rest of the buffalo. After they began to butcher them, it was found to be best to slit the belly lengthwise, and then to strip back the flanks without cutting them across. Women now began to make wooden pegs for stretching hides. The best tools and methods of work were discovered only by trial.

When the Arapaho were near the Rocky Mountains, they used snow-shoes for hunting buffalo in winter, when the snow was deep. These snow-shoes were oval and without a point. They were woven of strings of hide, like the netted hoops used to play with. The meat of a buffalo that was killed was packed into the hide, and thus dragged home over the snow.

If old men are smoking together, and a young man by mistake enters the tent, they say, "What are you doing here? You ought to be hunting." Then the young man goes out quickly.

People often went to war because they preferred to be killed in war and leave a good name rather than die old. When a war-party returned victoriously and without losses, they painted themselves black.

When the Sioux introduced the Omaha dance, they brought a bundle of sticks, cloth, etc., called tceäk'çaⁿ. This is a sign of friendship. If any tribe refuses it, they will surely be beaten in war by those who offer it. In recounting deeds of war (as is frequently done on ceremonial or social occasions), men told the truth, because if they lied they would surely be killed by the enemy. They even declined coups (blows struck an enemy, a high honor) that were mistakenly ascribed to them by others. Two men once found a (dead) Ute. There was question between them as to who was to strike him first. They pressed each other to take the honor of the first blow. One finally consented. Then they found the body already decomposed, and hence could not lay claim to having counted coup.

Property was formerly transported on dog-travois. Two

poles were harnessed to a dog, the lower ends dragging on the ground. The two poles were connected by sticks or slats, on which the load was packed. Later, horse-travois were made. These have now gone out of use among the Arapaho, but are sometimes used by the Gros Ventres, who lash a loosely netted frame to the two poles. Among the Assiniboine even dog-travois are still used (1901) by old people. The Arapaho had light cages of willows in which children were transported on travois. There is still a tradition of the time before there were horses. Some say that horses were first obtained from the whites, some that wild horses were caught. Dogs were not used for hunting.

Knives were formerly made of a narrow piece of the shoulder-blade of a buffalo, or of flint. For handles, the spines of buffalo vertebræ were used. Large tendons were used to wrap together blade and handle. As this became dry, it contracted. Hide-scrapers had their blades fastened in the same way to a handle made of the spine of a buffalo vertebra; or sometimes the blade was inserted in a slit in the handle. When bone knives were worn down, they were used for awls.

Fire was made by striking two stones together. Subsequently a piece of steel was used with flint. For tinder, dry, pithy cottonwood was used, which was kept in a horn. The fire-drill was also known. It was rubbed by hand. Sticks of siitcinãwaxu, a plant or shrub growing on the prairie, were used because very hard. The point had three sides. Buffalo-dung was used for tinder.

Bows are said sometimes to have been backed with five strips or layers of sinew; when made of cedar, they were covered with sinew on both sides. Iron for arrows and spear-points was first obtained from the Mexicans. Native copper was not used. There were some arrows with detachable fore-shafts or heads made of bone. Arrow-points, usually of flint, were sometimes made from the last rib of a buffalo. The bow and arrow are said to have been invented by the man who made the first knives; also by the father of the mythical twin monster-destroyers.

When a young man wants arrows, he secures the materials

for making them, provides food, and invites old men to his
tent.   These come and remain all day.   One makes points,
one feathers the shafts, one paints them, and so on.   Meanwhile they tell stories of war or of the buffalo-hunt, according
to the purpose for which the young man is to use the arrows.
They make six or twelve arrows, all painted with the same
marks.   The old man who does the painting shows the marks
to all the others, so that there can be no dispute as to the
ownership of the arrows.   Were any one else ever to claim
this young man's arrow as his own, the old men would recognize the marks, and settle the dispute.

In the time when old men wore their hair drawn in a bunch
over the forehead (*i. e.*, in the traditional, not mythic past),
baskets of flexible fibre were made.   They were used as
trays.   Some, more finely woven, and covered with pitch
inside, were used for drinking.   At present small trays of
coiled basketry are sometimes used for throwing dice.

Pottery was formerly made of mud (clay?) mixed with a
little white sand.   Several pieces were made and joined together until a round vessel was formed.   This was then
baked in the fire.   Another informant stated that to make
pottery, stone was pounded fine, and mixed with clay.   This
was worked by hand, just as a swallow builds its nest, until
a large vessel was made.   This was heated to make it hard.
Some vessels were merely dried.   The vessels were of various
sizes, and were used for cooking.   This art must have completely gone out of practice some time ago, as no traces of it
remain.   One old man denied that the Arapaho ever made
pottery.

Meat was boiled in rawhide.   A hole was made in the
ground, and rawhide pressed down into it, its edges being
weighted down with stones.   The sack-like rawhide was then
filled with water, which was made to boil by means of heated
stones.   Plates were made of rawhide.   Rawhide was used to
pound dried meat on.   Bowls were made of knots of cotton-
wood-trees.   A spherical knot was cut in halves, and then
hollowed out.   Spoons, as well as cups, were made of the
horns of mountain-sheep.

Several tools are in use for dressing skins. A chisel-shaped flesher (now generally made of iron, originally of a buffalo leg-bone) is used to clean the inner surface of hides from fat and flesh. If the hair is to be removed, which is almost always the case unless a blanket is being made, an instrument made of elk-antler is used. The end of this extends at right angles to the handle, and is provided with a metal blade. This instrument is at times made of wood, but then has exactly the shape of those made of antler. With this instrument the hair is cut from the skin with little difficulty. Sometimes a stone hammer is used to pound the hairy side of the skin until the hair comes off. With the elk-antler scraper the hide is generally thinned down more or less, the surface being flaked or planed off. All hides used for clothing are thinned to a certain extent. The scrapings obtained in this process are sometimes eaten. The elk-horn scrapers are usually marked with a number of parallel scratches or lines, which are a record of the ages of the children of the woman who owns the scraper. One woman kept count of the number of hides she had dressed with her instrument. Twenty-six scratches denoted so many buffalo-skins; forty small brass nails driven into the back of the instrument at the bend, signified forty skins of other animals that she had worked. These scrapers are sometimes used for digging roots.

After the hair has been removed, the skin is stretched on the ground by means of pegs, and dried until stiff, if rawhide is to be made. If soft hide is desired, as for clothing, the skin is soaked and then scraped or rubbed with a blunt edge until it is dry. Now, pieces of tin, whose scraping edge is slightly convex, are generally used for this purpose; formerly bone, horn, and perhaps stone, seem to have been used. Another form of scraper for softening or roughening hide consists of a slightly curved stick of wood a foot long; in the middle of the concave side of this is a metal blade. The whole object somewhat resembles a draw-knife. This instrument is used more particularly on buckskin, which is hung on an upright post or stick. A scraper of this kind is shown in Fig. 3. It has carved upon it in outline the figure of a deer viewed from the front. On the other side of the handle is a similarly carved figure of an antelope. The lines representing the flanks of the two animals are run into each other along the two sides of the handle. Buffalo-hides are also softened by being drawn over a rope, twisted of sinew, about one-third of an inch thick.

The Arapaho say that formerly the men parted their hair on each side; while in the middle, over the forehead, they left it standing upright. Over the temples it was cut into a zigzag edge. In front of the ears, the hair fell down; it was either braided or tied together. The hair was worn upright over the forehead in order to make the wearer look fierce. When the Arapaho adopted the present style of wearing the hair (braids or masses tied together over the ears, and the scalp-lock in the middle of the back of the head), the Crees, Shoshone, and other tribes adopted their old style. Some formerly tied all their hair together in a bunch at the back of the head. Very old men did not comb their hair; they rolled it, and, when it was sticky and matted, gathered it into a bunch over the forehead. "Our father directed that old men should do this," they said. Among the Gros Ventres, the keepers of the sacred pipes were not allowed to comb or cut their hair.

For women the old way was to wear the hair loose, with paint upon it. They painted streaks down their faces, on cheeks, forehead, and nose. This signified war. Old women wore their hair loose and generally tangled. They painted a spot on each cheek-bone, and one on the forehead. A spot between the eyes signified a buffalo calf, and a line from the mouth down

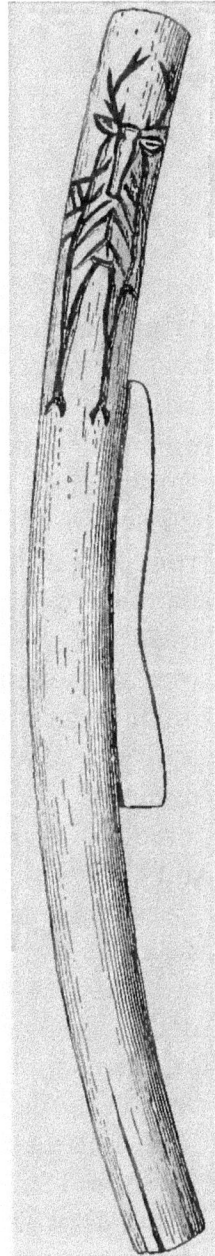

Fig. 3 ($\frac{50}{17}$). Skin scraper. Length, 39 cm.

the chin represented a road. This whole painting signified peace. Nowadays women wear two braids of hair from behind their ears, the hair being parted from forehead to nape; old women often wear their hair loose.

The face is painted in ceremonials regularly, almost always when any actions are performed that have any connection with what is supernatural, and often for decoration. Black is the paint to indicate victory. Of other colors, red is far the most frequently used. Old people confine themselves to red exclusively, so that red paint is often symbolic of old age. Paint on the face in general signifies happiness or wish for happiness. Mourners do not paint. Their first painting after the completion of mourning is with red, and is called "washing" or "cleansing." The paint along the part of the hair of both men and women is called "the path of the sun."

The dress of men consisted of a shirt, leggings reaching from the ankles to the hips, breech-cloth, moccasins, and a blanket of buffalo-skin. The women wore an open-sleeved dress not reaching the ankles, moccasins to which leggings were attached that extended to the knee, and a blanket. Small boys often wore nothing or only a shirt. One and the same word denotes the man's shirt and the woman's dress,—biixū'ut. The skin blankets were either painted or embroidered. There is a similarity between the designs on blankets and those on tents, bedding, and cradles.

Sewing was done with needles and awls of bone, and thread of shreds of dried sinew. Needles and awls are now of steel, but sinew is still mostly used for thread. Embroidery formerly consisted chiefly of colored and flattened porcupine-quills sewed firmly on the surface to be decorated. The quills were softened in the mouth and flattened with a bone. A dark fibrous water-plant was used to embroider in black. These materials, while still in use, have been largely replaced by small glass beads of many different colors. The quills are kept in pouches of gut, which they cannot penetrate (Plate x). The women have work-bags (Plate xv) in which they keep awls, sinew, quills, needles, bones for quill-flattening and for painting, incense, paint, medicine, and similar miscellaneous articles.   A bone used for flattening porcupine-quills and for painting skins is shown in Fig. 4.   It is said to represent a person.   The notches cut into the edges denote the age of a previous owner of the instrument.

The following are statements of an old woman.   When an inexperienced person tries for the first time to do quill-embroidery, failure ensues.   The points of the quills stick out, and the whole embroidery becomes loose.   When she was young, she once helped other women to embroider a robe.   She had never done this before.   The line of embroidery which she was working was spoiled, the quills would not stay fast, and the other women refused to work with her.   She arose and prayed that she might be able to work successfully, and said that she would make a whole robe in this style of embroidery.   An old woman who was present said that this was good.   After this the quills remained fast, and she was able to embroider.

A woman, thought to be the oldest woman in the Oklahoma portion of the tribe, kept a small stick with thirty notches.   These represented thirty robes that she had made in her lifetime.   She said that the usual buffalo-robe had twenty lines of quill-embroidery across it, and was called niisaⁿûxt. There were seventeen lines, and then three more close together along the bottom of the robe.   The lines were ordinarily yellow.   She made one robe with white quill-work, to signify old age.   The lines were formerly not made of red quills (as in some modern robes of children).   Only certain portions of designs on the lines were red.   Sometimes these were green instead of red.   Fifty small dew-claws of the buffalo were hung as pendants or rattles along the lower edge of a twenty-lined robe.   If the robe had only seventeen lines of quill-embroidery, forty hoof-pendants were attached.   She had made a robe for every member of her family but one.   Whenever she made and gave away a robe,

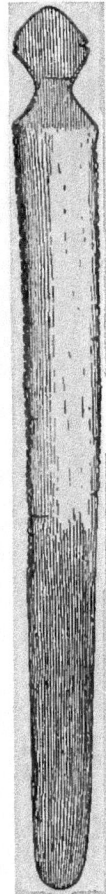

Fig. 4 ($\frac{1}{2}$).
Quill-flattener.
Length, 22 cm.

she received a horse for it.   She once began a robe with one
hundred lines (bătăăt°saⁿûxt), to be given to Left-Hand.
She had marked one hundred and worked thirty when her
son-in-law died.   She buried the robe with him.   Later she
learned that it was not right to bury this highest kind of
robe with any one.   It gives her vigor now to think of her
past life and what she has accomplished.

There are seven sacred bags owned by old women.   These
contain incense, paint, and implements for marking and sewing.   They are painted red, and kept wrapped.   They correspond to seven sacred bags kept by seven old men, and
containing rattles, paint, and perhaps other objects.   These
women's bags are used in ornamenting buffalo-robes and
tents, when certain ceremonies are gone through.

The following account was obtained from an old woman
who possessed one of the sacred bags.

"Backward, the mother of Little-Raven, was the owner of
my bag before it was transferred to me.   This bag was owned
successively by Night-Killer, Bihiihă ('Female Deer'?), Backward, and myself.   When I was about to obtain this bag, I
provided food, clothing, and horses (to be given away), and
called all the old women who then had bags.   There were
seven.   They were River-Woman, Large-Head, Thread-
Woman, Sore-Legs, Flying-Woman, another Thread-Woman,
and Backward.   A tent was put up.   The clothing was laid
all around the inside of the tent, the food was set near the
fire.   I also provided four knives and some fat.   The seven
old women sat around the tent, each with her bag.   I went
to each in turn, putting my hand on the top of her head, and
prayed.   I said that I wished to get a bag in the straight way.
Before they opened their bags they spit hăçawaanaxu on
them (this is a root which is chewed fine, and usually spit on
sacred objects before they are handled).   Then incense was
burned.   One of the women took fat and rubbed it with
paint; then, holding her hands palm to palm, and turning
them from side to side, she painted four spots on my face, and
a fifth (in the centre) on the nose; then she painted five spots
in similar position (that of a quincunx) on the top of my head.

The food had been placed southwest, northwest, northeast, and southeast of the fire (the tent always faces east, the fire being in the centre).   The food towards the southwest was taken up, carried around the tent, and set down in the same place as before, in front of one of the old women.   This woman then carried the other food around the tent in the same way, re-placing it all.   Then she took hăçawaanaxu, chewed it, and rubbed it over her body (a very frequent act in rituals).   Then she took food from four dishes and placed it on her hand in five spots.   Two of these pieces or heaps of food she placed on the ground, southwest and northwest of the fire; two she raised and laid on the ground, northeast and southeast of the fire; and the fifth she put into the fire.   Then she took (a dish of) blood-soup or pudding (bääk"). She touched it with a finger, touched this finger on the palm of her hand, and rubbed her hands together.   Then she moved her hands downward four times towards the southeast of the tent, repre-senting the planting in the ground of a tent-pole there.   Then she touched the pudding in three other places, after each time rubbing her hands, and successively motioning towards the southwest, northwest, and northeast.   The fifth time she made a scoop in the middle of the pudding; this she followed by motioning lower down, towards the pegs holding the edge of the tent.   While she was doing this, the others looked down, holding their left hand on the top of the head, the right hand on the ground.   A small dog had been cooked whole.   Backward took the dog by the head, and I took its hind-end, and we walked around the tent.   We walked around again, stopping on the southeast side and making a turn there, and then the same successively at the southwest, northwest, and northeast (i. e., going in a circle with the sun).   Then we made a turn before the door (inside the tent), and held the dog outside the door, moving its head, and telling it to look about at the people, the clothing, the food, the water, and so on.   Then we took pieces of meat from its four paws, its nose, the top of its head, and its tail, and put them on the ground four times, and a fifth time into the fire.   Then Backward [1]

---

[1] Possibly it was not Backward, but the narrator herself, who performed this action.

took the dog's tongue, and, holding it at the tip, touched one side of it, and then the other, to the ground at the southeast, southwest, northwest, and northeast successively; and at last, with a downward movement, touched the tongue against the wooden pins fastening the front of the tent above the door. Then the food was eaten. A dish standing southeast from the fire was first taken and passed to each in the tent, travelling in a circle; then the food at the southwest was taken; and so on around the fire until all the food had been passed around. Then friends were called, and the remnants given to them. After the dishes and plates had been taken out of the tent, incense was again burned inside. Then Backward told me to give her the four knives, and a board on which to cut medicine. I took niibaa^{n}tou (hemlock-leaves) and niisêna^n (part of a beaver) and cut them fine. Backward took biihtceihina^n (a yellow composita) and niäätä^n (a greasy carrot-like root) and cut them up together. The rest cut up and mixed niôx^u (sweet-grass) with niisêna^n, and niäätä^n with niisêna^n. This made four kinds of incense. Then Backward, with a spoon of mountain-sheep horn, took up the several incenses and put them into the small bags into which they belonged. Again she put incense on the coals. Then they all painted themselves with red paint and tallow. After that they painted their bags: they touched them with their palms in four places, and then in a spot in the middle of these four, and thereupon rubbed the whole bag with paint. They also painted the stones (used for holding coals for incense) and the pieces of bone (used for marking designs on robes) that were in the bags. The latter two incenses are used when a tent is decorated; the former two, with the stones and bones, when a robe is to be made. They replaced all these things in their bags and closed them. Then Backward told me to give her the cloth goods I had provided. I gave them to her. She touched the ground and put her finger to her tongue; then she rubbed me over with medicine from her mouth. She spit medicine on a piece of the goods, and put it under my dress from below, and, passing it under the dress to my other side, took it out there and laid it down. Then she passed another piece under my dress in the opposite direction. She repeated this three times more, so that at the end there were four pieces of goods lying on each side of me (those on one side having been interchanged with those on the other by passing them under the dress). Then she pushed two pieces under my dress on my stomach, and successively placed them below my shoulder, over the heart, and on my stomach again. There she left them. The other goods were given away. Backward told me to leave the pieces of cloth on my stomach for four days, while I fasted; then to prepare food and invite all the old women in again. I fasted and cried for four days; on the fourth, food was prepared, and the old women came again. After they had eaten, I received the bag, with instructions how to use it. Backward made a motion four times to give it to me; then, at a fifth motion with it from her heart, she gave it to me.

"A few days later, Yellow-Woman called me to make a buffalo-robe. The hide was already dressed and prepared. I entered the tent. At the back of the tent lay the buffalo-skin, folded and laid like a buffalo. Its head was toward the door. By it lay five pieces of goods as payment. I sat down at the middle of the back of the tent, behind the buffalo-skin. I told Yellow-Woman to call the other women. After they came, food was taken around (and sacrificed), as at the time when I received my bag. Then we ate, and the remainder was taken out for friends and the children. Then I burned incense. Then two of the women motioned toward the buffalo-skin with sticks, whipping it as if to make a buffalo rise. Then I spread the robe (the hair-side to the ground). I put a burning coal on the ground and placed incense upon it. I spit medicine on one of the marking-bones five times. I held the bone successively on four sides of the coal, near the ground; the fifth time I drew the bone across above the coal, to signify the marking (which is done by drawing the edge of the bone along the hide). Then all came close around the buffalo-robe and held it. Yellow-Woman with the marking-bone drew lines across it, which were to be embroidered with porcupine-quills. In her mouth she had häçawaanaxu, and she wet the end of the bone with saliva. When she had drawn the lines, she raised her right arm. I took the robe and four times I made a motion as if to give it to her; the fifth time I gave it to her, putting it under her arm. Then Yellow-Woman held out her hands, and I spit medicine on them four times. Then I laid on her hands four quills tied together, one each being red, yellow, white, and black; and with them I gave her sinew (thread) and needles. Yellow-Woman passed the quills between her lips, and then held them in her mouth. Then she began to embroider one line, beginning nearest the head of the skin. I watched her and gave her directions. When she had completely embroidered this line, she stopped. After this, one line was embroidered a day. It took a month to complete the robe. A line of embroidery must not be left unfinished over night. When the robe was completed, Yellow-Woman notified me. She invited me to come the next day to eat. The next day there was a feast like that given when the robe was begun. The robe was set up again to resemble a buffalo, and after being perfumed with incense, was touched as if to make it rise. Then it was spread out and five feathers laid upon it, — one at each corner and one in the centre. Then the women sewed the feathers in those places. Then Yellow-Woman announced the man for whom she had made the robe, and he was sent for. He was Bird-in-Tree. He came in, and sat down in front of me, looking toward the door. Yellow-Woman spit on the blanket four times, moved it toward him several times, then gave it to him. Then both he and the robe were perfumed with incense. Then he gave Yellow-Woman his best horse; she kissed him for it. Then he went out with his new robe.''

This robe made by Yellow-Woman had twenty lines of quill-work. The lowest three, as already described, were close together and somewhat separate from the rest. The lines represented buffalo-paths. The greater part of each of these lines was yellow. On each were three red marks, each of these red lengths being bordered by a shorter white portion, and each of these again being bounded on both sides

by still shorter black marks.   There was thus imposed on the
yellow background of the line an ornament composed of the
successive colors black, white, black, red, black, white, black;
the red being longest and the black areas shortest.   This
same arrangement of the four colors is found in other objects
ornamented in conventional quill-embroidery.   Between these
marks on the lines of this robe there were other smaller
marks in red and black, and in several places small tufts of
red feathers (see Plate xvi).   The four colors of this embroidery, taken collectively, signified the four lives since the
beginning of the world (generations or æons).   From the
lower end of the robe hung fifty pendants, at the ends of
which hung small hoofs, and loops covered with quill-work,
this bearing the same design of black, white, black, red, black,
white, black, that was embroidered on the robe.

The use of these sacred bags and the accompanying ceremonies are also referred to in connection with the tent-decora-
tions on pp. 70 *et seq.*

II.—DECORATIVE ART.

The present chapter is a description of the various objects of Arapaho manufacture and use, omitting, however, all objects whose use is ceremonial or religious. This account will deal largely with the ornamentation of the objects and with the significance attached to this decoration. The interpretation of these symbolic decorations was obtained, in every case dealt with, from the Indians. Almost always the information was secured from the possessor or the maker of the article. The specimens described are now in the American Museum of Natural History.

In the illustrations, colors are indicated by the following devices: red, by close vertical shading; yellow, by light dots; green, by horizontal shading. Light blue is indicated by diagonal shading. Black usually represents dark blue, but sometimes brown, very dark green, dark red, or black. Dark dots indicate orange.

Plate 1 is arranged to show the conventionality of ornamentation in moccasins. All the moccasins illustrated in this series are embroidered with the same fundamental decorative motive, — a longitudinal stripe extending from instep to toe. It will be seen that in this series of eight moccasins only three other decorative elements are used; and these, moreover, are similar to the fundamental element, in that they also are stripes, and bear a definite spatial relation to it, being either parallel or at right angles to it. These three elements are a transverse stripe at the instep, two short bars approximately parallel to the main central stripe, and a transverse stripe bisecting and duplicating this main stripe.

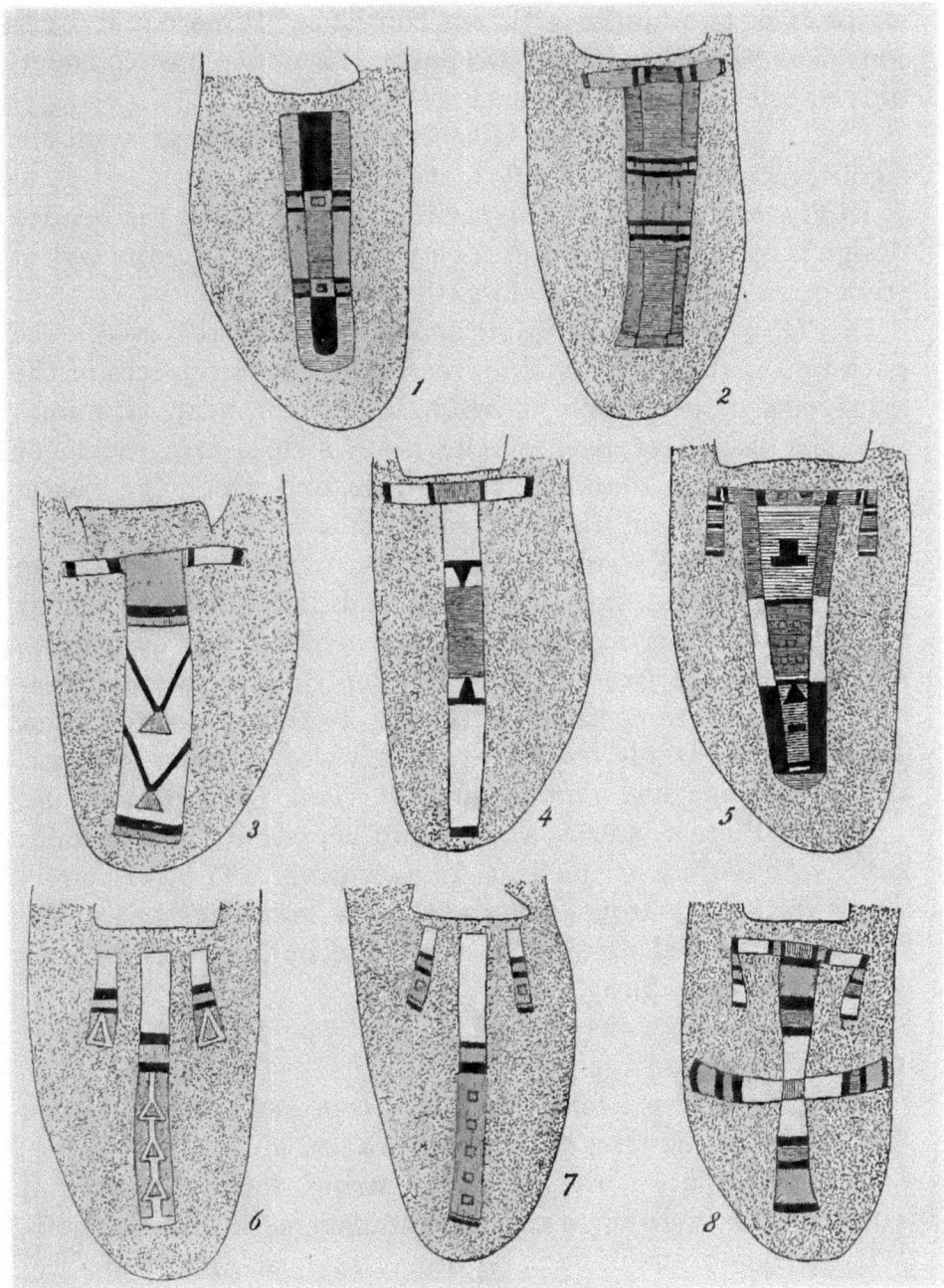

DESIGNS ON MOCCASINS.

The last element occurs only once (Fig. 8).[1] The longitudinal stripe is of two kinds: either it consists of three equal divisions or sections; or it has two parts, the upper one considerably shorter than the lower (Figs. 3, 6, 7).

Fig. 1 of Plate 1 shows a moccasin as to whose symbolic significance there is no information.[2]

In Fig. 2 of Plate 1 all the small stripes of which the beaded design is composed, whether their direction be longitudinal or transverse, represent buffalo-paths.

In Fig. 3 of the same plate the large stripe represents the path that is travelled (by the wearer). The two pieces of the transverse stripe (which, it will be noted, duplicate in miniature the design of part of the main stripe) are insects or worms which are found on the prairie, and which the wearer desired not to be in his path, but beside it. The upper portion of the large stripe is light blue, which signifies (as in many other cases) haze. The red and dark blue bands that edge the white portion of the stripe represent day and night. Red and black, or red and blue, frequently have this signification, both in ceremonial objects and in others not used thus. The winged triangle, which appears twice, signifies sunrise, also the passage over a mountain. It is called bāāeikŏtaha'ûû.

Fig. 4, Plate 1, shows a moccasin representing a buffalo-hunt. The white stripe is a buffalo-path. The green rectangle in this represents a buffalo. The two black triangular figures are barbed arrows shot into the buffalo. The transverse stripe is a bow.

As to the moccasins shown in Figs. 5 and 6 of this plate, information is wanting.

In Fig. 7, Plate 1, all the stripes represent buffalo-paths. The small blue squares are buffalo-tracks.

In Fig. 8, Plate 1, the two large stripes form a cross, and represent the morning star. The transverse line is the horizon. The two small bars represent rays of light from the star; i. e., its twinkling.

---

[1] Plate 1 is here repeated for the convenience of the reader.
[2] This moccasin, together with those shown in Plate 1, Fig. 6, and in text Fig. 5, a and c, was secured for the Museum by Rev. Walter C. Roe.

Fig. 5 shows another series of moccasins. The decorative motive which these all have in common is a border of bead-work around the edge of the foot. All but one (*a*) also possess the longitudinal stripe just described. This moccasin

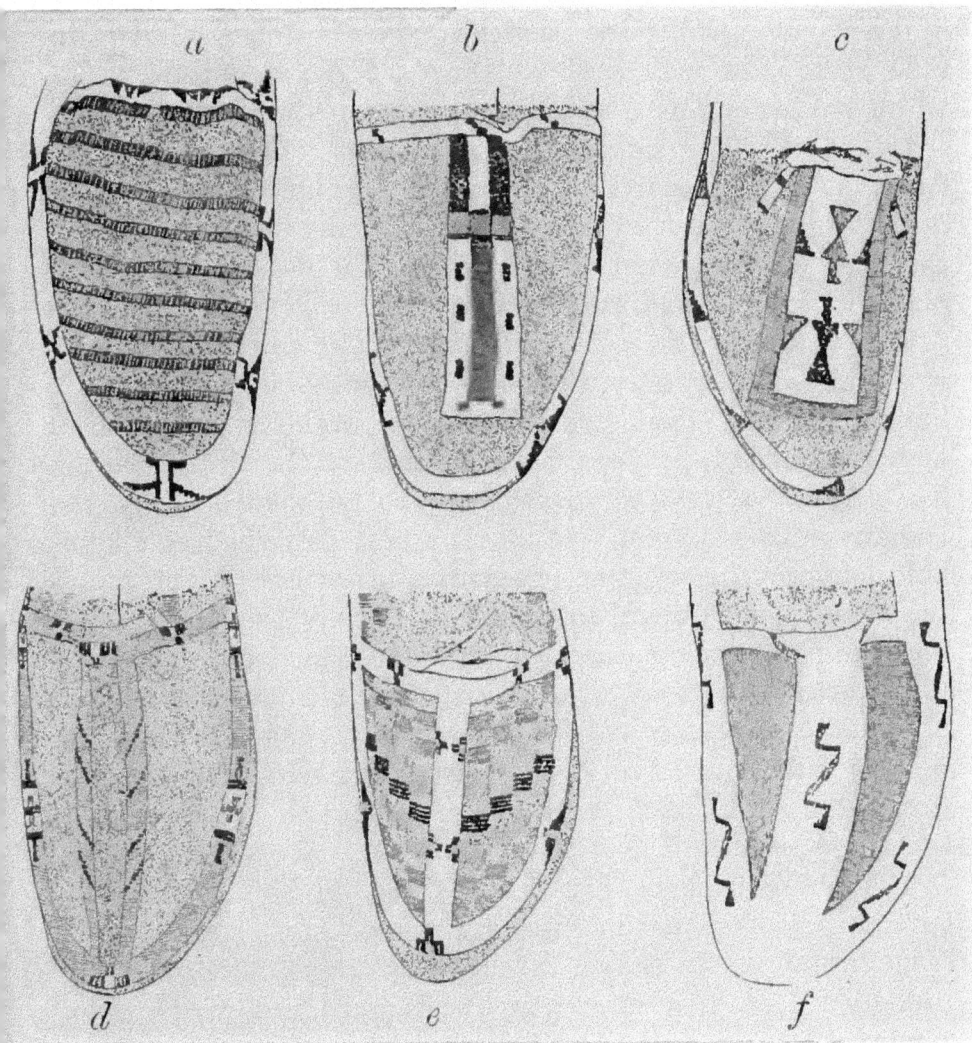

Fig. 5.   Designs on Moccasins.   *a* ($\frac{1}{5708}$), *b* ($\frac{50}{985}$), *c* ($\frac{1}{5780}$), *d* ($\frac{50}{888}$), *e* ($\frac{50}{827}$), *f* ($\frac{50}{1082}$).

has the entire area that is enclosed by the border, traversed by lines of red porcupine-quill embroidery. Information as to the meaning of this design is lacking.

On the moccasin shown in Fig. 5, *b*, the longitudinal stripe signifies häⁿçaeixaaⁿtin (the path to destination).

A small stripe at the heel of the moccasin (not shown in the figure) signifies the opposite idea, häät'xa'nin (whence one has come). The variety of colors in the large stripe represents the variety of things (which naturally are of many different colors) that one desires to possess. The small dark-blue rectangles are symbols that are called hiiteni. The white border of this moccasin, on account of its color, represents snow. The figures in it represent hills with upright trees. The stripe over the instep signifies "up hill and down again" (its middle portion being elevated above the ends by the instep of the foot). The dots in this stripe represent places left bare by melting snow.

The writer is unable to give the exact meaning of the word hiiteni, mentioned above. This symbol is said to signify life, abundance, food, prosperity, temporal blessings, desire or hope for food, prayer for abundance, or the things wished for. All these related ideas seem to be identified by the Indians in this symbol. It may be best described as a symbol of happy life, or, since in Arapaho symbolism the representation of an object or condition usually implies a desire for such object or condition, a symbol of the desire for happy life. Briefly, it may be called a life-symbol, and will be thus designated hereafter. It is the abstract symbol most frequently used, and will be often referred to. Its form is generally a trapezoid, rectangle, or square. A variety of forms is shown in Plates xxix, xxxi, Figs. 237–240, 417–422.

The symbolism in Fig. 5, c, is not known. Birds are evidently represented in the wide stripe.

Of the moccasin shown in Fig. 5, d, the symbolism is also unknown. In this specimen the longitudinal stripe is extended until it meets the border. The stripe, however, is beaded only at its edges, contrary to the style of embroidery in the other cases, and in its middle portion is merely painted red.

In the moccasin shown in Fig. 5, e, there are both the border and the stripe, triangular marks on which represent clouds along the horizon. The open areas are covered by a checker-board design, only every alternate square being

beaded.   This pattern represents the rough surface of buffalo-intestine.   The beads in this pattern are green, blue, and
pink;   these colors represent respectively grass, sky, and
ground.

The moccasin shown in Fig. 5, *f*, is completely beaded.
The border and stripe exist in the application of the beads,
and show in the coloring, being white.   On these white areas
are represented pipes.   The two large triangular areas are red
and green respectively.   Together they represent buffalo-
horns.   The red and green also denote respectively bare
ground (soil) and earth covered with grass; it is on these that
the buffalo walk and trample.   At the heel of the moccasin
(not shown in the figure) is a small square, which represents
a track.   At the instep there is a tongue (also not illustrated),
much like the tongue of a shoe, except that when the moccasin
is worn, the tongue falls over the front of the foot (a similar
tongue is seen in Plate III, Fig. 4).   This tongue is beaded in
light blue with dark-blue spots, is divided or forked, and has
small tin cylinders (rattles) attached to its ends.   It represents a rattlesnake.   The beading is the spotted skin;   the
two parts of the tongue, the forked tongue of the snake;   and
the tin cylinders, its rattle.

Plate II shows several moccasins that are entirely covered
with beads.   All of these except that shown in Fig. 1, the
pattern of which is unusual, are actually embroidered with
the border and the longitudinal stripe, though sometimes, as
in Figs. 2 and 5, these are not visible in the design because
the beads are all of the same color.

In Fig. 1 of Plate II the rows of triangles on the front of
the moccasins represent sharp rocks.   Two rows of alternating red and blue squares are hills.   Three red squares adjacent to each of these rows represent persons sitting on the
hills.   A light-blue line traversing the middle of the front
of the moccasin is a path; small squares adjacent to it are
rocks.   Two small detached bars, one at each side of the
entire design that has thus far been described, represent persons standing.   Along the edge of the sole, flat triangles with
small upright marks at each end, are hills and pines.   Marks

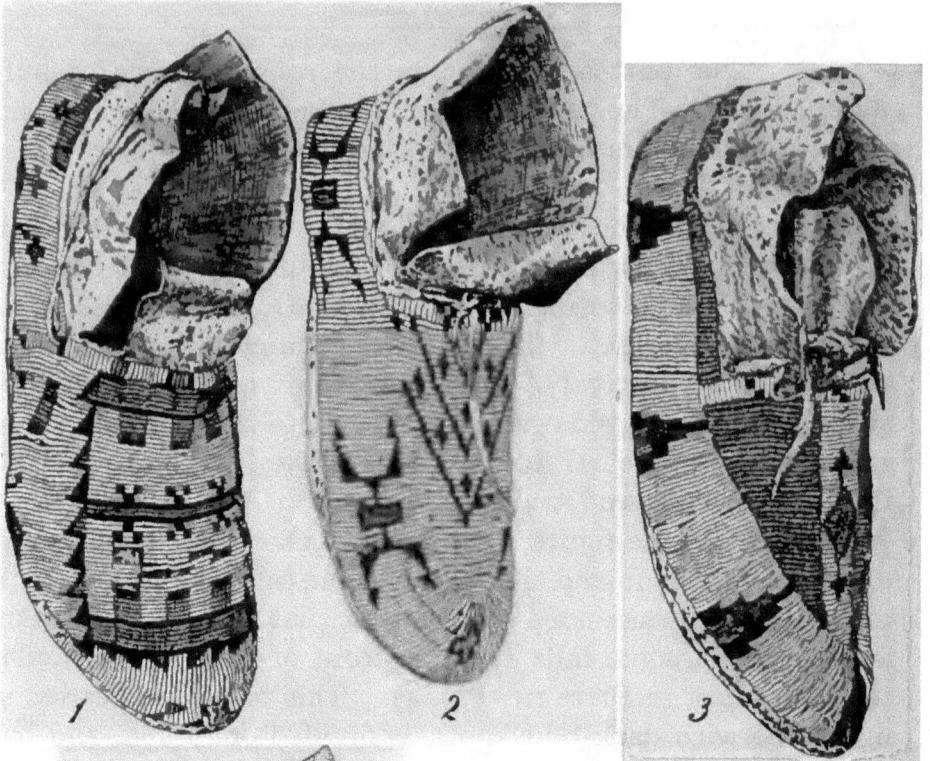

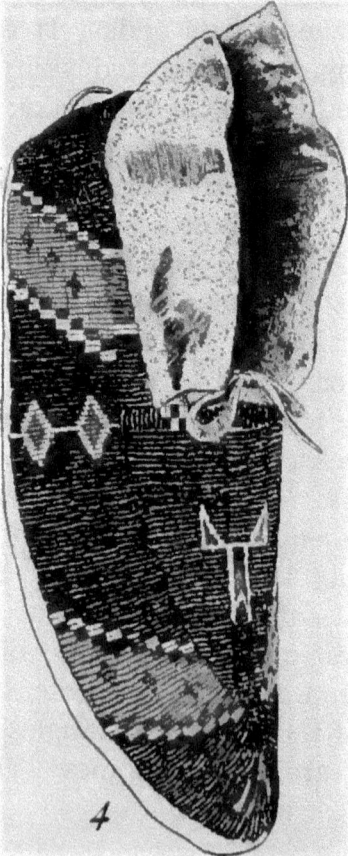

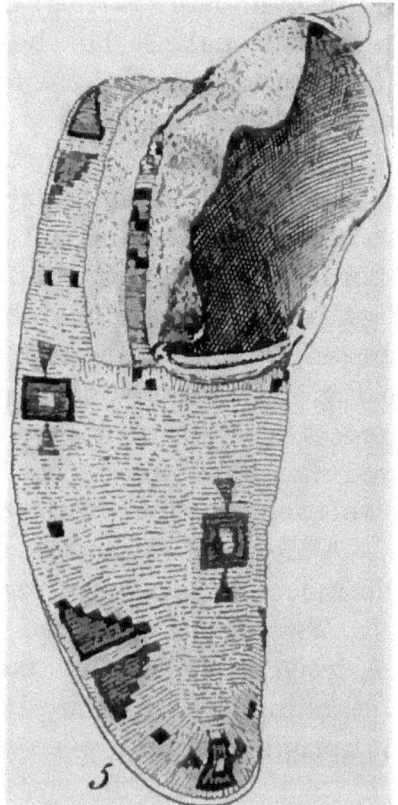

consisting of two triangles touching at their vertices, represent rough places in the path: those that are red denote prominences; those that are blue signify holes. Crosses are the morning star. A horizontal stripe at the heel represents a caterpillar.

On the moccasin shown in Fig. 2 of Plate II the white groundwork of beads represents sand. The parallel angles on the instep of the moccasin are tents. Small rhomboidal marks are stars. At the toe a wide cross is the morning star. At the sides claw-shaped figures represent hakîxta^n (buffalo-hoofs). Between each pair of these figures is a yellow and red rectangle, which represents an eye. Small squares on the transverse stripe at the instep, and at the heel, represent tracks.

On the moccasin shown in Fig. 3 of Plate II the white background represents snow. The dark-blue triangles with squares in them are tents and their doors. The two large, greenish-blue triangular areas on the instep represent lakes. Between them a diamond represents the navel (or perhaps a child's navel-amulet). Triangles at each end of this diamond are arrow-points. A greenish-blue stripe around the ankle represents both smoke and water. Small squares at the instep and at the heel represent tracks.

The moccasin illustrated in Fig. 4 of Plate II is one of the few solidly-beaded Arapaho moccasins of which the ground color is not white. It is a rich blue, and the figures upon it are chiefly pink and red. The blue represents the sky. The large parallelograms are clouds with white edges, piled up one on the other. Red crosses or diamonds in these are stars. Larger, white-edged rhombi in the blue are also stars. A triangle at the toe is a tent. In the middle of the front, a red figure represents a crayfish or scorpion.

Fig. 5 of Plate II shows another solidly-beaded moccasin. Green squares, enclosing a smaller square that is white and red, are life-symbols (hiiteni). Small red triangles in contact with the life-symbols are tents. Small black squares in several places on the white ground are rabbit-tracks in snow. The triangular figures represent seats (çiôku'utaana^n). The stripe around the ankle represents biisäⁿ, any snake or worm. Separate parts of this stripe have other additional significations. The forward portion is yellow, and denotes sunlight. Black squares are again rabbit-tracks. Five red squares in quincunx on a white ground are a turtle. The posterior portion of the stripe is green, and denotes the earth.

Three children's moccasins are shown in the first three figures of Plate III.

In Fig. 1, Plate III, the two lateral convexly triangular areas on the front of the moccasin are green, and represent horse-ears. It may be noted that analogous areas on other moccasins represent buffalo-horns, lakes, and fish. The figure between these two green areas represents a lizard. The head is supposed to be at the toe. Two blue slanting lines are legs. White and yellow spots on the red body are the markings of the animal. Below the ankle, a red stripe with two blue diagonal lines represents a butterfly.

Fig. 2 of Plate III shows a moccasin which is beaded around the edges, but has its front surface traversed by a number of quilled lines (*cf.* Fig. 5, *a*). The white beadwork represents the ground. Green zigzag lines upon it are snakes. The quilled lines represent sweat-house poles. These lines are red, blue, and yellow, and the colors represent stones of different colors, used for producing steam in the sweat-house. At the heel of the moccasin, which is not shown in the figure, are two small green squares. These represent the blankets with which the sweat-house is covered.

The design of a snake was embroidered on this moccasin in order that the child wearing it might not be bitten by snakes. The symbols referring to the sweat-house were embroidered on the moccasin in order that the child might grow to the age at which the sweat-house is principally used; namely, old age.

The moccasin shown in Fig. 3, Plate III, bears a design similar to several that have been described. All the stripes represent paths.

Fig. 4 of Plate III shows an unusually large moccasin. The two large convex, triangular areas on the front are barred

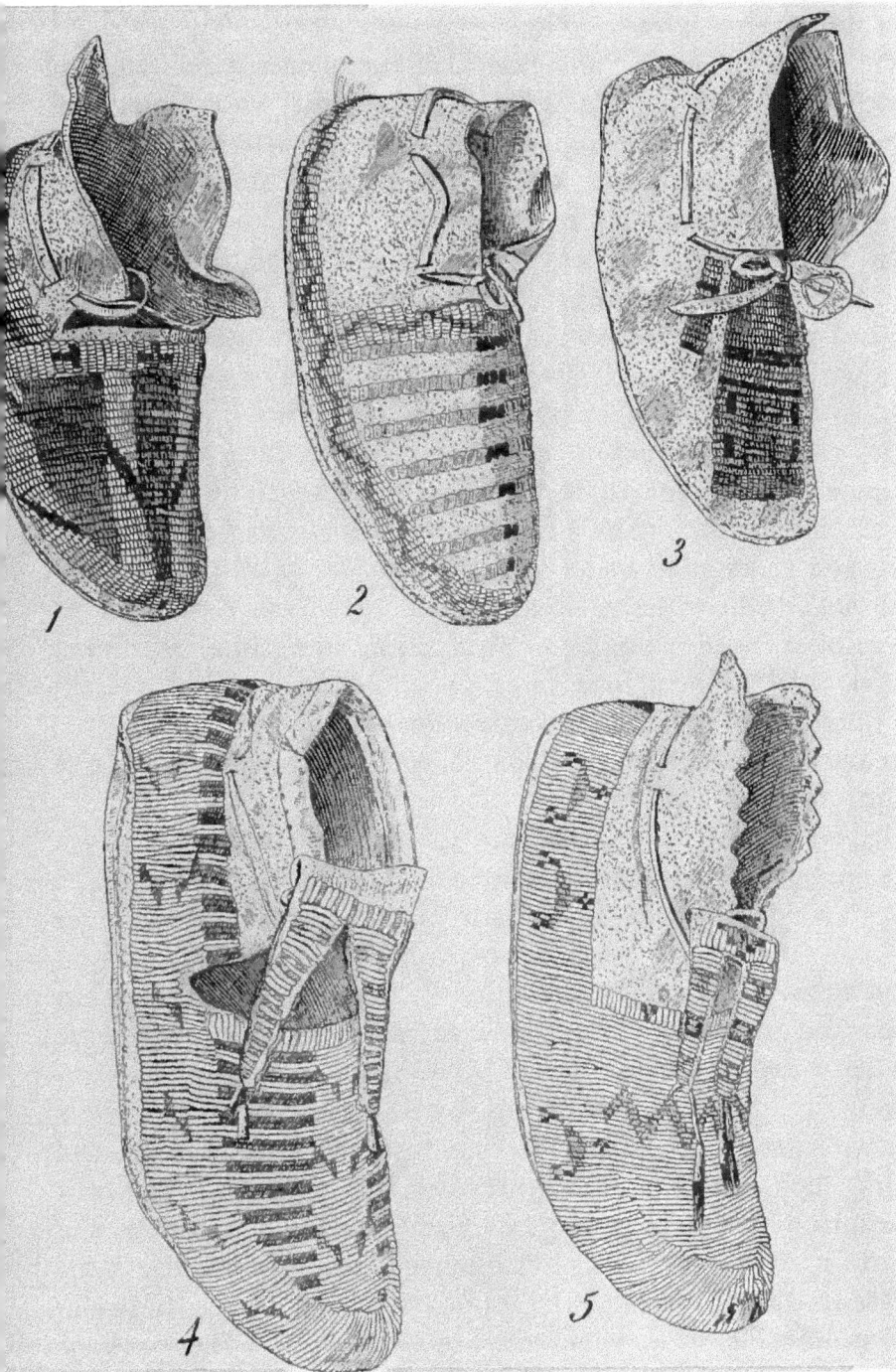

MOCCASINS.

dark blue and white. They represent fish. The similarly barred stripe around the ankle also represents a fish (or the markings on a fish). Small figures, some red, some blue, consisting of a pair of triangles joined at the vertices, represent butterflies. The double tongue over the instep represents a horned toad (*i. e.*, its markings).

On the moccasin shown in Fig. 5 of this plate the zigzag band across the front represents lightning.

What may be considered a typical solidly-beaded moccasin is shown in Plate IV. The white represents snow. The green, both in the triangular areas and in the stripe around the ankle, represents grass-covered earth. The blue and yellow figures consisting of three triangles represent the heart and lungs. The white stripe bisected by two shorter ones, inside the green triangular areas, is a dragon-fly. Groups of three small light-blue squares near the instep were described as halves of stars (five squares in quincunx sometimes represent a star). At the heel, four small green rectangles (invisible in the illustration) represent caterpillars. The design on this moccasin was embroidered as it was previously seen in a dream.

Fig. 6 shows two views of one of the leggings worn by a little girl. The moccasin is attached to the legging. The skin of which the legging is made is painted yellow wherever it is not covered by beads, excepting in the white-bordered stripe running alongside the shin of the leg; in this the skin is painted red. The designs worked on the legging were seen in a dream or vision. This pair of leggings was considered exceptionally handsome by the Arapaho; it always attracted attention at once. The design on each side of the legging, consisting of two connected triangles, represents a mountain with the morning star above it. (The figure of the mountain is symmetrically duplicated, which gives the star, represented by a cross, the appearance of being between two mountains, the upper one inverted.) At the back of the legging the rhombus represents the morning star when it is rising; the two crosses are the morning star when it is high up above the horizon. The contact of the crosses with the

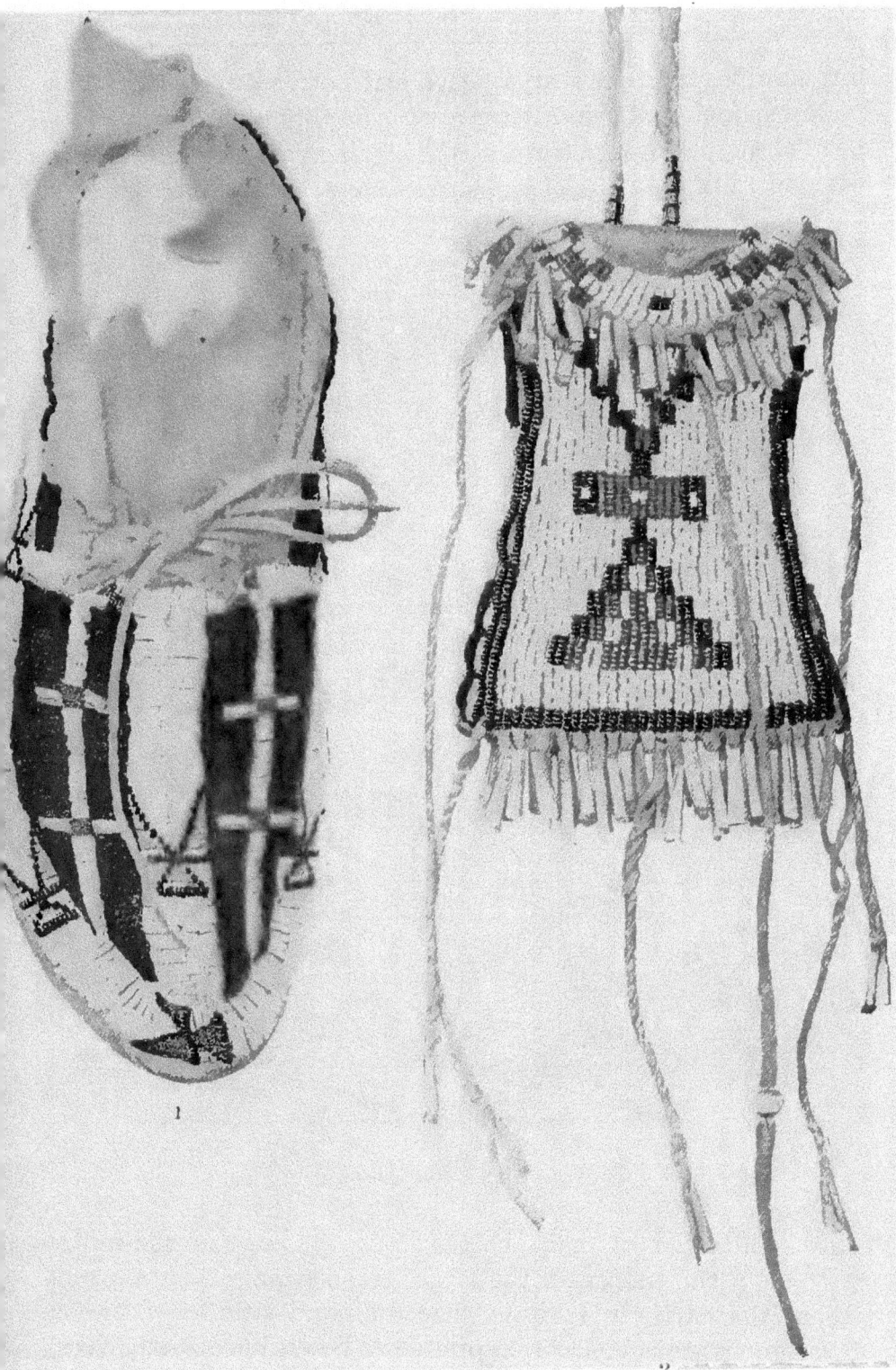

1

2

MOCCASIN AND POUCH.

line signifies that the star appears just before daybreak. The yellow painting of the skin represents daylight. The two white beaded stripes up the front of the legging represent the partly divided milky way. The colored designs in these stripes de-

Fig. 6 (₅₀₁₄). Girl's Leggings.

note small stars of many colors along the edge of the milky way. On the moccasin the large, green triangular areas represent the earth in spring. The diamond situated between these green areas is a star supposed to be visible directly overhead at noon. The six diamonds connected by a line passing

PARTS OF GIRLS' AND WOMEN'S LEGGINGS.

around the edge of the moccasin are a ring of stars, probably the constellation Corona.

Another legging worn by a little girl is shown in Fig. 1 of Plate v. The moccasin has been removed. The design appears twice, once on the vertical band, and again on the horizontal band extending around the ankle. The two rows of small triangles represent ranges of hills. The red stripe along the middle of the white band of beads represents ground. Two green squares in this are springs. Four blue lines issuing from each of these squares are streams flowing from the springs. A small yellow bar bisecting the red stripe is a river; its dark-blue border is timber along its course. A row of green and blue beads along the edges of the legging represents game of various kinds.

Fig. 2 of Plate v shows another girl's legging and moccasin. The three diamonds in the centre of the figure that is on the side of the legging are the life-symbols. Above and below the three diamonds are figures, each consisting of two dark-blue right-angled triangles. These represent deer-tracks. Two similar figures, wider and green in color, touch the middle one of the three diamonds; they represent elk-tracks. This whole design is repeated on the opposite side of the legging. At the back, also invisible in the illustration, is a long red line crossed by nine short lines; this represents a centipede. Along the front of the legging the triangular designs are tents; and the red rectangles, life-symbols. The tin rattles are attached to the legging in order that by their noise they may frighten away insects or snakes that would bite the child wearing the legging. On the lower border of the moccasin are rectangles of red and green beads. These are again life-symbols. This symbol thus has three different forms on one object. Dark-blue triangles, two of which are near each of the life-symbols last mentioned, represent the designs, largely composed of triangles, with which rawhide bags and parfleches are painted. The red lines of quill-work extending across the toe of the moccasin represent the paths of children.

Embroidered portions of girls' and women's leggings are

shown in Figs. 3, 4, 5, of Plate v.   In Fig. 3 the triangles
represent arrow-points.   Those that have three small dark
triangles at their base also represent tents.   The cross is the
morning star. The line with which it is in contact is a path. At
the back of the legging, invisible in the illustration, is a figure
of a buffalo-leg, symmetrically duplicated; the hoof of this resembles the deer-track design on the legging last described.

In Fig. 4, Plate v, the triangles denote tents.   Between
the two triangles on the side of the legging, whose points are
directed toward each other, are two figures which coalesce in
the middle.   These figures represent the hăⁿtcăciihi teihiihaⁿ,
a powerful dwarf cannibal people several times mentioned in
Arapaho myths.   The tents are supposed to belong to them.
The blue bar at the base of the wide vertical stripe of embroidery indicates the range or limit of habitation of the
dwarfs.   The dark Y-shaped marks are horse-tracks; they
imply (in this connection) human beings (as opposed to
monstrous or supernatural people).   At the back of the legging there is a vertical row of these horse-tracks.   The green
beads at the edges of this legging represent vegetation.

In Fig. 5 of Plate v the yellow and green right-angled triangles, each with a small square of the opposite color at the
base, represent tents.   The white stripe dividing them is a
path.   Between the figures of tents, a green and a yellow
isosceles triangle are each a cactus-plant.   The projections
arising from them represent the cactus-spines.   On one of the
figures these projections are red, and therefore represent also
the red edible fruit of the cactus.   This whole design is repeated on the opposite side of the legging.   At the back of
the legging is a vertical row of seventeen (green and red)
isosceles triangles, the base of one resting upon the point of
the next lower one.   These represent ant-hills.   They are not
shown in the illustration.   Along the front of the legging the
flat triangles represent brush-shelters.   The small upright
marks at the ends of each figure are the tent-pegs at the sides
of the shelter.[1]   The rows of beads along the edges of the legging represent animals or variety of game.

---

[1] The brush-shelter is often partially covered with canvas.   Formerly hides were
used for this purpose.   This cover may be pegged down like a tent.

Fig. 7, *a*, represents one of a pair of armlets covered with beadwork. Such armlets or sleeve-holders are generally worn chiefly on gala occasions; that is, at dances. The red and green bisected squares represent black beetles with hard *elytræ*. Small loops of beads along the edge represent worms or maggots. The large beads on the two attached strings rep-

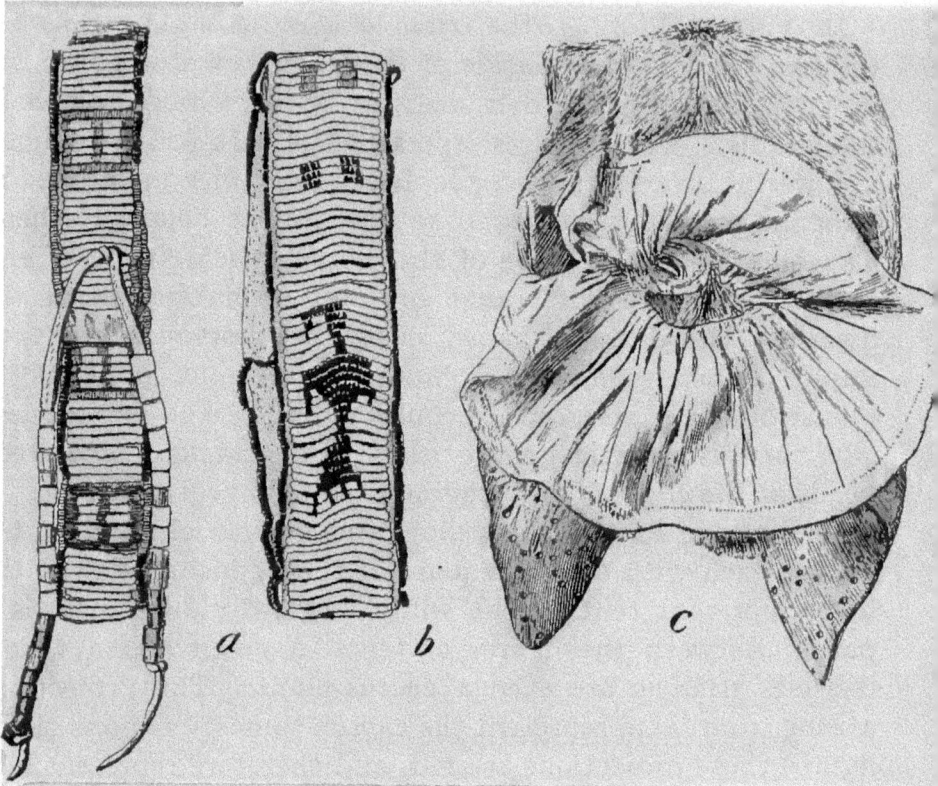

Fig. 7, *a* ($\frac{50}{585}$), *b* ($\frac{50}{1100}$), *c* ($\frac{50}{875}$). Armlets.

resent ants. These various insects were represented because they are constantly moving and crawling, just as the people travelled and roamed over the earth.

One of another pair of armlets is shown in Fig. 7, *b*. The figure of a bird represents both an eagle (on account of the crooked beak) and a swallow (on account of the forked tail). The squares, both blue and red, are stars. The white ground-work of beads represents haze or smoke; the blue beading at the edge represents clouds or the sky.

Fig. 7, c, shows an unembroidered armlet, made of the skin from an elk-foot. A round piece of green cloth attached to the skin represents the sun. The two pieces of hoof represent the long, curving nails of old persons. The small holes in these hoofs represent the various things possessed by the owner of this armlet. These holes also have another signification: those around the edges of the hoofs denote stars; and five holes in quincunx in the middle of each hoof represent (the five fingers of) the hand, which is symbolically equivalent to possession of property.

One of a pair of red quill-embroidered armlets is shown in Fig. 1 of Plate vi. It was worn in the ghost-dance. The black squares represent buffalo. The red quill-wound strings falling from the armlet are kakau'çetcana^n (thoughts, reason, imagination, hope, desires, or anything mental). The ornaments at their ends represent näii'täte'ihi (fulfilment of desire).

Fig. 2 of Plate vi shows a woman's ghost-dance armlet, embroidered with yellow quill-work. The bird embroidered in green quills represents a magpie. The red cross is the morning star. The red rectangle is the symbol of life. The fringe of green-dyed buckskin represents rays of light, and (on account of its color) the earth. The attached magpie-feathers represent persons (presumably spirits); and small yellow plumes attached to these represent the sun.

Fig. 3 of Plate vi shows a head-dress. It consists of a small hoop wound with yellow quills. Two owl-feathers are attached to it. It is worn on the side of the head. The circular quill-wrapped portion with four black spots on it represents a sun-dog.

A peculiar head-dress, which is found among many of the Plains tribes, consists of a strip of skin, measuring about two inches by eight, which is covered with beads or quills, and has various strings or appendages attached to it. It is worn hanging from the scalp-lock, at the back of the head. Among the Arapaho, a horse-tail is generally attached to the lower end of this head-dress. It is worn by young men on festive occasions and at ceremonials at which uniform regalia are not prescribed. Many of these head-dresses represent animals.

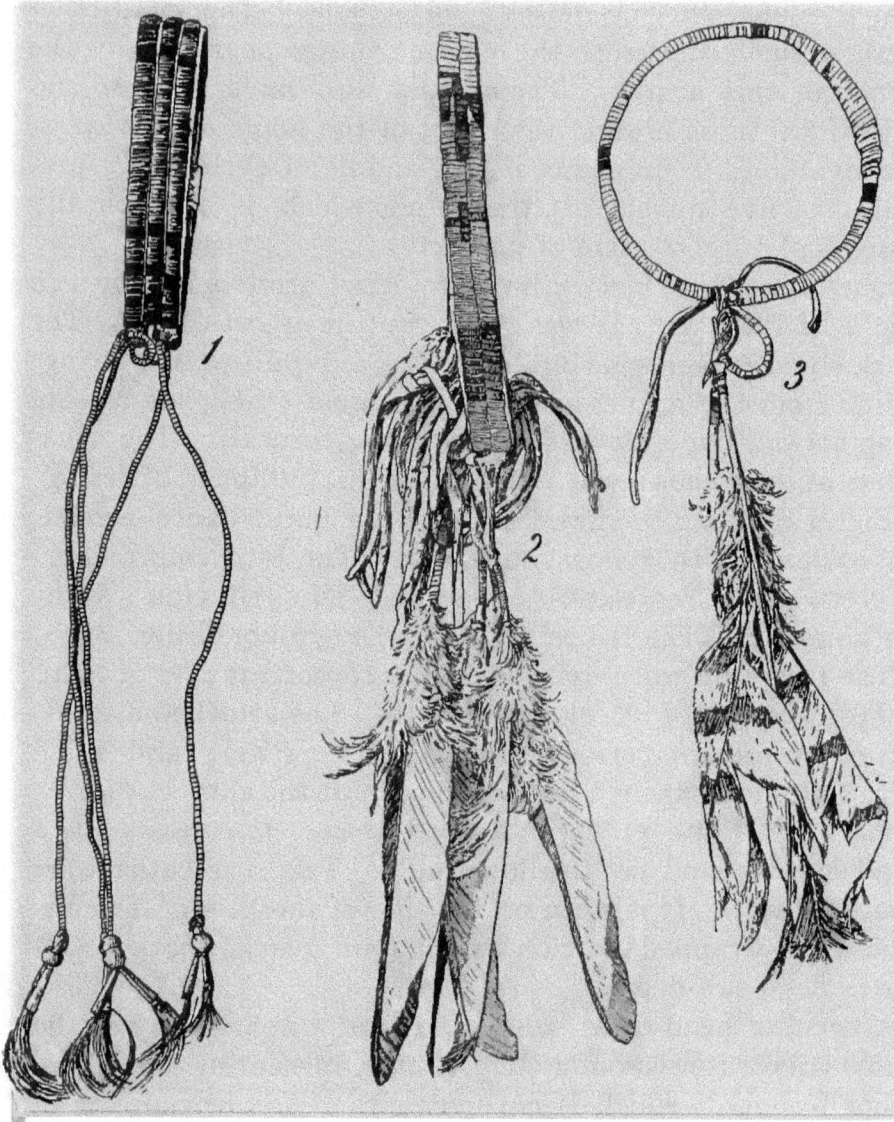

ARMLETS AND HEAD-DRESS.

The specimen shown in Plate VII, Fig. 1, represents a rat. The possessor and maker of this head-dress explained his choice of this animal as an object of representation, by the occurrence of the rat in a number of tales about the mythic personage Nih'a^{n}ça^n. It is a fact, however, that all the objects of Arapaho manufacture which represent animals at all, denote small animals such as the lizard, frog, fish, or rat. The cross on this specimen is the conventional na^{n}kaox, or morning star.

Fig. 2 of the same plate shows one of these head-dresses worked in quills. The horse-tail is dyed golden-yellow. This color was chosen by the wearer of the head-dress because he was desirous of possessing a horse of this color. The horse-hair is also a symbol of good luck, because horses are the usual gifts when presents are made.

The animal symbolism is fairly well worked out in this specimen. The quill-work is the body of a rat; the horse-tail, its tail. The long pendants at the four corners are of course the legs. Two loops at the top of the head-dress are the rat-ears, and two strings of red beads at the top represent the pointed mouth. Down the middle of the red quill-work runs a green stripe, which is a path. Blue, yellow, and green squares at the sides of this stripe represent (the tracks of?) rats running into the path.

Fig. 3 of Plate VII shows a similar head-dress representing a lizard. It is worked in beads, and the tail is twisted and dyed red. The bead-work design is the morning-star cross.

The navel-strings of Arapaho girls are preserved and sewed into small pouches stuffed with grass. These pouches are usually diamond-shaped and covered on both sides with beads. The child wears this amulet, which contains its navel-string, on its belt until it is worn out.

Such amulets are found among many tribes. Among some they are worn by boys as well as girls, or two are worn by one child. Among the Sioux these amulets sometimes have the shape of horned toads. Among the Assiniboine they are generally diamond-shaped, but less elongated than among the Arapaho. Among the Gros Ventres they are often diamond-

HEAD-DRESSES.

shaped; they sometimes represent a person, but more usually a horned toad, and sometimes have the figure of this animal. Among the Utes these navel-amulets are also diamond-shaped, but they are attached to the infant's cradle. Among the Arapaho they usually represent a small animal.

In connection with the usual diamond shape of these amulets, it may be observed that throughout the decorative symbolism of the Arapaho the navel is represented by a diamond-shaped symbol.

Fig. 1 of Plate VIII shows the only example of navel-amulets possessing realistic shape, seen among the Arapaho. It is further unique in not being beaded on the under side. It represents a lizard (säni'wa^n). This word, in Gros Ventre, means "horned toad," but in Arapaho seems to signify "lizard." The Arapaho regard the horned toad, which they call by the same name as a mule (bihiiha^{n}x), as a good animal, and do not kill it.

The more decoratively conventionalized form of navel-amulet is seen in Fig. 2 of Plate VIII. This object represents a fish. The diagonal lines indicate its appearance (*i. e.*, the markings of the fish).

The amulet shown in Fig. 3, Plate VIII, represents a tadpole (hiseinôtä^n, literally "woman's belly"). Two figures upon it in dark-blue beadwork represent stars. These forms appear to be modifications of the cross, which usually denotes the morning star. The red ornament in the middle represents the butterfly, or possibly the dragon-fly; it could not be determined which. The white beaded background represents snow.

Fig. 4 of Plate VIII illustrates another amulet representing a lizard (säni'wa^n). The dark blue and yellow areas signify its markings, while the bisecting lines represent paths.

The previous specimens are alike on both sides. Figs. 5 and 6 of Plate VIII, however, represent the two differing sides of one navel-amulet. The whole object represents the navel itself, also a frog. The two dark-blue trapezoidal ornaments in Fig. 5 represent miniature or toy bags, resembling those ordinarily used, but made for children. Below, a (red and

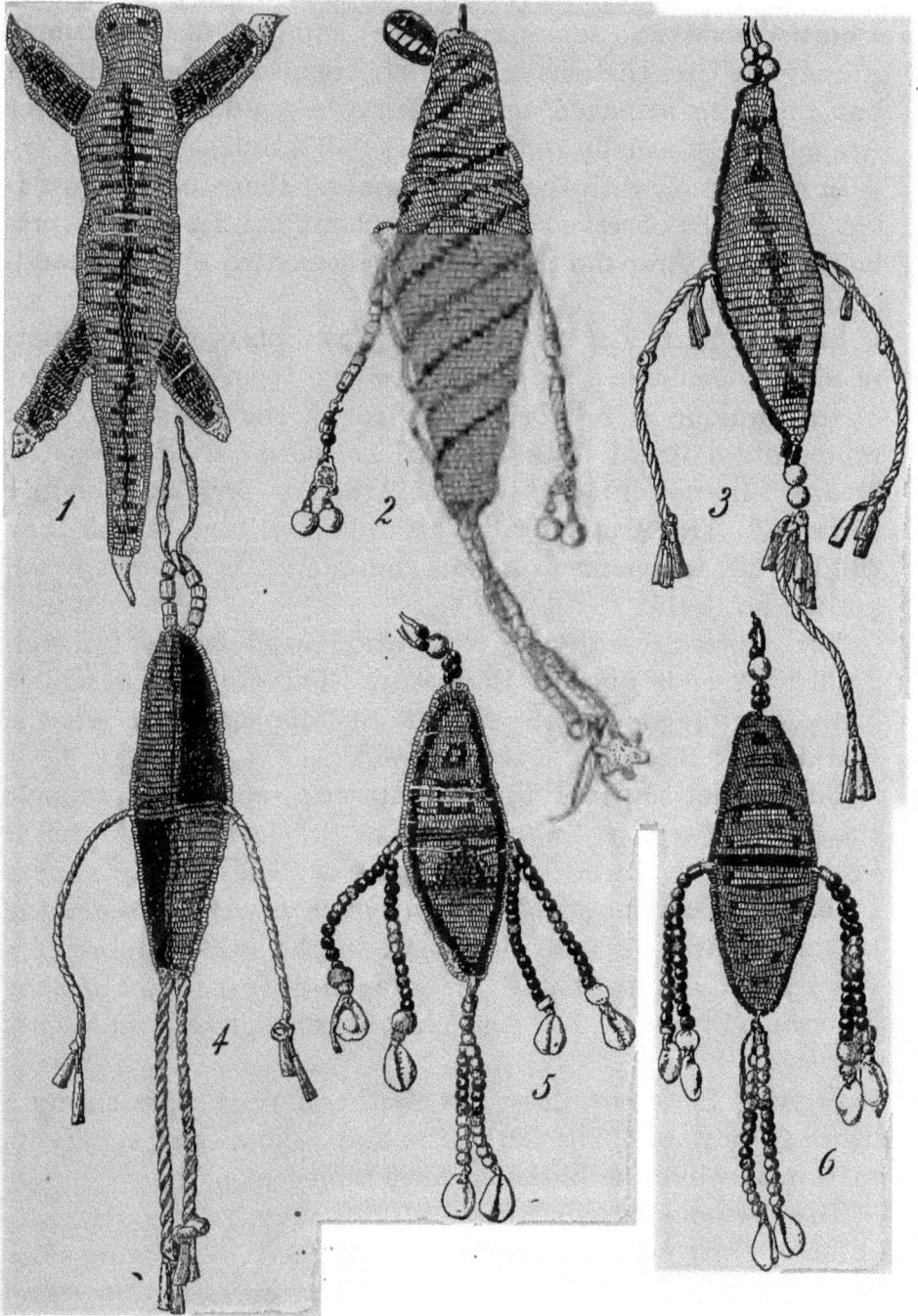

NAVEL-AMULETS.

pale-blue) triangle with a stripe across its point represents a female dress (evidently that of the little girl who wore the amulet). The golden-yellow background and the black stripe around it represent (the color of) the girl's hair respectively as it is now in her youth (her hair being light brown) and as it will be when she has grown older. On the other side (Fig. 6) the stripes or lines represent navel-strings. The green and blue single lines of beads at the seam or edge of the pouch represent sinew. The loose pendants of large beads represent navel-strings; the shells at their ends represent teeth.

In addition to the representation of a frog, there are three lines of symbolism in this object. First, teeth and color of hair are often used in symbolism to denote age, and express a wish for old age; the toy bags, and possibly the dress and navel-strings, also refer to the age of childhood. Secondly, the dress, and perhaps the sinew (which serves as thread, and therefore denotes sewing, woman's occupation), symbolize sex. Thirdly, the navel, and therefore also the navel-strings, symbolize the human being (ini'tä^n).

It will be seen from these figures that the navel-amulet of the conventional diamond form has a pair of strings at the sides, which denote the legs or fins of the animal represented. When a lizard, frog, or fish is represented, these strings aid the slight similarity of the pouch to the animal; but when a tadpole is represented, as in Fig. 3, it is evident that their effect is the opposite, and that their presence is due to the prevalence, in this point, of stylistic convention over accuracy of symbolism. But a specimen like the first one described (Fig. 1) shows the opposite predominance of representative accuracy over decorative convention. From this it would seem that there is always some tendency toward realistic symbolism, and some toward ornamental convention, but that the relative proportion of the two varies considerably in different individuals making decorated objects.

One-half of the front of a bead-covered waistcoat is shown in Fig. 8. This garment is of course modern. The figures that may be described as inverted Y's are sticks or racks set up inside the tent to hang saddles and blankets upon. The designs above them are saddle-blankets. The cross is the morning star. A row of blue squares represents rocks. A blue stripe represents a rope. Below this are ornaments consisting of a line with a hollow square at the bottom. These represent men's stirrups. On the back of the waistcoat, instead of these ornaments, are others consisting of a line with a triangle at the bottom. These represent women's stirrups. The Arapaho at present use saddles of their own manufacture for women. These have triangular stirrups of wood and rawhide. The men ride American saddles, which usually have oval wooden stirrups. Thus, as in many other cases (the sky, the earth, the sacred hoop), the square or rectangle here represents something circular or oval. In symbolism anything four-sided or four-cornered is equivalent to a circle, and anything circular is considered to have four ends.

Tents, even now that canvas has replaced buffalo-hides, are still often decorated with a conventional set of ornaments. These ornaments are the following.

Fig. 8 ($\frac{50}{1889}$). Front of Beaded Waistcoat.

1. A circular piece of hide about eight inches in diameter, covered with embroidery of beads or quills (Plate IX, Fig. 2). This is sewed to the back of the tent at its very top, just below the place where it is fastened to the hiinana′kaya^n, — the pole in the middle of the back which is used to raise the tent into position. To the bottom of this ornament are

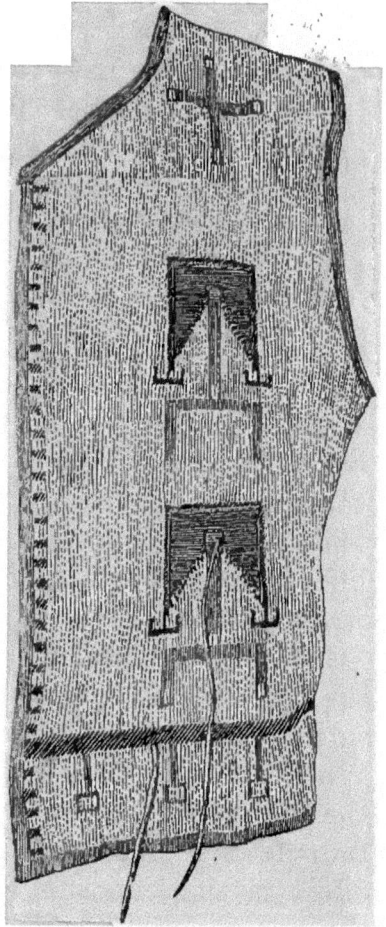

attached two buffalo (or cattle) tails. This ornament is called ka°eibiihi.

2. Four similarly embroidered pieces of skin considerably smaller (Plate IX, Fig. 1). These are attached to the sides of the tent, several feet above the bottom, at the southeast, southwest, northwest, and northeast (the tent always facing east). To the middle of each of these ornaments is attached a buffalo-tail and a pendant consisting of three quill-wrapped strings which have at their ends the small dew-claws of buffalo and a quill-wrapped loop.

3. A series of pendants, each triple, with dew-claws and loops at the ends (Plate IX, Fig. 3). These resemble the pendants just described, except that instead of strings, wider strips of skin are wound with porcupine-quills. When quills are not to be had, corn-husk or plant-fibres are used. These pendants, called xaxanāāhihi, are attached in two vertical rows to the front of the tent, where it is fastened together above the door; also to the edge of the two flaps or ears at the top (which give light and ventilation, but can be closed when it rains).

These three sets of objects constitute the regular ornamentation of a tent.

These tent-ornaments are of three different kinds, the patterns in the circular embroidery varying slightly.

Fig. 9, *a*, shows one of the three kinds. The design consists of alternating black and yellow concentric circles and of four black-edged white radii.

Fig. 9, *b*, shows a second style, which contains four colors, whereas the first contains three. This may be described as similar to the preceding, excepting that the two sectors enclosed by the four radii are solidly red instead of continuing the black and yellow circles that cover the main part of the surface. The specimen figured has teeth around its edge. Such teeth may be either present or absent in any of the three styles.

The black and yellow concentric rings represent the whirlwind, or perhaps more exactly the course of Whirlwind-Woman. When the earth was first made (and was still small),

Näyāⁿxati'sei (Whirlwind-Woman) did not know where to stop (to rest), and went from place to place.   As she circled,

the earth grew until it reached its present extent. When she stopped, she had gone over the whole earth. It was she who first made this tent-ornament, which represents what she did.

The two preceding styles are both known as "black" on account of their black circles. The third style lacks these, and is therefore called "white." It is also called xanāⁿkū'bää, *i. e.*, "straight-standing-red," on account of its two opposite red sectors. This third style is like the second except that instead of being banded black and yellow, it is solid yellow.

The specimen shown in Fig. 2 of Plate IX is of this third kind. It represents the sun, on account of both its shape and its prevailing yellow color.   The two red sectors are tents containing persons (red sometimes signifies mankind in Arapaho color-symbolism).   The teeth at the circumference represent persons.

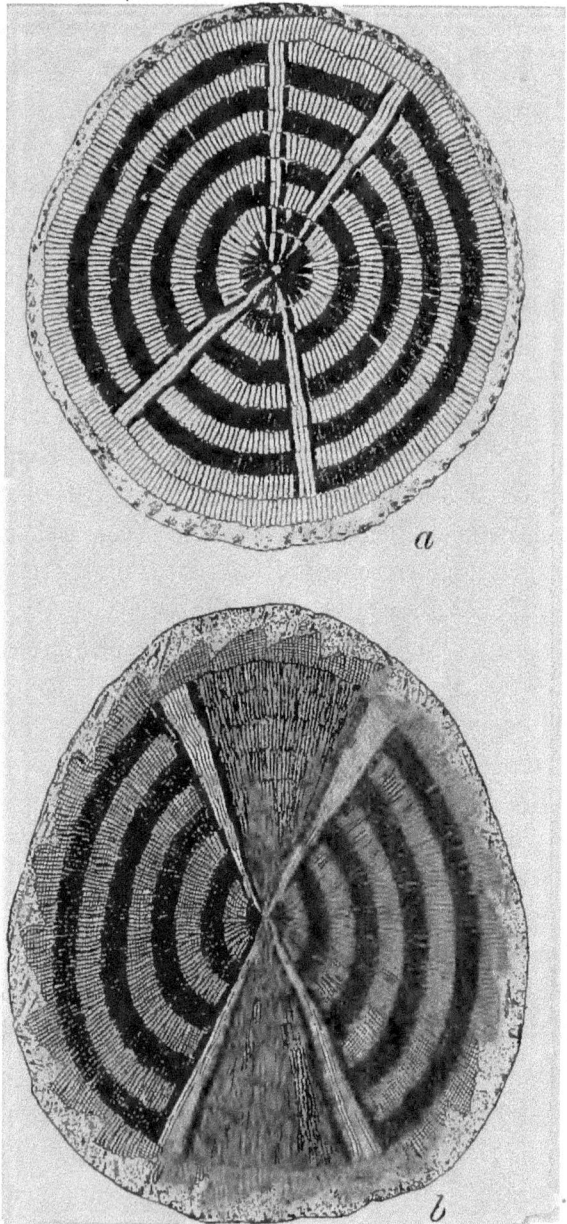

Fig. 9, *a* (₃₈₈⁵⁰), *b* (₂₀₂⁵⁰a).   Tent-ornaments.   Longest diameter, 19 cm., 26 cm.

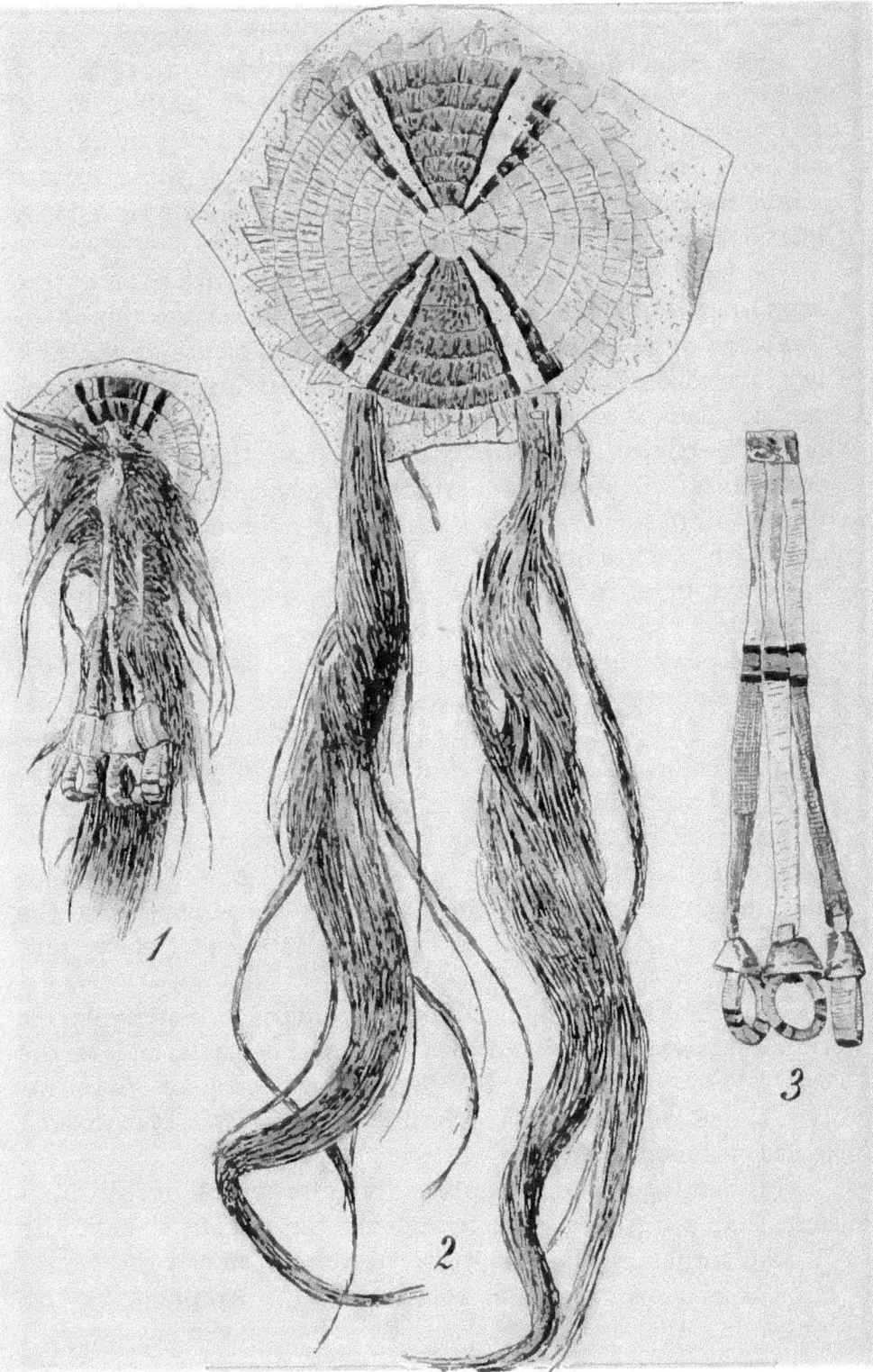

TENT-ORNAMENTS.

Another specimen of this third kind, worked in beads, was said to represent, as a whole, the sun. The red sectors, at the opposite sides (ends) of the circle, are the red of sunrise and sunset. The white and black radii bordering these sectors can be regarded as two intersecting diameters, forming a cross. Therefore they are the morning star.

The four small circular ornaments going with each of the large ones that have been described are miniature reproductions of these, except that the small ornaments of the first two styles omit radii and sectors, consisting only of concentric black and yellow circles.

The pendants are more variable than the circular tent-ornaments. Sometimes they are entirely yellow. Generally they contain some red. Very frequently there is a white portion with black edgings. The one shown in Plate ix, Fig. 3, has green upon it. The rule seems to be to employ only the four colors red, yellow, black, and white.

One kind of pendant is entirely orange; another (Fig. 10), from the upper part downward, yellow, purple, white, purple, orange. The purple probably stands for black. The arrangement of colors in Fig. 10 is similar to that shown in Plate ix, Fig. 3, except that the middle strip is white and of greater width. Generally the upper part, at which the three pendants hang together, is wrapped with quills of the same color as the upper parts of the pendants. The rings at the lower ends of the present specimen are red, white, and black.

Instead of the large circular embroidery, a rectangular or trapezoidal figure of beadwork is sometimes attached to the top of the back of the tent. Fig. 11 shows such an ornament. It is called nīhā^{n}xā$'^n$hayā^n ("yellow-oblong"?). It is worked in red, yellow, black, and white.[1]

This rectangular form is probably more typical of the Cheyenne than of the Arapaho, though the Cheyenne also have the circular ornaments. The Gros Ventres formerly possessed circular ornaments similar to those of the Arapaho, but no longer use them; merely a few detached specimens are still

---

[1] By mistake the yellow in this specimen is indicated as green in the illustration.

in existence.   Among the Shoshone, Bannock, and Ute, the writer has not seen any tent-ornaments.   The Blackfeet also did not use them.

A Cheyenne tent-ornament in the American Museum of Natural History exactly resembles the Arapaho one illustrated in Plate IX, Fig. 2, except that blue is substituted for the white.   Another Cheyenne tent-ornament seen by the

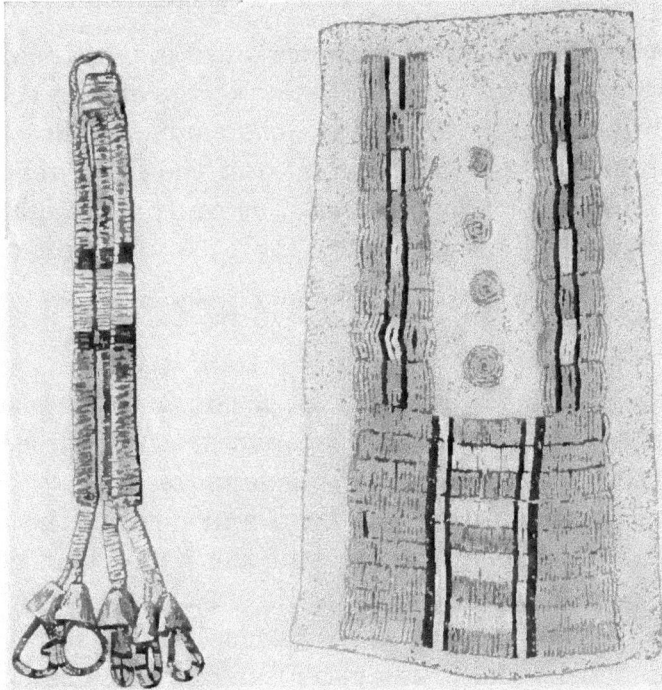

Fig. 10.   Fig. 11.

Figs. 10 ($\frac{50}{1800}$b), 11 ($\frac{50}{600}$).   Tent-ornaments.   Length, 27 cm., 23 cm.

writer was identical with these two, except that it was green where these were respectively white and blue.

It appears that the combination of red, yellow, black, and white, while not confined to the Arapaho, is more characteristic of their tribal ornamentation than of that of their neighbors.   When green is used by the Arapaho in the embroidery of such tribally-decorated objects, it may replace either red or white.

Designs and color combinations very similar to those of tent-ornaments are found on other objects in which a highly conventional style of quill-embroidery formerly prevailed.

These objects are particularly buffalo-robes, buffalo-skin blankets or pillows, and cradles.

Fig. 12 shows one of twenty lines embroidered in quills across a buffalo-robe, previously mentioned on p. 34. The line represents a buffalo-path. The four colors — the conventional red, yellow, black, and white — represent the four lives (generations or periods) since the beginning of the world, one for each color.

If one follows the circumference of one of the circular tent-ornaments (as of Fig. 2, Plate IX), excepting the first style, which lacks red, one meets in the course of this circumference the same succession of colors, and the same relative amount or proportional width of each, as on this straight line on the buffalo-robe. In each case the bulk or body of the line is

Fig. 12. Quill-embroidered Line.

yellow; there are red spaces of considerable size; these are bordered by smaller white spaces; and these, finally, are bordered by still narrower black spaces.

Buffalo-skins, from the head and neck of the animal, were used to hang over the head of the bed. One of these skins seen by the writer was ornamented in the following manner. 1. The horns were not attached to the skin. Where the eye had been there was sewed one of the small circular tent-ornaments consisting of yellow and black concentric rings. 2. The place of the top of the head was covered by a quill-work ornament called the "brain," which was nothing else than one of the large circular tent-ornaments of the style that lacks the black concentric rings. 3. The place of the ear was covered by a figure embroidered in beads and quills. This was trapezoidal, the smaller of the bases being convexly rounded. This ornament is shown in Fig. 13. Most of it is yellow. The middle portion is red; this is bordered by two white stripes, which are edged by black lines. 4. Along the "throat," that is, along one of the sides of the piece of skin, was a fourth ornament. This consisted of two strips of hide extending the length of the skin, parallel to each other at a

distance of about six inches.   Connecting these were about
thirty short strips of hide, each about half an inch wide.   These
strips were wound with corn-husk of the four colors,— red,
yellow, black, and white.   The arrangement and proportion
of colors on these strips were identical with those on the ornament representing the ear.   In addition, three or four smaller
strips, with the same color-pattern, were put on each of the
long pieces of hide, extending in the same direction as these;
that is, vertically.   This entire ornament, in its general character, somewhat resembled the long orna-
ment hanging from the cradle shown in
Fig. 14, *b.*

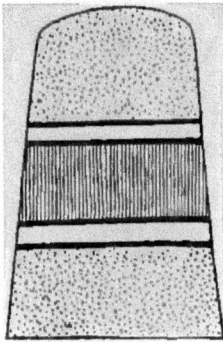

Fig. 13.   Buffalo-skin
Ornament.

These buffalo-skin pillows with the tribal
ornamentation were decorated, like tents
and robes, under the direction of the old
women possessing the sacred seven work-
bags.   It is probable that the last specimen
of this kind has now perished.

Cradles, or infant-carriers, are also decorated in a style similar to tent-ornaments.
The embroidery is altogether in quills.
Sometimes, however, only three colors are used on these
cradles, instead of four.   There are two chief lines of symbolism connected with this ornamentation.   According to
one interpretation, the various ornaments represent the child
that is in the cradle.   According to the other interpretation,
these ornaments represent parts of the tent.   When the child
grows up, it will inhabit its own tent as now it inhabits the
cradle.   Therefore this symbolism serves to express a wish
that the child may reach the age of manhood or womanhood.

Fig. 14, *b*, shows such a cradle.   The round ornament near
the top of the cradle, situated over the top of the child's head,
represents the head or skull of the child.   The long ornament,
consisting of two strips of hide connected by red, black, and
white quill-wrapped strips, represents the child's hair.   The
smooth, slippery quills denote the greasy hair of the child.
At the lower part of the cradle the long quill-covered thongs
represent ribs.   The lowest pair, however, are the legs.   Of

the three colors in the embroidery, red represents blood; black, the hair (of youth and middle age); white, (the hair of) old age. Of the sticks forming the framework inside the cradle, one is unpeeled, the other peeled. The unpeeled one denotes that the child is as yet helpless and dirty in its cradle;

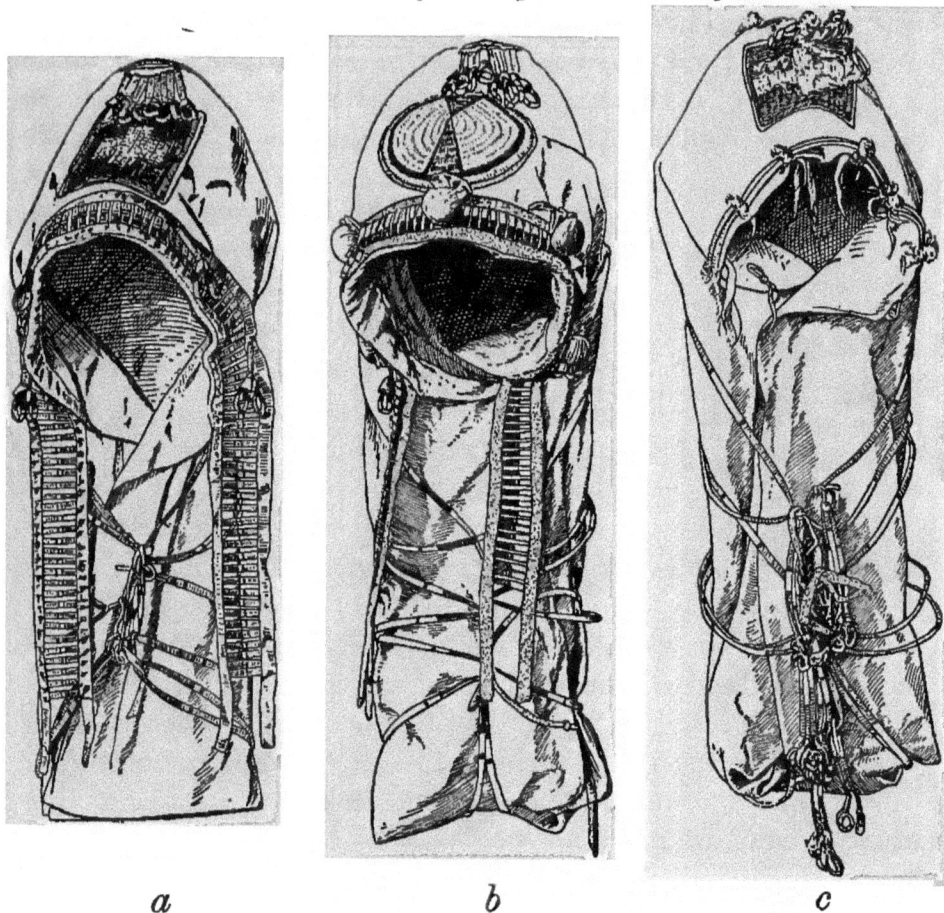

Fig. 14, *a* (⅕⁰⁷⁰), *b* (⁸⁸⁵), *c* (⅕⁰⁸⁰). Cradles.

a   b   c

the peeled stick represents its subsequent more cleanly condition.

The round ornament at the top of this cradle, besides denoting the head of the child, represents also a tent-ornament, which indeed it closely resembles. The tent-ornament signifies that the child, when it has grown up, will have a tent. Above the round ornament are pendants having small hoofs and quill-wrapped loops at their ends. These represent the pendants or rattles above the door of the tent. Still higher up than these on the cradle, are two quill-wound strips lying parallel to each other. These represent man and woman, since a man and a woman own a tent together. On the ornament representing hair are several pairs of pendants having loops at their ends. These loops represent the holes in the bottom of the tent through which the tent-pegs pass. The whole cradle, owing to its shape and the fact of its being stretched on a framework of sticks, resembles a tent-door, and therefore represents it.

Both of these extensive symbolic interpretations were given by one and the same person to the ornamentation of one cradle.

Fig. 14, *a*, shows a cradle like the preceding, except that in place of the round ornament over the head there is a rectangular one of red quill-work on which is a white cross. The shape of this probably has reference to the rectangular tent-ornaments sometimes used.

Very similar to the two cradles just described are two in the Field Columbian Museum in Chicago. One of these contains green in its quill-work.

Fig. 14, *c*, shows a cradle worked in yellow quill-embroidery instead of red. The rectangular ornament containing a white cross is similar to that on the cradle last described, but in several other respects this cradle differs in ornamentation.

The oblong ornament at the top represents the head of the child. Yellow wool embroidered upon it is hair. A stripe of blue beads surrounding this ornament represents face-paint. At the lower part of the cradle are the ribs of the child.

The oblong ornament also represents a tent-ornament. The pendants above it are the rattles at the top of the tent. They signify that it is wished that the child may become old enough to possess a tent. Yellow strips surrounding the opening of the cradle represent the circumference of the base of the tent. Tufts of wool at intervals between these strips represent the places of the tent-pegs. The ornaments that are called ribs are also the pins used for fastening together the front of the tent, just above the door. Rattle-pendants attached to them represent the pendants on the tent alongside of these pins, lower down than those referred to at the top of the tent.

Quill-embroidered cradles have been seen by the writer only among the northern Arapaho. Beaded cradles, which are used among both portions of the tribe, are very different in design and symbolism.

A beaded cradle is shown in Fig. 15. Dark-blue triangles represent tents. Green rectangles, with three projections at each end, represent brush-shelters or sun-shades, with the poles on which they stand. A long red stripe is a path. Around the edge of the cradle are marks that are blue, red, and yellow. These represent piles of stones marking the extent of the camp-circle. At the bottom a border passing completely around the cradle represents the camp-circle of tents. At the very top an attached square with a broad cross in it represents the morning star. In a similar square from the top of a Cheyenne cradle, Ehrenreich[1] found designs that had a highly abstract significance.

A Sioux cradle in the American Museum of Natural History bears a resemblance to this one that is very remarkable. Nothing is known of the symbolism attached to this cradle by the Sioux.

Fig. 15 (₅₀/₅₀). Beaded Cradle. Length, 69 cm.

Fig. 16 shows a figure in the shape of a tent-ornament, which was intended to be attached to the head of a cradle.

---

[1] Ethnologisches Notizblatt, 1899, II, 1, p. 27.

Fig. 17 shows the tent-ornament design slightly altered, and used to cover one side of a ball.

Tent-ornaments are generally attached to the tent with a certain amount of ceremony.   This is done by an assemblage of old women, one or more of whom are possessors of one of the seven sacred women's bags that have been referred to. The ceremonies are similar to those that have been described as taking place in connection with the transfer of one of the sacred bags or with the embroidering of a robe (pp. 30 et seq.).

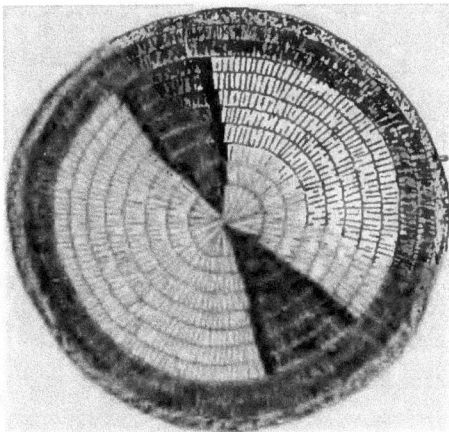

Fig. 16 (₁₀₀₇⁷). Cradle-ornament.
Diam., 14.5 cm.

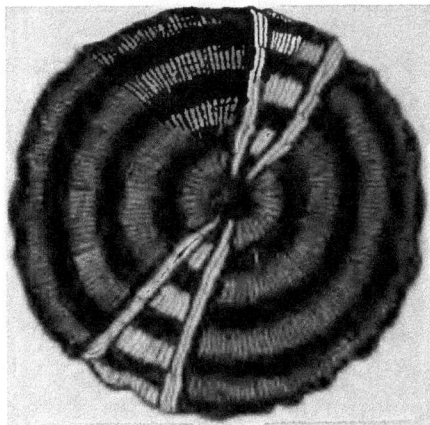

Fig. 17 (₁₀₁⁸). Beaded Ornament for Ball.
Diam., 15 cm.

The following is a description of the ceremonies accompanying the ornamentation of a tent, as witnessed by the writer.

A middle-aged woman who wished her tent decorated had prepared the ornaments.. These consisted, when the ceremony began, of a piece of skin on which the large circular ornament had been beaded; of the four smaller ornaments, also of embroidered hide; of cow-tails to be attached to the circular ornaments; of four sets of thin pendants, to be attached, with the tails, to the four small circles; of fourteen quill-wound yellow pendants, bearing small hoofs at the ends; of sixteen similar yellow pendants which were ornamented with the design black, white, black, red, black, white, black, that has been previously described (p. 34); and of red flannel to be cut into pieces to be hung on the pendants next to the hoofs.   The canvas tent which was to be ornamented had been taken down, but the poles had been left standing, and all the household property was still in place under them. The ceremonial attachment of the ornaments took place in another tent, perhaps a hundred feet away from the bare framework of poles. The camp broke and moved that morning, and soon these two tents were the only ones left standing. The woman who had been called to preside over the ceremony was the one from whom the account of the use of the sacred bags was obtained by the writer (see p. 30). She was called Cedar-Woman.

The owner of the tent that was to be ornamented sent a wagon to bring Cedar-Woman. She, however, was not ready, and remained in her tent, painting herself and putting on a good dress. Finally she came on foot, followed by another old woman who possessed a sacred bag, and by a third elderly woman. The food, which is a requisite of the ceremony, was already in the tent, set on the ground around the fireplace. There was now a delay in order that more elderly women might be secured. At last enough were found. With the last comers the writer entered the tent, from which men are ordinarily supposed to be excluded. Cedar-Woman, the head of the ceremony, sat at the back of the tent (*i. e.*, opposite the door, which, as always, faced east). At each side of the tent sat four women, the owner of the tent sitting next to the door. The women were cutting the red cloth into strips and attaching it to the ends of the pendants. The entirely yellow pendants were being worked upon on one side of the tent, the four-colored ones by the women on the other side. Cedar-Woman had the piece of hide on which the large circular beaded ornament was embroidered, and was cutting out the ornament from it. Later she fastened the thin pendants to the cow-tails. While at work putting the ornaments together, all the women seemed to speak and laugh freely. The owner of the tent once went out to get an awl.

The owner of the tent now arose from her place by the door and kneeled before Cedar-Woman, who took medicine from her sacred bag and began to chew it. The kneeling woman held out her two palms together. Cedar-Woman touched her

finger to the ground, and then placed it five times on the
other woman's joined palms, in four spots forming a circle. and
then in the middle.   The course of her finger was from right
to left, contrary to the usual ceremonial order.   Then she spit
a minute quantity of medicine on the same places on the
woman's two hands; the latter then rubbed herself all over
with her hands.[1]   Cedar-Woman spit on her two cheeks, and
then on her own hand, which she placed on the kneeling
woman's breast and then on the top of her head.   She also
took some of the medicine from her own mouth and put it
into the other's.   The woman then rose and walked around
past the fire and the dishes (which occupied the centre of the
tent) to the door.   Then she took up a dish of food that stood
towards the southeast (*i. e.*, not far from the door), and, holding it just above the ground, walked around the fireplace
from left to right.   Then she gave it to the woman before
whom it had stood.   Going to the southwest quarter of the
tent, she took up a dish there, and, after having made a complete circuit with it, gave it to the woman nearest whom it
had stood.   Then she did the same at the northwest and
northeast.   The rest of the food, other than these four dishes,
was not moved.   The women all produced plates or kettles,
and the owner of the tent ladled out food to them from one
dish.   The remaining dishes she set before Cedar-Woman.
Cedar-Woman took five crumbs from one of the dishes and
laid them on the tent-owner's palm.   This woman then went
around the tent, laying one crumb on the ground at each of
the four ends or sides (southeast, etc.) of the tent.   The fifth
she placed on the fire in the middle.   Then she came back to
Cedar-Woman, who placed five pieces from another dish on
her palm.   The woman then rubbed her hands together, and,
going around the fire, stood before a tent-pole on the southeast side of the tent.   She moved her hands down in front of
it with a motion as if she held it and were letting her hands
glide down along it.   She went successively to the southwest,
northwest, and northeast of the tent, and made the same mo-

---

[1] This is a common practice in ceremonials; a root called hâçawaanaxu is used for
the purpose

tion before the tent-poles there. The fifth motion she made in the same way before the door. Then, going to Cedar-Woman a third time, she received five grains of corn on her hand, and placed them on the ground and on the fire, just as she had placed the first food given her by Cedar-Woman. The fourth time, Cedar-Woman put pieces of a soft food on her hands, which she "fed" to the poles as previously. Then she brought Cedar-Woman a pot of food standing northeast of the centre (*i. e.*, to the left of the door, viewed from inside the tent), and, having had a little of the contents placed on her hands, made the same motions in front of the four tent-poles and the door as before. From a dish at the southeast (to the right of the door), she then again "fed" the ground. Occasionally she mistook the place or made a wrong motion, whereupon all the other women laughed at her. After she had sat down, a young woman, apparently her daughter, entered the tent and kneeled before Cedar-Woman. She also had her palms touched by the old woman's finger after it had been placed on the ground, and she also had chewed medicine spit upon her. Then Cedar-Woman fed her with a spoon; she passed her hand lightly down over Cedar-Woman's arm several times, apparently as a sign of thanks. Rising, she carried several dishes of food to the door; then took a dish from Cedar-Woman to the other old woman who possessed a sacred bag. Leaving the tent, the young woman returned with plates on which the food in the dish last mentioned was distributed. She went out for more plates, and all the food was dished out. Then she sat down against the door. All now ate. The second old woman with the sacred bag once held up a piece of food and said a short prayer, and one of the other women did the same. When they had nearly finished eating, the young woman left the tent, taking several dishes with her. Several women were now called in from outside, and food was given to them to carry away. At last all the food had been removed from the tent.

Then the owner of the tent, who had again been sitting near the door, went out and brought in live coals, which she put on the fireplace. (As it was summer, there was no fire in the tent.)   Cedar-Woman took out from her bag a root which looked like that called niäätä", and sliced pieces from it.   The owner of the tent now took two forked sticks and with them picked up two live coals from the heap which she had brought in; she laid them on the bare ground before Cedar-Woman, and kneeled before her.   With her arm guided by Cedar-Woman, she slowly took a small amount of the finely-cut root from Cedar-Woman's other, outspread hand.   Still guided by Cedar-Woman, she moved her arm up and down four times, then four times made a motion as if dropping the root on the two coals, and with the last of these motions dropped it.   Then she returned to her seat by the door. Cedar-Woman put the remainder of the finely-cut root on the two coals, and, as the smoke rose, began to pray.   She prayed a long time.   All the women in the tent bowed their heads, and some covered their eyes.   Most of them wept a little. The owner of the tent then replaced the two coals in the fireplace.

This done, she brought in the cover of her tent.   It was laid on the ground, to the south of the fireplace, folded so that it was about a foot wide and perhaps twelve feet long.   The head was next to Cedar-Woman, the other end near the door. Cedar-Woman rose, and, followed closely by the owner of the tent, walked around the fire, touching the canvas with the two forked sticks that had been used to pick up the coals. Again she circled around the fire, followed by the woman owning the tent, who carried the ornaments that were to be attached.   This time, in walking around the fire, they stepped over the tent four times (see Fig. 18).   Then the top of the tent was spread out.   The owner of the tent stood up, motioned four times with the bundle of ornaments, and threw them on the canvas.   Cedar-Woman gathered them together, and holding them up, spoke a short prayer.   Then she handed the four smaller circular ornaments to four women. All now gathered around the canvas, which was rolled out somewhat, though not fully spread.   All the participants were now on the south side of the fire, where the canvas lay, except Cedar-Woman, who kept her place at the middle of

the back of the tent, west of the fire, and one woman who
remained idle on the other side of the tent, north of the fire.
The five circular ornaments were now sewed on the canvas.
The large one at the top of the tent was attached under Cedar-
Woman's direct supervision, but neither she nor the other
old woman possessing a bag sewed. The owner of the tent
also did not sew. As one woman remained idle, there thus
were five who were sewing on five ornaments. While they
worked, they conversed freely. Cedar-Woman never exposed
her bag plainly, but kept it covered and wrapped even while
taking something from it. This caution may have been
due to the presence of the writer.
When the circular ornaments had
all been sewed to the canvas, Cedar-
Woman took two of the cow-tails,
and directed one of the women
how to attach them to the large
ornament. When this had been
done, the part of the canvas that
would be at the front of the top of
the tent was spread out and held
flat on the ground. Then seven
of the yellow pendants were laid
in a row upon it, and their places

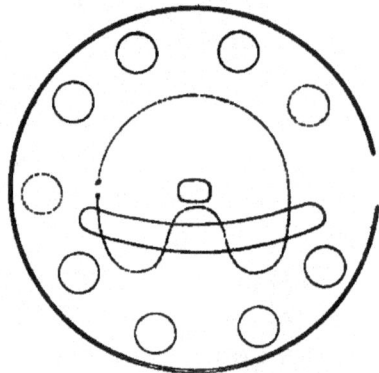

Fig. 18.   Diagram illustrating
Ceremonial.

marked with a bit of charcoal. In these places holes were
then made in the canvas with an awl. The tent had been
folded so that it was pierced twice, which made two rows
of seven holes. By means of strings of buckskin and small
squares of hide, the fourteen yellow pendants were then
attached in these places. Then the four-colored pendants
were attached in the same manner, below the others, and
just above the door; they formed two vertical rows of eight
each.

The tent was now bundled together and taken out by the
woman who owned it. Together with her daughter, she at
once began to put it up on the poles that were already standing. This was done, as usual, by taking out the pole at the
middle of the back (called hiinana'kaya^n), laying it on the

ground, and tying the canvas to it near its top, so that by raising the pole the canvas was elevated to the proper height. The other women now all came out from the tent in which they had been. Cedar-Woman took the pole that was lying on the canvas and partially raised it four times. Then the owner of the tent, unassisted, raised it altogether, put it in its place, and spread the canvas around the framework of poles, though without fastening it either in front, over the door, or at the bottom edge; so that it sagged and hung loosely.

Cedar-Woman now took the four tails which had had embroidered pendants attached to them, and which were to be fastened to the four small circular ornaments that were a few feet above the ground on the southeast, southwest, northwest, and northeast sides of the tent. Starting from before the door, and followed by the owner of the tent, she took a complex course that finally brought her before the northeast side of the tent, where one of the tails was to be attached to the beaded ornament. Her course is shown in Fig. 19.

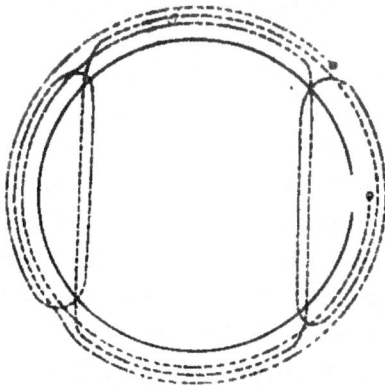

Fig. 19. Diagram showing Ceremonial Circuit around Tent.

Altogether she walked past every part of the circumference of the tent three times (excepting the distance between the place where she stopped and the door from which she started); crossed the tent four times from north to south or south to north, lifting up the canvas once at each of the places where the ornaments were, going under it, and emerging under the ornament directly to the north or south; and in all her course kept turning from left to right, making five complete revolutions. When the two women had stopped on the northeast of the tent, the owner pierced the ornament with an awl, and Cedar-Woman fastened the tail to it. The remaining participants in the ceremony, together with several other persons who had been watching outside, looked on from a distance, sitting on the ground.   The two women then went to the ornament on the southeast side of the tent, and, having fastened a tail to it in the same manner, did the same at the southwest and then at the northwest.   Then Cedar-Woman sat down with the others; and the owner of the tent, assisted by her daughter, took down the now completely ornamented tent.

Ordinarily this would have ended the ceremony; but the same woman had another tent to be ornamented.   Accordingly the women re-entered the tent in which they had been, and the owner brought in to them a second canvas.   Presumably this was decorated and set up like the first, although without another meal preceding.

This ends the account of the tribal decoration of the Arapaho.

Plate x represents two of the gut cases or pouches used to hold porcupine-quills.   Generally these pouches are not embroidered.   On the larger one (Fig. 2) the blue and yellow triangles in the beadwork at each end represent rocks.   On the other one (Fig. 1) red and blue lines on the white beadwork represent leeches.

The Arapaho keep the dry finely pulverized paint, which they use to put on their persons, in small pouches of soft skin. Old people may have plain little sacks without any decoration.   Generally, however, the pouches are about half covered with beadwork.   They take two main forms.   One has a fringe hanging from the bottom of the pouch.   The other typical form has, in place of the fringe, a pointed triangular flap of skin about as long as the pouch itself.   These paint-bags are usually intended to represent other objects.   Many represent one half of a saddle-bag.   Saddle-bags were made of soft skin, deep, beaded, and with a long fringe.   They were double, so that one end hung on each side of the horse. One half of a saddle-bag had much the shape and appearance of many of the paint-pouches.   Others of these paint-pouches represent small animals.   The pouch itself is the body of the animal, its opening is the mouth, the strings with which the

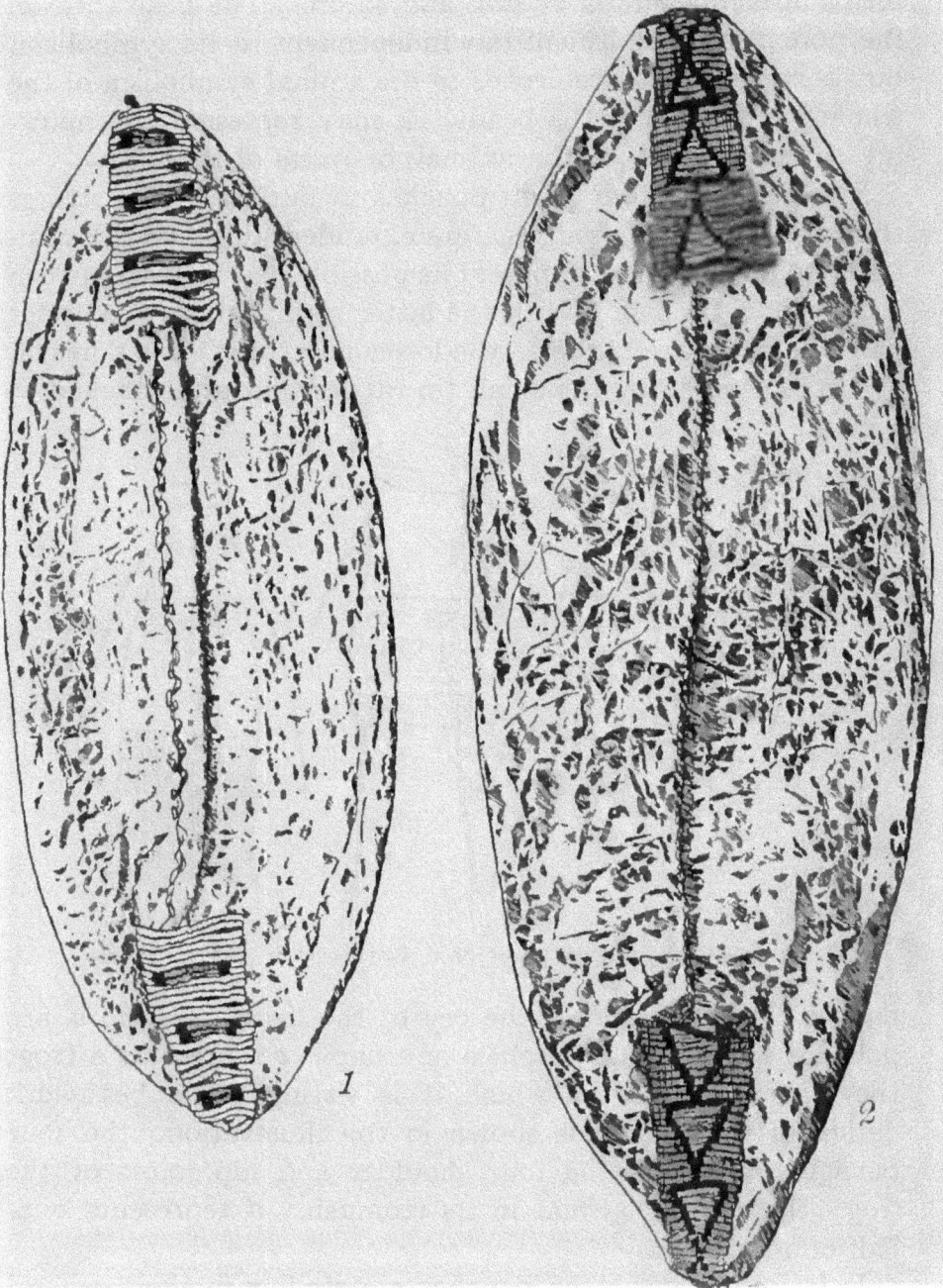

POUCHES FOR HOLDING PORCUPINE-QUILLS.

opening is tied together are limbs, other strings or attachments are hind-limbs or tail, and so on. The beadwork on
the pouch is generally entirely independent in its symbolism,
but sometimes has reference to the animal symbolism of the
whole pouch. Thus the beadwork may represent the markings or habitation of the animal, or parts of its body.

Fig. 20 shows four paint-pouches in outline. The strings
that represent legs, fins, etc., are extended, to make the similarity to an animal as apparent as possible. *a* represents both
a beaver and a fish. With the latter signification, the upper
pair of strings are barbels; the lower pair, fins. *b* is a lizard.
The sound made by the small tin rattles that are attached to

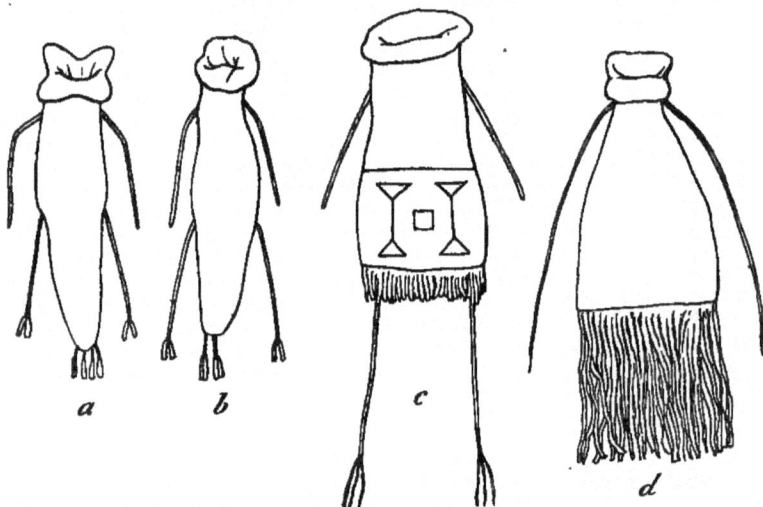

Fig. 20, *a* (₅₀₁/₈₀), *b* (₅₀₂/₈₀), *c* (₄₄₂/₅₀), *d* (₅₀₁/₈₀). Paint-pouches   About ⅓ nat. size.

flap and strings denotes the cry of the lizard. *c* and *d* are
pouches with a fringe in place of a flap. *c* represents a frog;
the fringe is grass in which it is sitting. The beadwork
design of this pouch is shown in the illustration; the four
triangles represent the four shoulder and hip joints of the
frog; the square is food in its stomach. *d* represents one-
half of a saddle-bag.

It is evident that the pouches are similar in their general
pattern, however diverse their symbolic significance.

Unless otherwise specified, the paint-bags to be referred to
are ornamented alike on both sides.

The paint-pouch shown in Plate XI, Fig. 1, represents a saddle-bag. The triangular design upon it is a tent. The stripe along the side of the pouch is a snake. The beads at the edge of the opening are variously-colored rocks. The five-pointed mouth of the pouch represents a star.

The pouch shown in Figs. 2 and 3, Plate XI, represents a beaver. The triangular design in beadwork is a tent. It rests upon a green horizontal line, which represents the ground when the grass is green. On the other side of the pouch is another, differently-colored triangular design, which is also a tent. This rests upon a yellow band, which represents the ground in autumn, when the grass is yellow. Light-blue stripes at the two sides of the pouch represent the sky. On the flap, the two converging white stripes are an arrow-head. The small dark-blue triangles are also arrow-heads. The line of beads projecting from the edge of the flap represents the scales on the beaver's tail. It will be seen that one side of this flap is left bare, which is unusual.

In the pouch shown in Fig. 4 of Plate XI the opening is four-pointed, and represents the morning star.

The pouch shown in Fig. 5 of Plate XI represents a saddle-bag. The triangular design is a mountain. The gray-blue area on which it is imposed is hazy atmosphere. The blue-and-yellow border represents mountain-ranges. This pouch is beaded on one side only.

The pouch shown in Fig. 6 of Plate XI represents a greenish lizard. For this reason the ground-color of the beadwork is green. In most pouches it is white. The design represents a mountain: this species of lizard lives mostly on mountains. The whole bag with its opening, besides being the lizard itself, is also the hole in which the animal lives; and the vertical green stripe with two bands across it represents the lizard with the markings of its skin. The opening of the pouch is also the lizard's mouth; and the projections at the opening, its ears.

The bag shown in Figs. 1 and 2 of Plate XII represents a lizard. The rectangular design (Fig. 1) with six projections represents a cricket. Below it, the crosses are stars, and the

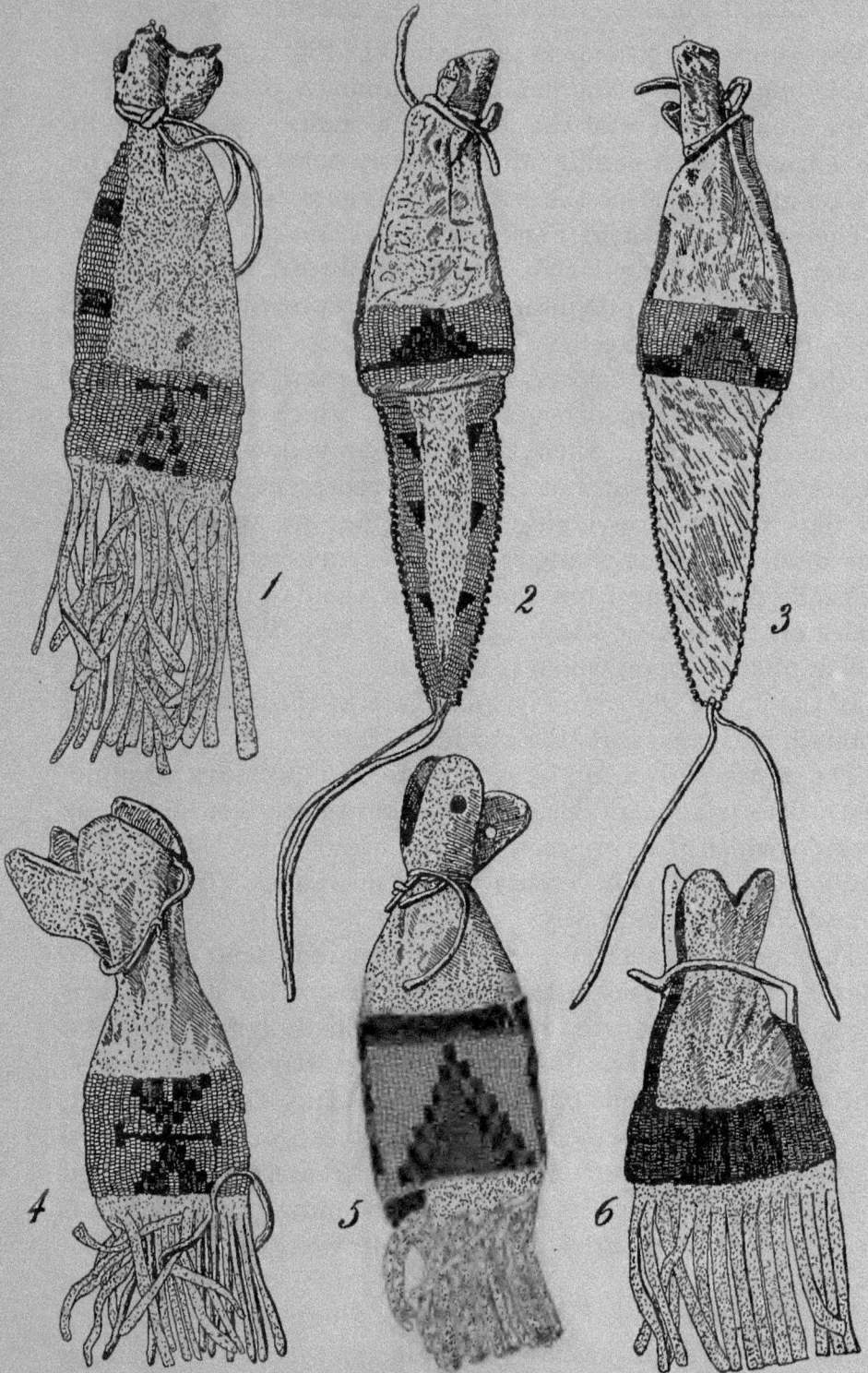

PAINT-POUCHES.

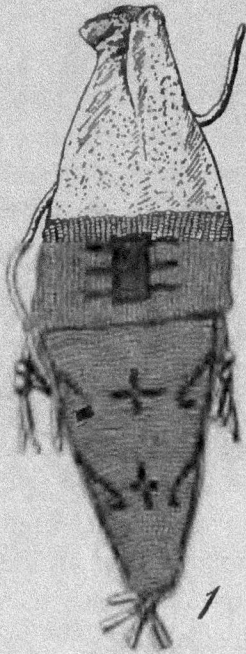

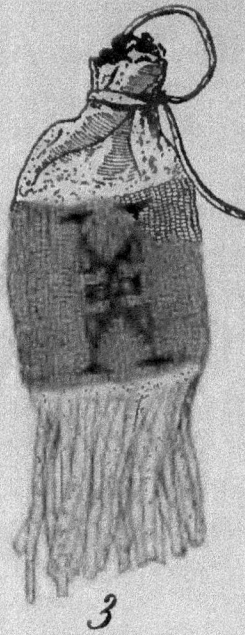

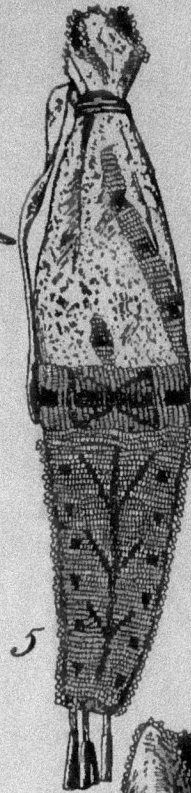

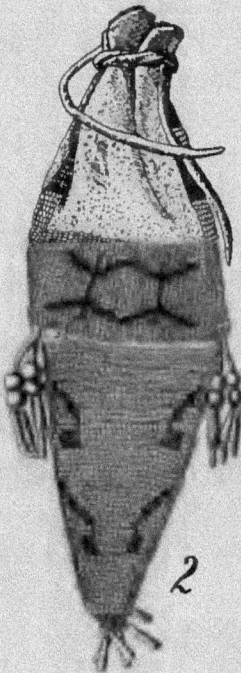

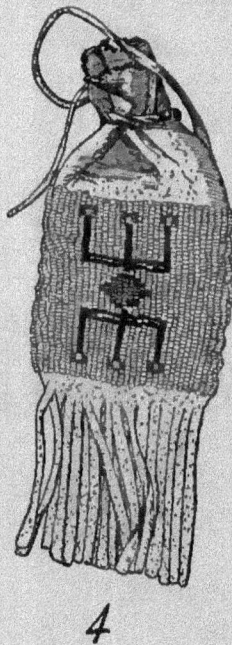

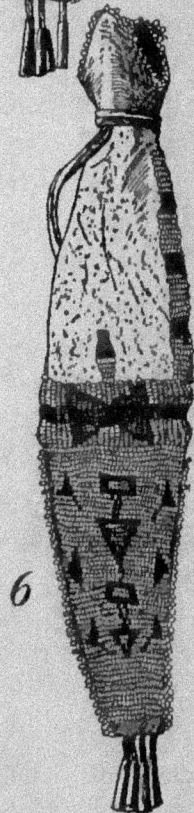

PAINT-POUCHES.

lateral figures pipes. On the other side (Fig. 2) is a representation of a turtle and of several pipes. The two narrow stripes extending to the mouth of the pouch are caterpillars.

The bag shown in Figs. 3 and 4 of Plate XII represents both a saddle-bag and a prairie-dog. On one side (Fig. 3), four right-angled triangles represent mountain-peaks. Small white patches on these represent snow. Dark figures at the points of these triangles are eagles on the mountains. The figure between the mountains represents the crossing of two paths. On the other side (Fig. 4), the diamond in the middle represents a turtle. The two three-pronged figures are turtle-claws. Small white spots on these are turtle-eggs.

It will be noticed that identical white spots mean on different sides of the bag respectively snow-patches and turtle-eggs. What signification they have depends in each case on the symbolic context. Similarly a three-pronged figure like that on this bag often signifies the bear's foot, but here, when adjacent to a turtle-symbol, a turtle's foot. Such representation of different objects by the same symbol — or such different interpretation of the same figure, according as one may wish to state it — is constantly found in the decorative art of this tribe. '

The pouch shown in Figs. 5 and 6, Plate XII, again represents a lizard. The large ornament about the middle of the bag (Fig. 5) represents a butterfly. The two triangles are its wings, and the rhomboidal figure of beadwork projecting on the leather surface is its body. On the flap is represented the centipede. The rows of small squares are its tracks. On the other side (Fig. 6) there is the butterfly again. On the flap is a dragon-fly, or perhaps two. The detached, somewhat triangular figures, at the sides of the dragon-fly, are its wings.

The pouch shown in Fig. 21, *a*, represents a saddle-bag. The design is a tent. The conventional stripe towards the opening, only part of which is shown in the illustration, is a snake.

In the paint-pouch shown in Fig. 21, *b*, each of the triangles with the two lines at its ends represents a tent. The space

enclosed by the triangle and the two lines represents the place
where the tent is.   In the stripe reaching to the opening of
the bag are representations of worms, each row or thread of

Fig. 21.   Paint-pouches.   About ⅔ nat. size.

a (₆₆₇), *b* (₁₁₁₂), *c* (₆₆₆), *d* (₁₈₈₃), *e* (₆₆₆), *f* (₁₁₁₂), *g* (₁₆₆₁), *h* (₆₆₆), *i* (₁₈₈₆).

beads being a worm.   The beading at the edge also represents worms.

The bag shown in Fig. 21, *c*, represents a saddle-bag.   The
large diamond, as well as the crosses on the vertical stripes,

are the morning star. Metallic beads in these figures express the lustre of the star.

The pouch shown in Fig. 21, *d*, represents a horned toad. The design represents caterpillars (*cf.* Plate XVII). The white represents snow.

The pouch shown in Fig. 21, *e*, also represents a horned toad. The triangles are mushrooms.

On the paint-pouch shown in Fig. 21, *f*, the ground-color is yellow, instead of the usual white, and represents ground. The pattern represents rocks. More accurately, dark blue in this design indicates rocks; red and pink, earth; and green, grass among the rocks. The stripe toward the opening symbolizes a narrow range of hills, and dark blue on this stripe is again rock.

The pouch shown in Fig. 21, *g*, represents a rat. Two triangular pink marks just below the mouth are ears. The rest of the design is very dilapidated, most of the beads having been worn off.[1]

The paint-pouch shown in Fig. 21, *h*, represents a saddle-bag. The ornamental design represents a lizard. Stripes along the sides, toward the opening of the pouch, are worms. Red squares on these stripes are the holes of the worms. The beading at the edge of the opening represents light and dark colored maggots.

The paint-pouch shown in Fig. 21, *i*, represents a reddish bivalve mollusk, probably a mussel.

Representation of an animal by an entire object which bears little visual resemblance to the animal, is not confined to paint-pouches or navel-amulets. An awl-case, made of hide wound with black and white beads, was intended to represent a lizard (Plate XIII, Fig. 1). Here, as in other cases, the particular animal represented could not well be recognized even by an Indian; and that this awl-case represents a lizard, and not a snake or fish or rat, is a matter of the individual purpose or interpretation of the maker. Perhaps even a distinct motive or intention for this symbolism was lacking in

---

[1] By mistake the design shown in the figure below the ears is the one on the opposite side of the pouch; that on the same side as the ears is similar but less dilapidated.

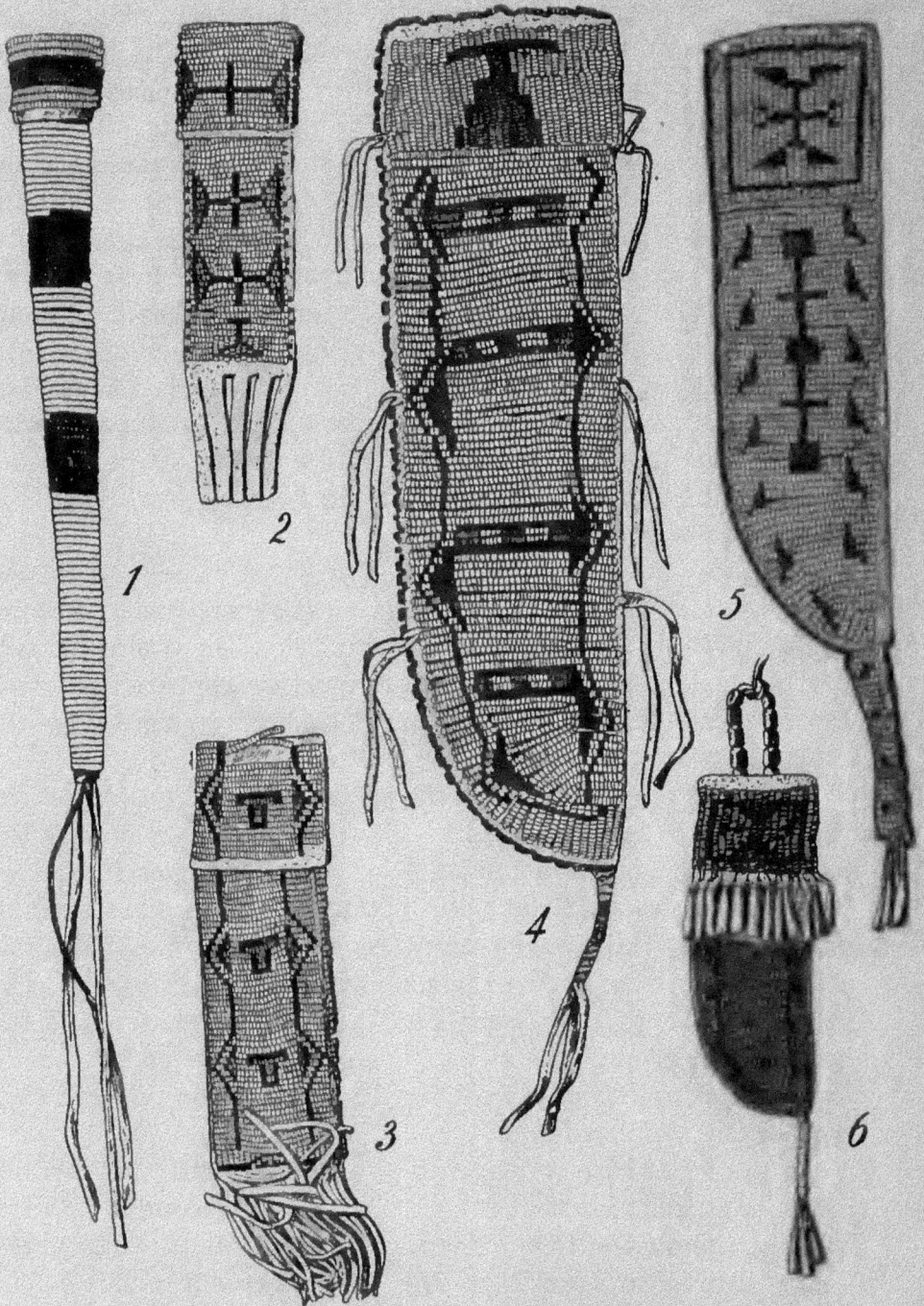

KNIFE AND AWL CASES.

this person's mind, for the lizard is the most common of all animals represented in this way; so that the symbolism of this awl-case may have been as conventional as its form.

A small knife-case is shown in Plate XIII, Fig. 2. The crosses have the usual meaning of the morning star. The triangles are tents. At the bottom end of the case is a small design that looks like half of the double figure occurring above it three times. The triangle in this design again represents a tent, but the T-shaped figure denotes the sun overhead, with its rays shining into the tent. All the figures are repeated in different colors, but with the same signification, on the other side. The white background represents sand or light-colored soil; the separate green beads along the edge are biisääna^n (insects or worms); and a yellow stripe of beadwork at the side of the case, which, however, is invisible in the figure, is a path.

A similar knife-case (Fig. 3 of the same plate) represents, as a whole, a fish. The design upon it represents mountain-ranges. The T-shaped figures are trees. On the other side of the specimen the mountain-ranges are repeated in other colors, while the trees are replaced by crosses, signifying the morning star.

A larger knife-scabbard is shown in Fig. 4 of Plate XIII. At the top is the figure of a tent. A wavy red line enclosing the rest of the design is a path. The green triangles inside are buffalo-wallows, and the stripes connecting them are buffalo-paths. The white background represents snow. The little attachment at the end of the scabbard is called the tail. The other loose thongs represent small streams of water. At the upper edge, around the rim of the opening, are red beads, to signify that the bloody knife used in butchering reddens that part of the scabbard.

On the knife-case shown in Fig. 5 of Plate XIII, the symbolism is so incoherent that it must have been secondary, in the mind of the owner, to the decorative appearance. The green lines forming a square at the top represent rivers. The figure within it is an eagle. The two larger dark portions of this figure are also cattle-tracks. The two rows of triangles on the body of the scabbard represent arrow-points. The squares in the middle are boxes, and the lines between them are the conventional morning-star cross. The small squares on the pendant attached to the point of the scabbard are cattle-tracks.

The signification of the ornamentation on another knife-case (Fig. 6, Plate XIII) is as follows. The yellow background is the ground. The dark blade-shaped line is a mountain, its small projections being rocks. The light-blue squares are lakes. The lines forming the rectangle at the top and the horizontal line within it are rivers, The two triangles are tents.

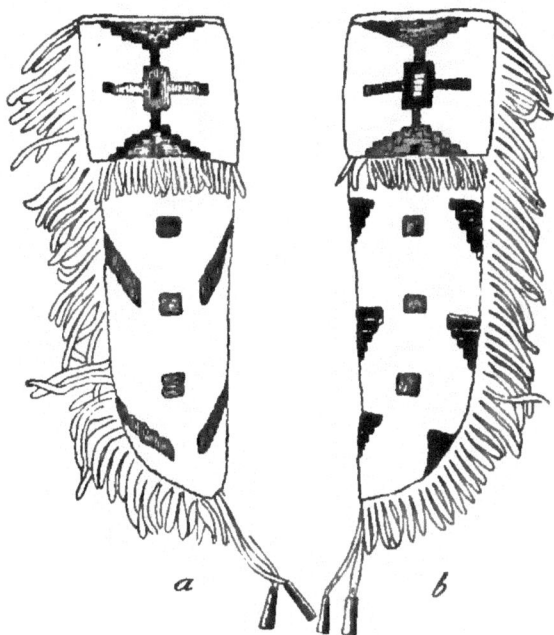

Fig. 22 (т⅞⅞). Beaded Knife-scabbard. Length, 12 cm.

Fig. 22 shows two sides of a small beaded knife-scabbard. At the top is the cross, naⁿkaox. In this case it represents a person. Adjacent to it are two triangles, which represent mountains. Below, are three green squares. These are the symbol of life or abundance. Red slanting lines pointing toward the squares are thoughts or wishes (kakauçetcanaⁿ), which are directed toward the desired objects, represented by the life-symbols. On the other side the colors are different, but the design is identical, except that instead of the red lines there are blue triangles, which represent knife-scabbards such as this specimen itself.

Small pouches are worn by the women, hanging from their belts. In these they keep matches, money, or other small articles. These bags are generally partly covered with bead-work, and are often further decorated by the attachment of leather fringes, tin cylinders, or buttons. A number of these belt-pouches are illustrated in Fig. 23 and Plate XIV.[1]

In Fig. 23, *a*, the white beadwork represents ground. The ornament in the middle represents mountains. The two dark-blue rectangles connected with this ornament symbolize rocks on the mountains. On the flap that closes the pouch, red and blue squares denote piles of rock or monuments (çiayaana^n).

In Fig. 23, *b*, the large triangular figure, the red lines forming a rectangle, and the variously-colored beading along the

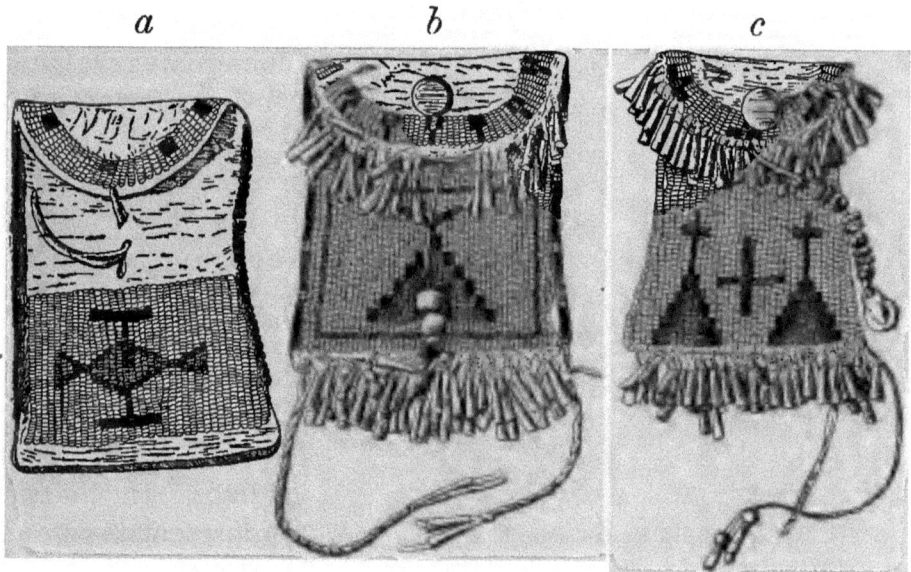

Fig. 23, *a* ($\frac{50}{3410}$), *b* ($\frac{50}{3343}$), *c* ($\frac{50}{1083}$). Women's Small Belt-pouches. ⅓ nat. size.

edge of the pouch, all represent rocks. Red and blue are often employed to denote rocks. On the point of the large triangular rock is a representation of an eagle. On the flap of the pouch is a white stripe which represents rocks, and blue figures on this are eagles sitting on the high rocks where they nest.

Similarly, on the pouch shown in Fig. 23, *c*, two triangles represent tents, while cross-like figures at their ends represent

---

[1] These pouches, as well as the larger ones shown in Figs. 25–28, are made of dark leather, while the body of the beadwork is white. In the illustrations the leather appears lighter in color than the beadwork.

eagles sitting on the tent-poles.   Between them is the morning-star cross.   Above, covered in the illustration by the
fringe of tin rattles, is a beaded design representing a rack on
which meat is dried.   It consists of a stripe of blue beads,
from which three inverted T-shaped figures descend, the stem
of the T being composed of four beads, while the cross-bar has
three beads.   The figures in the white stripe on the flap
denote stars.

In Fig. 24, *a*, the large design near the lower edge is the
bear's foot, generally conventionally represented by the

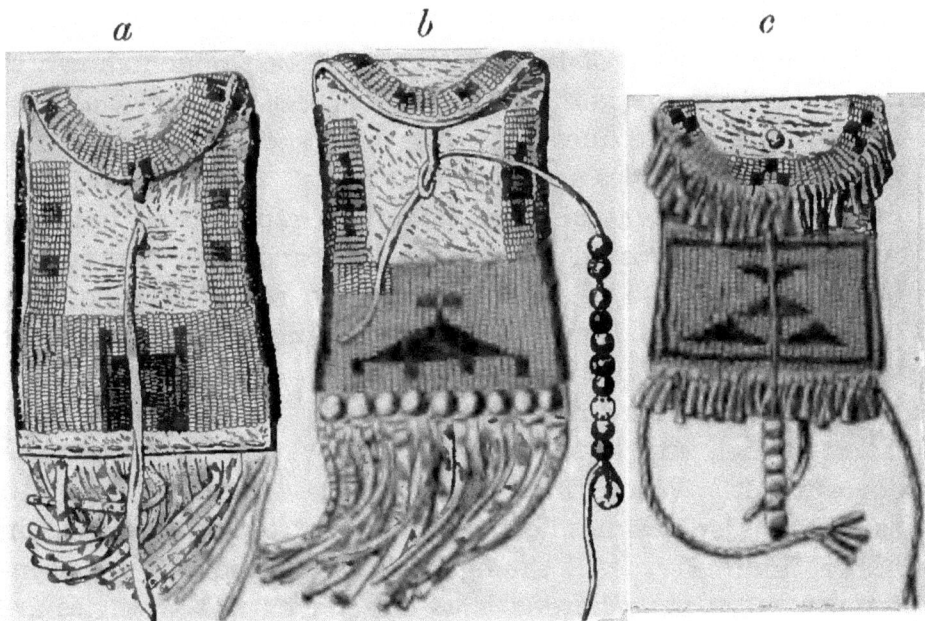

Fig. 24, *a* (₅₀₋₇), *b* (₅₀₋₇), *c* (₅₀₋₆).   Women's Small Belt-pouches.   ¼ nat. size.

Arapaho with only three claws.   Square pink spots on the
body of the design are the bare skin on the sole of the foot.
The white beadwork is sand or soil.   The curved band on
the flap is a mountain.   The leather fringe at the bottom of
the pouch represents trees.

On another pouch (Fig. 24, *b*) the white is sand.   Green
beading at the edges, on account of its color, denotes timber.
Two designs that may be described as compressed crosses represent the morning star.   Squares on the flap are rocks.   The

large figure near the bottom is a mountain, with a tree on its summit; below it are four small red and blue rectangles which denote little streams flowing from a spring near the foot of the mountain. This spring is represented by a green square in the large triangle.

In Fig. 24, *c*, the rectangle of beadwork on the front of the pouch represents the earth or the world.[1] The white denotes snow; and the red and blue triangles, rocks. The stripe on the flap is continued around the edge of the back of the pouch. It represents an ant-hill. The small squares on it represent dirt. The tin cylinders are ants. Stripes at the two sides of the pouch are ant-paths.

The signification of the design on the belt-pouch shown in Fig. 1 of Plate xiv is the following. The six triangles all represent tents. The lines enclosing the trapezoidal area within which these triangles are, represent trails. In the two stripes immediately above this area, stars are represented both by red rectangles crossed by a green line, and by green crosses on a red field. The white zigzag line on the flap of the pouch is a snake; the beaded stripes along the seams denote rivers.

Sometimes these small bags are made to hold the cards or tickets which entitle the bearer to the rations issued by the government. When this is the purpose of the bag, the flap or cover is sometimes left off. Such a pouch is shown in Fig. 2, Plate xiv. All the figures are geographical representations. The pink border is a large river, the triangles are islands in it. The green area within this represents the earth. Two large red A-shaped marks represent a stream, called by the Arapaho Fox-Tent Creek. The two rectangles represent mountains, called by the Arapaho House Mountains. The short yellow stripe connecting these represents Yellow Canyon. All these natural features are said to be situated to the north or northeast of the present location of the tribe in central Wyoming. Such representation of actual specific mountains, valleys, and rivers, is uncommon, though this case is not unique. It will be noted that the ornamentation is

---

[1] The same word means "world," "earth," "land," "ground," "soil."

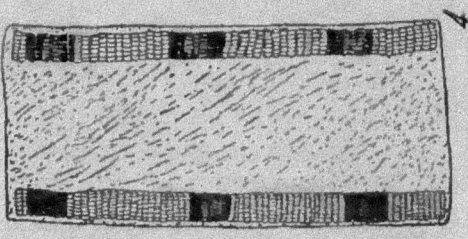

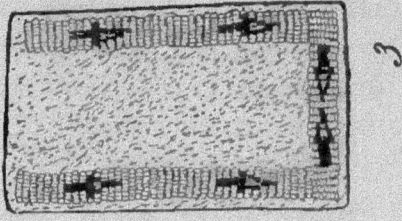
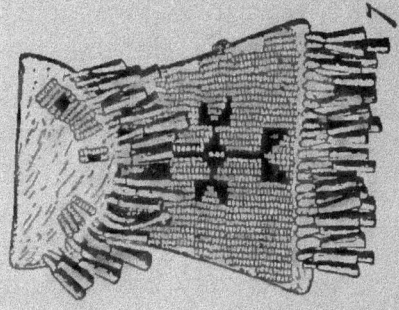
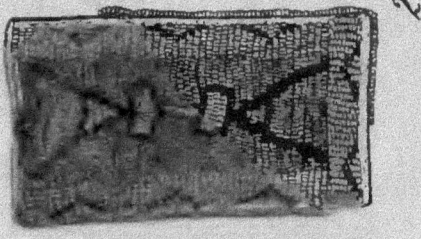
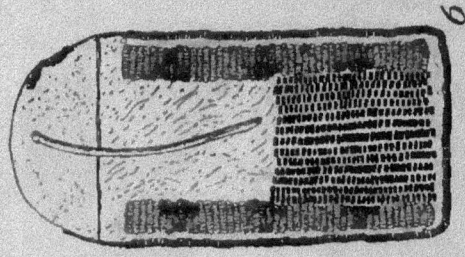
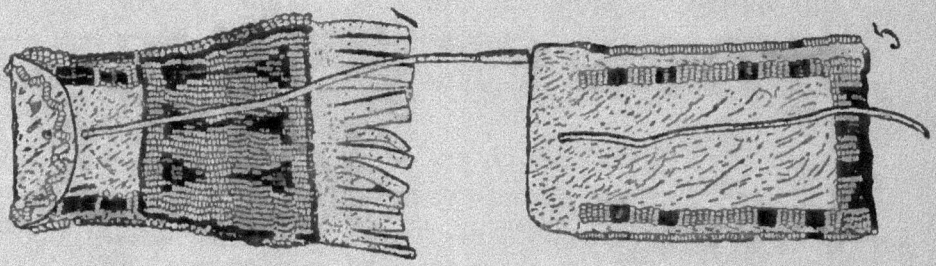

POUCHES.

symmetrically duplicated, in spite of the quasi-map-like nature of the design.

Another of these ration-ticket pouches is that shown in Figs. 3 and 4, Plate xiv. On the front are represented flint arrow-points. On the other side (back and flap) the stripes represent arrow-shafts, the colored portions being the property-marks with which arrow-shafts are painted. Arrows are the means of securing game; game is used as food; so is the beef that is issued by the government, and this is obtained by means of the ration-card kept in the pouch. Such is the reason for representing arrows by the ornament on this little bag. Associations of this sort (arrows, game, meat, beef, ration-card) are not uncommon among the Arapaho, especially among the speculative and the old. They remind one strikingly of the symbolic identification, on account of analogies in single respects, that is so prominent in the religion of the Indians of the Southwest, and which has been treated of extensively by Cushing among the Zuñi, and lately, in more detail, by Lumholtz among the Huichols.

Another pouch is shown in Fig. 5, Plate xiv. The squares along the sides are bee-holes. The figure at the bottom is a bee. The red beads at the lower edge of the pouch are bees. The white edges on the sides are trails, the red spots denoting holes.

Fig. 6, Plate xiv, shows another pouch in which ration-cards were kept. The black beads covering the lower half of the bag represent coffee, which is obtained at the ration-issue. The light-blue bands at the sides, on account of their color, represent the sky. The ornaments upon them are mountains. The single lines of dark-blue beads along the edges represent wolves.

On the tasteful pouch shown in Fig. 7, Plate xiv, the red diamond in the centre of the design represents a person. The four forked ornaments surrounding it are buffalo hoofs or tracks.

In Fig. 8 of Plate xiv the main ornament is a tent. The rectangle above the apex of the triangle represents the spreading upper flaps or ears of the tent, and the two lateral hand-shaped designs are buffalo-tails attached to the top of the tent. The white background denotes ground; its red border, water (evidently streams). On the cover is a design which is continued as a border on the back of the pouch. This is mostly red, and, on account of this color, denotes flame, and therefore, by a series of symbolic equations, matches, which are kept in the pouch. White marks upon this border represent ashes.

Fig. 2, Plate IV, shows a belt-pouch. The white background represents snow. The blue lines enclosing the design are mountains, while lines of green beads at the very edge of the pouch represent trees. On the face of the pouch, two triangles are tents; a rectangle or stripe between them is a stream of water. On the flap, a blue spot is a rock, and two groups of red squares are two stars.

Bags about a foot in length, made of dark leather, and nearly covered with beads on the front, are used to hold combs, paint-bags, and other more modern articles of toilet use.

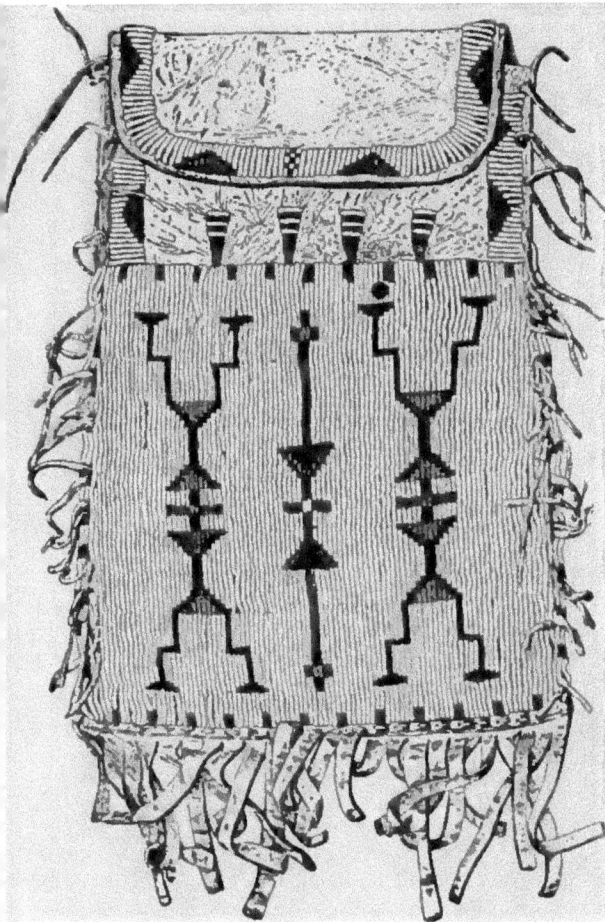

Fig. 25 (₁₈₈₄). Toilet-bag. Height, 38 cm.

Fig. 25 shows a typical bag of this kind. The large ornament that is duplicated on each side of the design represents persons. The narrower ornament in the middle represents two dragon-flies. Both the persons and the dragon-flies are to be conceived as having their heads joined. Rectangular red marks all around the edge of the beaded area represent a fence, symbolized by its posts. The four ornaments standing up above this beaded field represent worms. On the flap of the cover, and just below, are white stripes. On these are designs of mountains; in the middle of the stripe on the cover is a small checkered ornament which represents rocks.

In another toilet-pouch (Fig. 26) three crosses represent, as usual, the morning star, and four three-pronged ornaments denote bear-claws. In two square areas, situated between the bear-foot ornaments, pink triangular surfaces represent tents, while the blue and white diagonals separating them are trails. A dark-blue line enclosing all the ornaments that have been mentioned signifies mountain-ranges. Two H-shaped marks near the top of the pouch

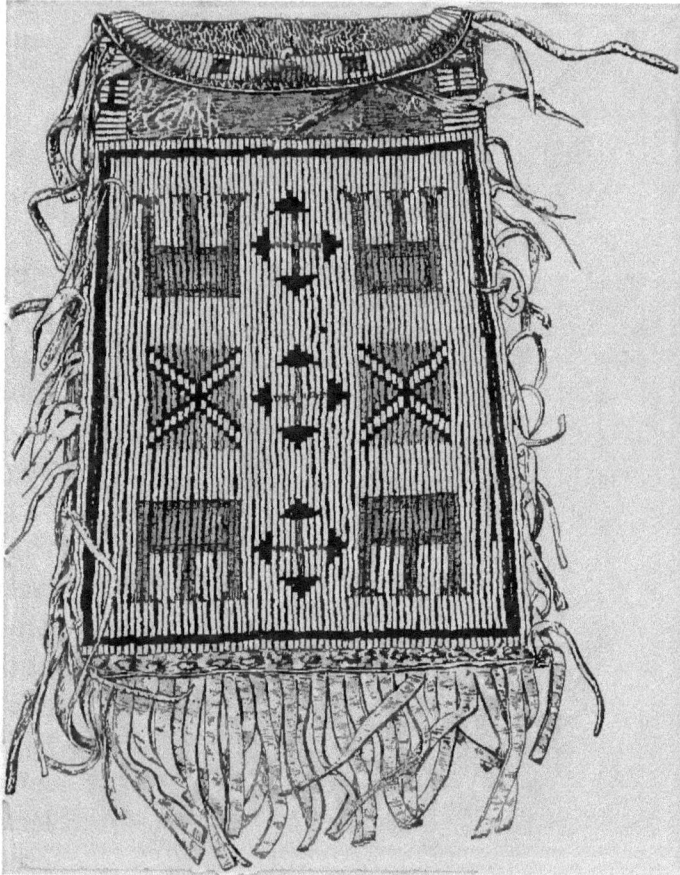

Fig. 26 ($\frac{50}{7472}$).   Toilet-pouch.   Height, 39 cm.

represent racks for drying meat. On the white stripe upon the cover are mountains (represented by triangles) and lakes (represented by squares).

Fig. 27 illustrates a toilet-pouch[1] somewhat larger than most

---

[1] In the specimen itself there is a pleasing contrast between the brown leather and the white beadwork, which is not indicated in the illustration.

others, and more delicate in ornamentation. The two ornaments, placed symmetrically, one on each side of the square
white field, are worked chiefly in green; the design between
them is mostly blue. At the centre of this last design there
is a cross, the Arapaho word for which means also "morning

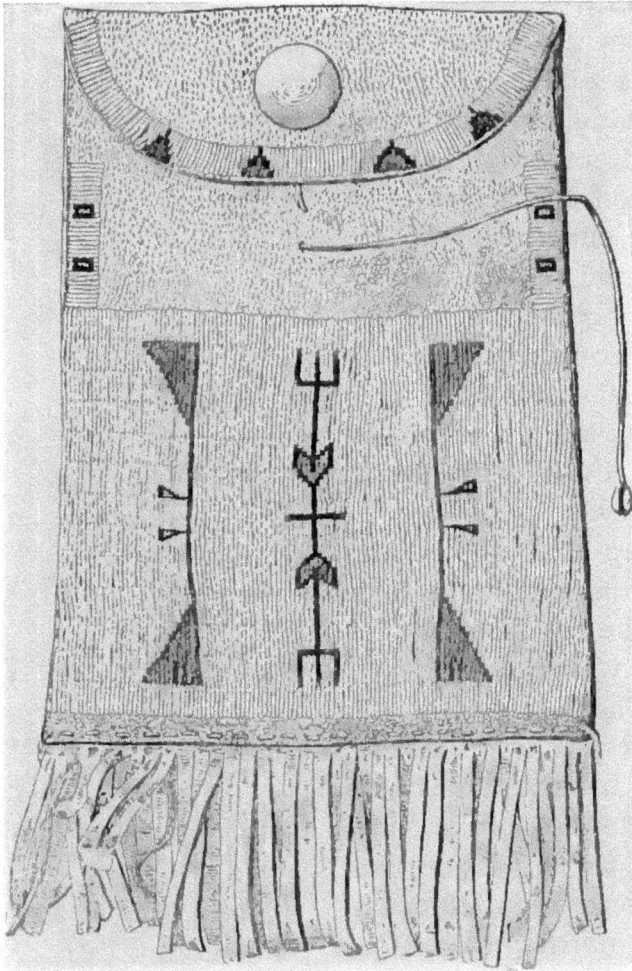

Fig. 27 (₁⁸⁶⁄₂₅). Toilet-pouch. Height, 42.5 cm.

star." The notched marks adjacent to this represent clouds,
also the heart. A few brass beads within these figures denote
the gleaming of the cloud. The three-pronged figures at the
ends are bear's claws (wasixta). The line connecting this with
the cloud-symbol is the bear's leg. In the lateral figures, the

green triangles and red lines represent respectively the leaves and stems of yellow-weed (nihaᵑnaxuⁱn), a common plant used as medicine. Within the leaves are small red rectangles which represent face-paint. Two small blue triangles, just touching the representations of the stems, are eyes. Brass beads within these denote the gleam of the eye. Outside of this decorative area, on the two white stripes at the edge above, are small rectangles, also of blue and metallic beads, which also denote eyes. The entire white background of beadwork symbolizes clouds. On the cover, triangles represent tents; because they are arranged on the curved white band, they also symbolize the camp-circle. The leather fringe at the bottom of the bag denotes various trails.

The last bag of this series is shown in Fig. 28. In the middle of the white decorative field are three red crosses, representing, as usual, the morning star. The four ornaments on the bordering stripes above

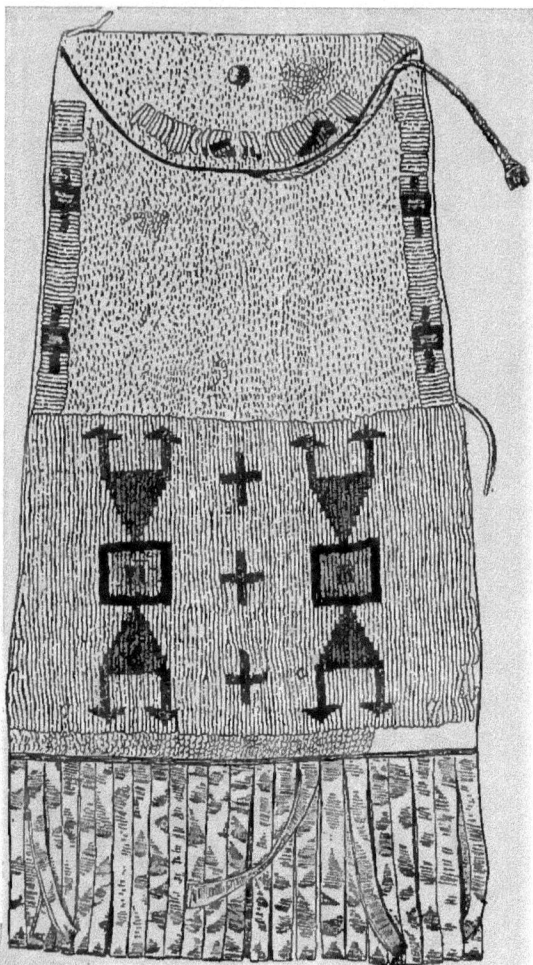

Fig. 28 (1/81). Toilet-bag. Height, 43 cm.

are also crosses, or the morning star. Four large green triangles, each with two projections, represent frogs. The two squares between these triangles represent floating scum in which the frogs have their heads. The centre of these squares is red; this symbolizes the face-paint which is kept

in the pouch.   The white represents clouds.   On the cover
are hills, rising and falling along the horizon.

It is noteworthy that, with all the diversity of symbolism
on these four pouches, their designs should be so similar.   On
all of them there is a large white decorative field, approximately square.   Above this the leather is left bare except for
a narrow strip upward along each side.   The convex edge of
the cover is also bordered by a band of white beadwork.   On
the main decorative area there are three figures or groups of
figures, extending vertically.   The outer two of these three
figures are alike, which gives symmetry to the whole design.
The middle figure is always different from the two others, and
narrower.   Each of these three figures falls into three parts,
which may be connected or separate.   The resemblance can
be traced still farther, as in the shape of these parts of the
three figures.   A glance at the illustrations will show this
better than a verbal description.[1]

Yet with this general unity of decorative scheme there go
hand in hand, first, an astounding diversity of detail; and,
secondly, an equally great diversity of symbolism.   Ornaments that are analogously placed and somewhat similar in
form represent, on different pouches, objects as different as
men, bear-feet, leaves, and frogs; or, again, dragon-flies, stars,
bear-feet, and clouds and stars.   The diversity in ornamental
detail is as noticeable as the general decorative similarity.
The co-existence of these two apparently contrary traits is due
to the fact that the Indians, while strongly impressed with
certain conventional styles or patterns of decoration, do not
directly copy the ornamentation of one pouch in making
another, but always exercise their inventive powers in design-
ing ornamental forms.   This constant variability of detail
within narrow limits has been shown above to exist in ornamented moccasins, and is perhaps still more striking as regards
the painted rawhide bags and the parfleches treated below
(see pp. 104 et seq.).

[1] These bags are of course not specially selected to show similarity of design, but
comprise all the toilet-pouches from the Wyoming Arapaho that the American Museum
of Natural History possesses.   A pouch from the Oklahoma Arapaho, with a different
style of design, was described and illustrated in Symbolism of the Arapaho Indians
(Bulletin A M. N. H., Vol. XIII, 1900, pp. 82, 83).

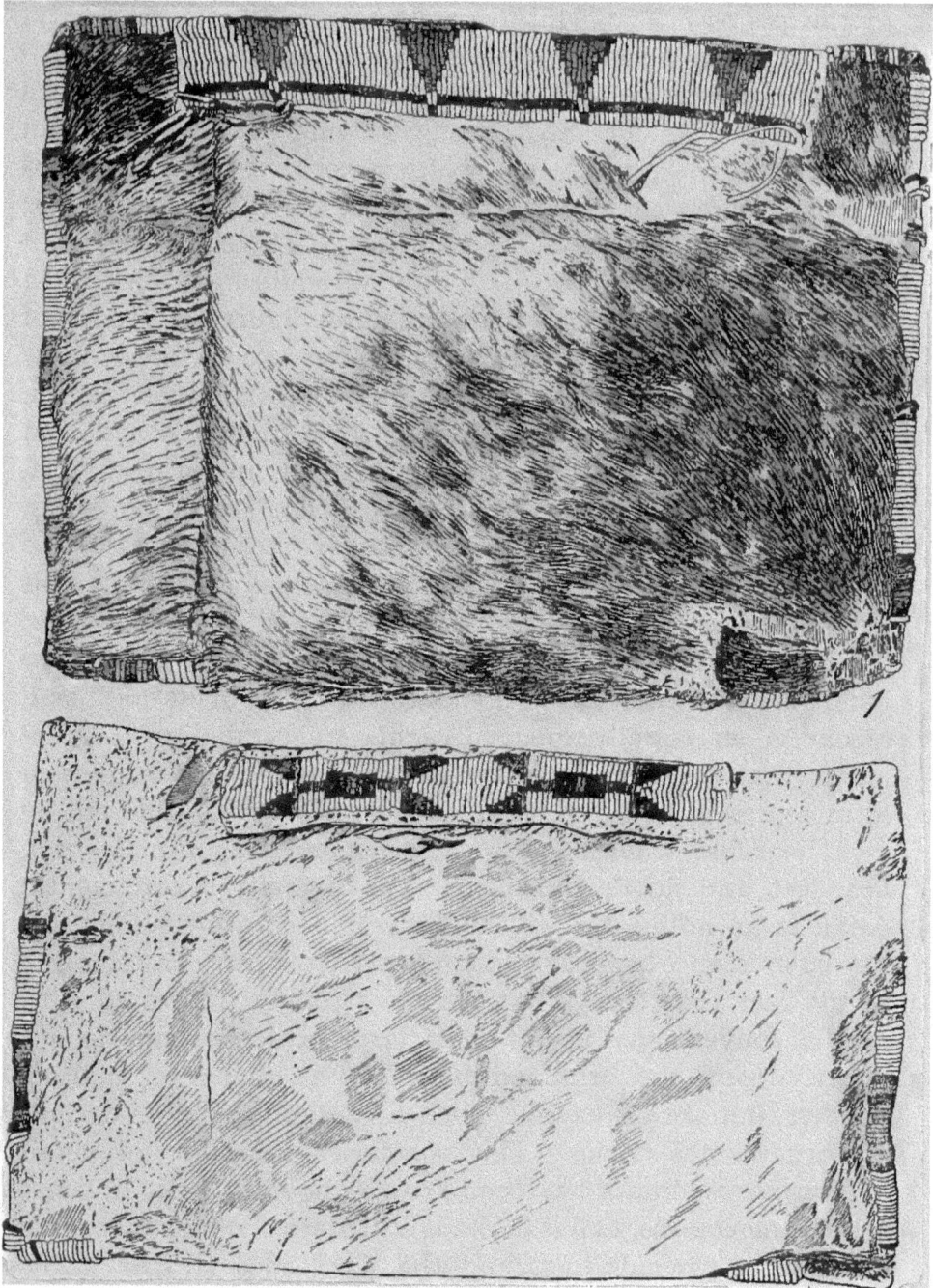

WOMEN'S WORK-BAGS.

Plate xv shows two women's work-bags. These are made of hide on which the hair has been left. The opening extends at the top along the border of beadwork. Both the bags are much worn. The first (Fig. 1) is ornamented with designs of tents and a path, represented by green triangles and a dark-blue line at the top. White beading around the edge represents mountains. Green and yellow marks on this represent springs. From the second bag (Fig. 2) the hair is almost completely worn off. The white stripe at the top is a trail. The marks on this denote four elk-legs. Just below this stripe are the remnants of a line of quill-work, which was embroidered there in order to symbolize quill-embroidery (perhaps because the bag was used to hold sewing-appliances). The borders at the other edges represent paths.

These ordinary sewing-bags must not be confounded with the women's seven sacred bags that have already been mentioned (see p. 30). The sacred bags are quite different in appearance.

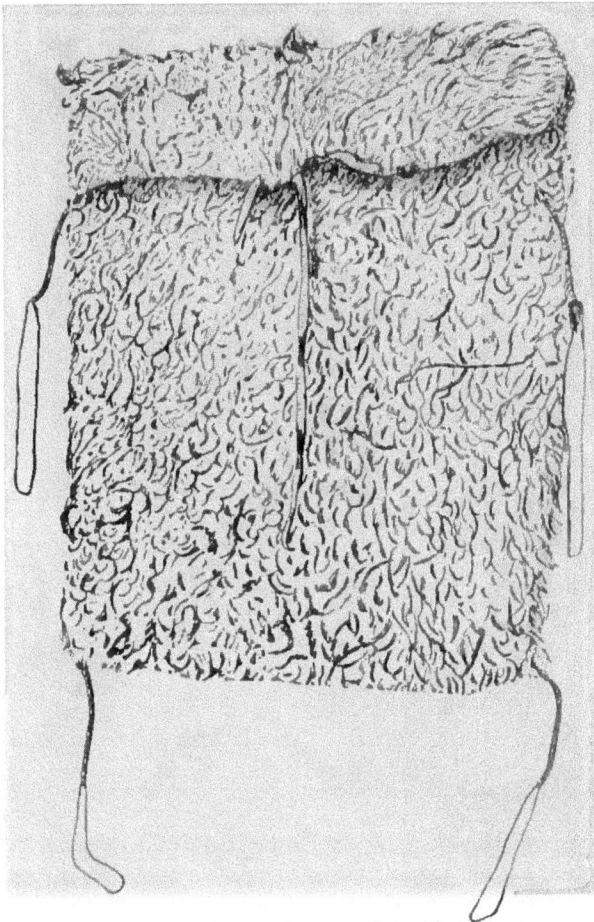

Fig. 29 ($\frac{50}{1088}$). Bag of Buffalo-skin. Height, 32 cm.

Two bags that are made of skin that has the hair left on it are shown in Figs. 29 and 30. The one shown in Fig. 29 is made of woolly buffalo-skin. It represents, in its entirety, a

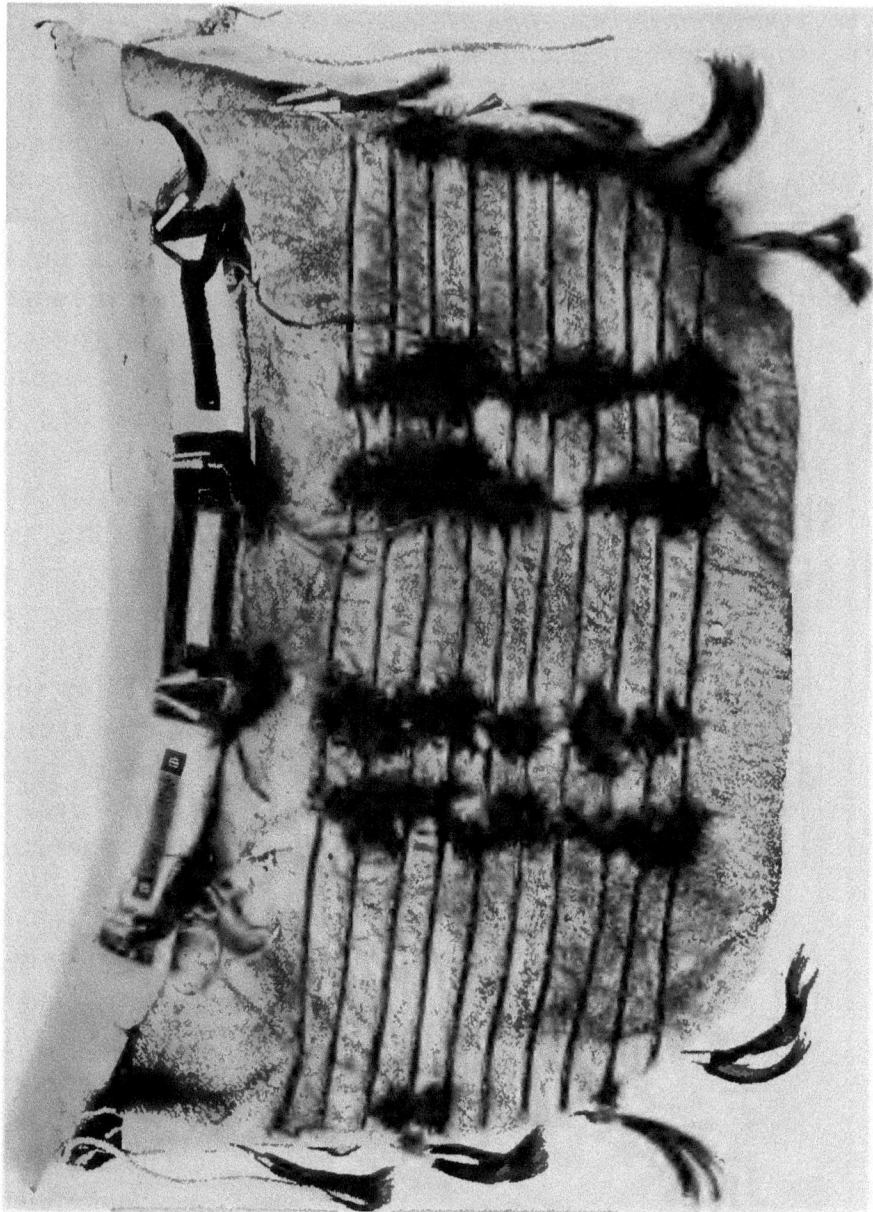

Soft Bag, Front and Side Views.

beaver. That shown in Fig. 30 is made of the skin of a buffalo calf. Around the opening, a band of beadwork, with red
squares in it, represents the camp-circle. Plum-pits attached
to the bag near this beadwork represent burrs sticking in the
hair of buffalo. At the lower end, a small beaded attachment
represents the tail of a buffalo.

Bags of soft pliable hide are used for keeping and transporting clothing and similar arti-
cles. They are beaded along
two edges and on the cover.
Sometimes the front is also
covered with embroidery in
beads or quills. These bags
must be distinguished from
rawhide bags, which are stiff
and hard, and painted instead
of embroidered. Rawhide
bags and parfleches are sometimes used to hold clothing
and household articles, but
seem primarily intended for
food.

Plate XVI shows such a
bag. The five-colored pattern
which extends along each
end of the bag is typical.
In this specimen the longitudinal stripes were said to
represent the marks of tent-
poles on the ground; that is,
camp - trails. The shorter
transverse stripes are ravines; that is, camping-places.

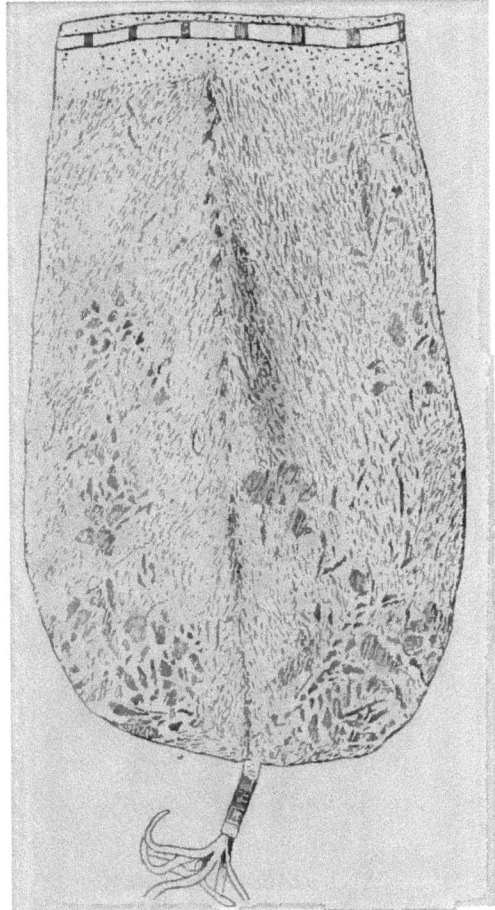

Fig. 30 ($\frac{50}{1001}$). Hide Bag. Height, 69 cm.

The squares are life-symbols.
On the flap forming the cover the symbolism is the same.
On the front of the bag the horizontal lines of quill-work,
which resemble the lines on buffalo-robes, are paths.
Bunches of feathers on these lines represent buffalo-meat
hung up to dry. Adjoining the beadwork are small tin

cylinders with tufts of red hair; these represent pendants or rattles on tents.

Fig. 31 shows the beadwork on the end of another soft hide

bag. This design, like the last, represents camp-trails and camping-places. Another individual explained the analogous design on another bag as representing buffalo-paths.

Plate XVII shows a bag of soft hide with considerable beadwork.[1] On the front each of the two large figures, with four pairs of projections each, represents a centipede. They are also caterpillars and leaves, the green rectangles with the cleft figures at their ends being the caterpillars; and the intermediate yellow rectangles, leaves. In the middle of this side of the bag are four figures representing butterflies.

The design at the end of the bag, while resembling those which represent paths in previous specimens, represents worms; each of the stripes, longitudinal or transverse, being one animal. At the centre of this design, a square, green outside, then yellow, then red, and light blue inside, represents an ant-hill.

Fig. 31 ($\frac{50}{100}$). Beadwork on End of Bag. Length, 46 cm.

---

[1] In the illustration of this specimen, red is represented by horizontal, yellow by diagonal, and green by vertical shading.

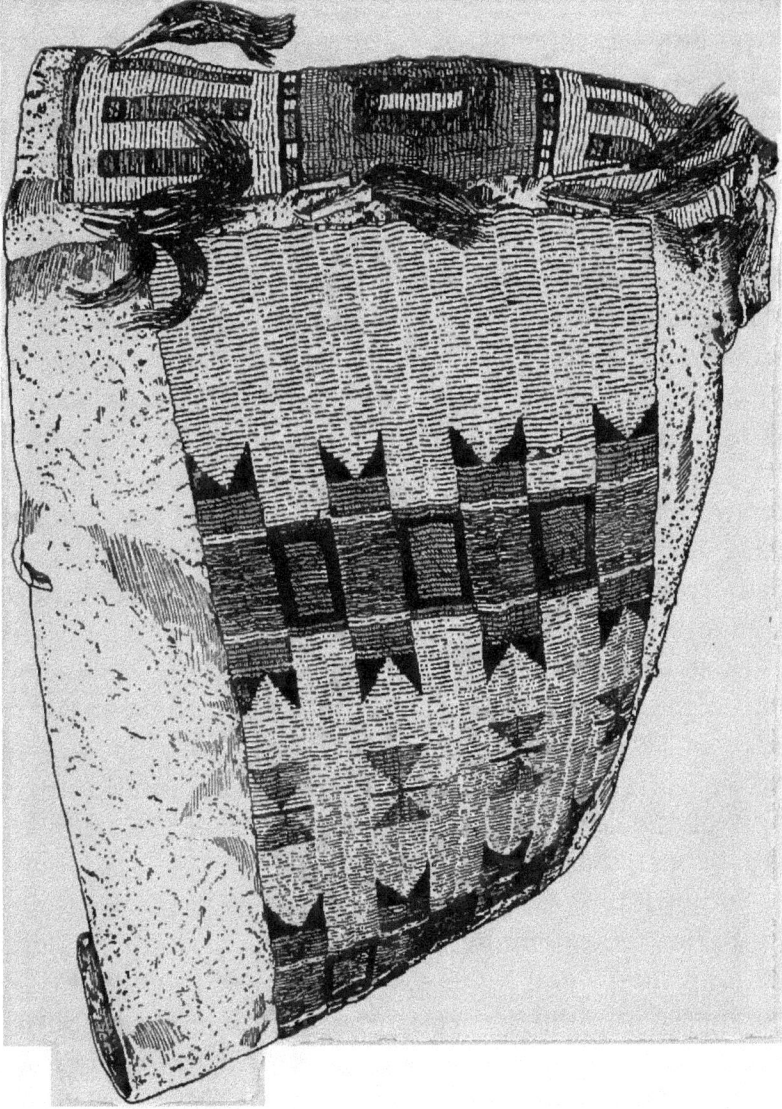

Beaded Bag.

Many bags, pouches, and receptacles of the Arapaho are made of stiff white skin, from which the hair has been scraped. The most typical form is that called "parfleche." This consists of a single piece of rawhide, generally half a buffalo-skin, approximately rectangular. The two long sides are folded inward to meet in the middle. The opening where the two long edges come together is closed by turning over the two short ends of the folded hide so that they also meet in the middle, where they are tied together (see Fig. 3, Plate XVIII). The rawhide is stiff and keeps its folded shape, but is elastic enough to allow of the parfleche being pressed very flat when empty, and widely distended when filled. The two upper covers of the parfleche are painted each with the same design, which is rectangular in shape, and composed chiefly of triangles. The parfleches are used particularly for storing and transporting dried meat. They are also convenient and much used for holding clothing and household articles. They are usually made in pairs. In travelling, one is hung on each side of a horse, the painted side of course being outside.

Bags or pouches, when made of rawhide, are also made of one piece. There is a fold along what constitutes the lower edge of the bag; the edges along the two sides are sewed together. The top is covered by a triangular flap, which is part of the back, and is drawn down over the front of the bag (Plate XXI, Fig. 1).

Sometimes a somewhat larger bag is made without the flap to cover the opening. The fold in the hide is along one of its long sides; the other edge is stitched. Or the bag may be composed of two pieces sewed together along both of their long edges. The two ends are composed of soft hide or cloth. The opening is merely a slit in one of these ends. This kind of bag is more distendible than the simple pouch-like form. It is used chiefly to store food. One is shown in Fig. 3, Plate XXI. The more common form of rawhide bag is used for gathering berries and fruits.

Almost all rawhide bags are painted on the back, though the design is simpler than that on the front. Parfleches, however, are unpainted on the back or bottom.

In the following illustrations, only one of the painted flaps of each parfleche is shown; but of bags, the back and cover, as well as the front, are in most cases represented. The bags are illustrated as if the stitches at their edges had been removed and the piece of hide composing the bag spread out flat.

Fig. 1 of Plate XVIII shows the design on the flap of a parfleche. The red areas along each side of the design represent a red bank along a stream. The adjacent unpainted space represents sand. Adjacent to this, a triangle formed by blue lines is a hill. The upper part of this is green, and represents grass; the basal portion, yellow, and represents earth of that color. On the other half of the symmetrical design, the figures of course have the same significance. Between these two halves is a longitudinal stripe which is red in the middle, but white at the ends. This represents a trail. As a road cannot be alike in all its length, this representation of it also has more colors than one. The entire rectangle of the design is the earth.

While bags of rawhide open along one edge, parfleches, as explained, open in the middle. The two covering flaps of hide are there tied together by strings. These strings pass through holes near the ends of the two covering pieces (*cf.* Fig. 3 of this plate). In this specimen (Fig. 1) there are two such holes near the edge of the design, where the symbol of the road ends. Through these holes the fastening-strings are passed. Therefore they control access to the contents of the parfleche. As the parfleche does not open except at this place, it is necessary, in order to obtain its contents, to reach these holes; therefore the road is painted leading to them (see Fig. 3 of this plate). Moreover, the white sections of this road are oblong, which is the shape of the parfleche itself. The two hills and the road between them form a roughly rhombic figure; and very nearly such is the shape of the hide of which this parfleche is made, when it is unfolded and spread out (ordinarily this piece of rawhide is more nearly rectangular than rhombic).

The maker of this parfleche, an old woman, said that it was made to resemble another one. It represents the land as it is, as nearly as it can be represented. People try to paint

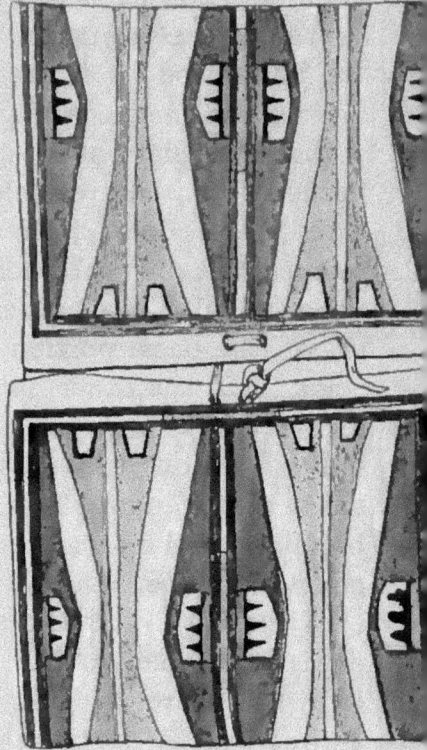

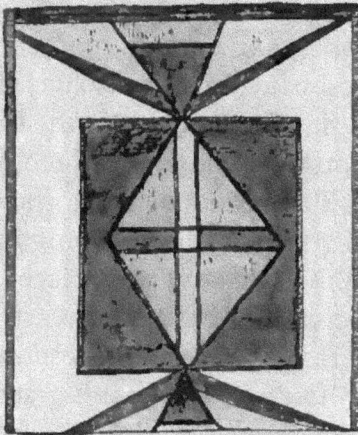

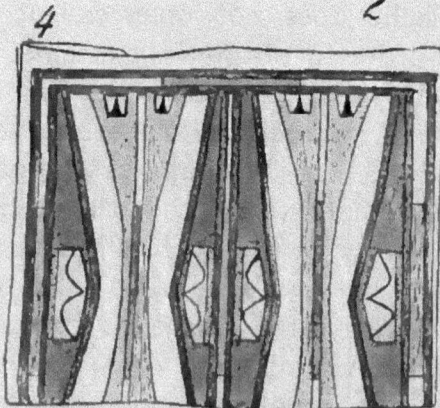

DESIGNS ON PARFLECHES.

their parfleches so as to be as pretty as possible.   Often they dream of the designs.

Fig. 2 of Plate xviii shows the design on another parfleche. In the centre of this design is a green rectangle, which denotes the earth.   A yellow stripe traversing this longitudinally represents a large river; a blue stripe bisected by it, streams of water flowing into the river.   The small white unpainted square at the intersection of these stripes is called the centre.   The red triangles forming a diamond in the green rectangle represent mountains.   At the two ends of the design are two triangular areas, also representing mountains. In each there is an equilateral triangle, which denotes a tent; the lower part of this triangle, which is red, is the door of the tent.   Yellow, outside of this tent-symbol but adjacent to it, denotes day or sunlight.   Four green lines which enclose the whole area represent the camp-circle.

Fig. 3 of Plate xviii shows an entire parfleche with its two flaps painted with the same design.   The long triangular areas, which are blue, represent, of course wholly on account of their color, the sky.   The white areas in them, having rounded tops, are sweat-houses; the black tooth-like marks are people in the sweat-house.   A red stripe at the foot of the sweat-house represents red earth or paint.   Between each pair of the long, blue sky-triangles is a pair of figures stretching the whole length of the design; one of each pair is red, the other yellow.   These figures denote four sticks such as are used in painting parfleche designs like this one.   White trapezoidal areas at the ends of these stick-figures are life-symbols. The longitudinal curved spaces left unpainted between the sky-symbols and the stick-figures represent thongs or ropes of rawhide, such as that used to fasten this parfleche.   The narrow white stripes, of which there are several, are trails.   The green lines enclosing each design represent grass.   On each of the four sides near the edge, as well as in the very middle, of the design, is a yellow stripe; these stripes, on account of their color, represent sunlight and yellow clouds (literally, "yellow day").   These yellow stripes are bounded at their ends by small dark-brown (black) rectangular marks, invisible in the illustration; these represent black water-beetles, called in Arapaho "buffalo-bulls" (the buffalo is at times also represented by a black rectangle).

A parfleche design very similar to the last is shown in Fig. 4 of Plate xviii. The four long flat triangles are again blue, and the figures between them are half yellow and half red. The blue triangles also again enclose a white area with rounded top, within which is a figure with three points. In spite of this similarity to the design last described, the symbolism differs considerably. In the present specimen the flat blue triangles are mountains; the red three-toothed figures are red hills, the white spaces between their projections being basins or valleys; a yellow stripe at the base of this hill-and-valley figure represents a flat or plain; the red-and-yellow figures, which taper toward the middle, are tents; the trapezoidal white areas enclosed at their bases are life-symbols; and the black marks bisecting the life-symbols are tent-pegs, this interpretation being probably suggested by their shape and by their position at the foot of the tents; the straight lines or narrow stripes, whether red, blue, or unpainted, are paths. On account of its four-sided shape, the whole design represents the earth.

A parfleche which, both in the color and the shapes of its design, is unusual, though a pattern somewhat resembling the more common one is recognizable in it, is shown in Fig. 5 of Plate xviii. The six rectangles are yellow; they are exteriorly bordered by red, as are the four triangles interiorly. The rest of the designs consists of black lines. The six rectangles are bear-feet (the claws, sometimes the most prominent feature, being omitted). The triangles are flint arrow-points. The black lines are ropes. The black lines enclosing the entire design are (because forming a rectangle) the earth. At each corner are two short red stripes, forming an angle. These are life-symbols. Evidently each stripe is regarded as an elongated quadrilateral, the square or trapezoid being the regular figure for the life-symbol.

On the parfleche shown in Fig. 1, Plate xix, the triangles represent tents. Strictly, the equilateral triangles and the

1

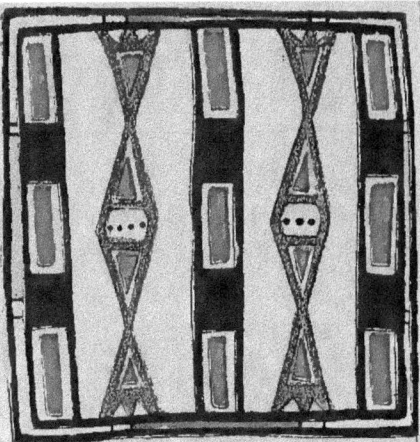

2

3

4

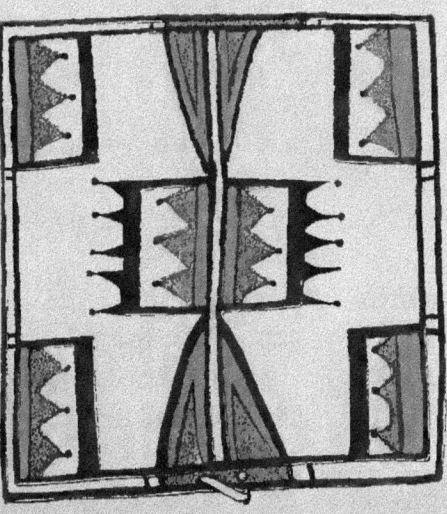

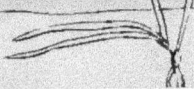

pairs of right-angled triangles represent tents; but the four blue right-angled triangles at the corners of the design, half of a tent. Their colors denote the colors (red, yellow, blue, or green, but not black) with which tents were formerly painted. The design is longitudinally trisected by two white stripes, which represent paths. Black dots in them are coyote-tracks. These stripes are edged on one side by red, and on the other by blue; these colors denote night and day, and, because night and day are opposite, are on opposite sides of the white stripe. The blue lines enclosing the whole design represent tent-pegs. The white stripes which they enclose are rivers; the red and yellow stripes which they enclose are camp-sites. The small squares in the corners of the design are the ends of the earth (hǎneisa^n biitaawu). The white areas within the design, consisting each of a high narrow trapezoid surmounted by an equilateral triangle, represent women. This design (*i. e.*, style of design), as well as that called wasixta ("bear-foot"), was first made by the mythic cosmological character, Whirlwind-Woman.

In the parfleche design shown in Fig. 2, Plate XIX, the three wide blue stripes represent rivers. Evidently both form and color are symbolic. The red rectangles in them are islands, and the white border around these is sand. The triangles are bear-feet (wasixta). The red portions of the triangles represent the bare skin of the sole of the foot; the projections at the base of the triangles are the claws. The white hexagonal areas represent the prairie (*i. e.*, land, ground); the black spots in them are coyotes. Enclosing the whole design are the customary lines or stripes. These signify paths. Those of them that are blue represent buffalo-paths; the white, antelope-paths; the yellow, elk-paths; and the red, deer-paths.

In the parfleche design of Fig. 3, Plate XIX, the large yellow triangles, one along each long side of the rectangular design, represent mountains or the earth; the red stripes at their bases are red banks along rivers; the white squares at the ends of these red stripes are lakes; the blue areas adjoining the squares represent smoke, haze, and heavy atmosphere; the large white areas represent bare ground. In the middle, the entire hourglass-shaped figure is a bed. The green portion is grass-covered ground. The red stripe is a path. The red triangles at the end are again red banks. The small yellow triangles at the ends represent a hill on the Wind River Reservation in Wyoming, which is said to be yellow in appearance, and at which a fight once occurred. It is called nihaⁿnōû'tăⁿ.

In the parfleche shown in Fig. 4, Plate xix, color is more important than form, so far as symbolism is concerned. The blue represents mountains; this is presumably both on account of its color and because the blue areas are all obtuse iosoceles triangles, the usual symbol for a mountain. The red represents fruit or berries. The yellow, wherever it occurs on the parfleche, represents wood, especially willow on account of its yellowish-green bark. In addition, the colors used here also represent all objects having those colors. The acute red triangles also represent flame. The red, yellow, and blue acute triangles represent tents. The white and red pentagonal areas within the blue represent the door or opening in the mountain from which the buffalo originally issued on the earth. The long straight lines represent rivers.

Fig. 5, Plate xix, shows a parfleche design that is not very frequent, but old. It is called wasixta ("bear-foot"). It was said to be the oldest of the parfleche designs, and to have been invented by Whirlwind-Woman, the first woman on earth. All the points or projections represent bear-claws. The lines enclosing the whole design, and forming a square, represent the camp-circle.

In the parfleche design shown in Fig. 6, Plate xix, the two long isosceles triangles along the sides represent mountains. At each end of the design are three acute triangles, which represent tents. To each belongs one half of the diamond adjoining its vertex, this half-diamond being the projecting tent-poles. At the corners of the middle diamond are two small black triangular marks, which represent the rope passed around the poles near their tops to hold them together. The two middle tents also have their doors shown. In the other triangles, blue circular spots denote the place or situation of the tent. The entire square of the design is the earth. The stripes enclosing the design are rivers, red portions of them denoting river-banks of red soil. Minute black marks crossing these stripes represent paths.

Fig. 1 of Plate xx shows a bag which appears to have been made out of one end of a parfleche. The design is also a typical parfleche design. In the middle are two long flat triangles which are green; these represent grass-covered mountains. In each there is a pentagonal white area, which denotes a cave or hole in the mountain, and black pointed marks, which represent buffalo in the cave, from which they are supposed originally to have come. At the two sides of the pattern, mountains are also represented. The yellow acute triangles represent tents, and three red teeth at the base of each are its pegs. Lines and stripes denote paths, and the white portions of the design signify water.

In the parfleche design shown in Fig. 2, Plate xx, the circles, a very unusual ornamental figure in rawhide painting, represent lakes. They also represent buffalo-eyes. Near them, the triangles with the three-toothed bases are tents with their tent-pegs. A row of black dots just above the base of the tent represents people inside. Two small green triangles just above this row of dots are the dew-claws of buffalo. Along the two sides of the design, right-angled and equilateral triangles represent mountains. The double blue lines surrounding the whole design are rivers; the white and red stripes between the blue ones are paths. In the middle of the design, extending longitudinally, are two tents. The stripe bisecting them is a path, black dots in which signify tracks. The lower part of each of these middle triangles is divided off by a black line, and forms a white quadrilateral area resembling the life-symbol. These areas represent bears' ears, which are used as amulets. Two small black points in each of these figures are also bears' ears.

Fig. 3 of Plate xx shows the design on a very small parfleche. The design is bordered by a pattern in four colors. In this border-design red lines, forming an edging, are paths. The body of the border is green, and represents the earth.

DESIGNS ON RAWHIDE BAGS.

Blue triangles on this are mountains; and small yellow triangles enclosed within the blue are yellowish rocks on the
mountains.   Inside of this border the white unpainted skin
represents earth or ground.   The triangles are all tents, whatever their colors.   Some of them have two small dark-brown
marks at their bases; others, one such mark at the vertex.
These small figures represent respectively tent-pegs and projecting tent-poles.   Straight red lines are again paths, while
white lines with black rectangular spots on them represent a
row of buffalo-tracks.

Fig. 4 of Plate xx shows the design on another unusually
small parfleche.   The green lines enclosing the whole design
are the camp-circle.   The long flat triangles are hills.   The
six acute triangles are all tents: the interior red is the fire
inside; the yellow line, next to the red, is the tent itself,
i. e., the skins of which it consists; and the green outer border
of the triangle is the ground on which the tent stands.   Four
black tooth-figures at the base of some of the triangles are
tent-pegs.   The rhombus in the centre of the design represents both the eye and the navel.   In each of the hills there
is an oblong area, in which a red stripe denotes earth, a yellow
stripe sunlight, and two white trapezoids the symbol of life.
In general, without reference to their location in particular
places in the design, the colors on this parfleche have the following signification: green is the earth, yellow is day or light,
red is humanity, black is the sky.

In the parfleche design shown in Fig. 5 of Plate xx, two
elongated central diamonds, which were originally red, represent lizards.   Green lines in them, forming a cross, are their
bones.   The red diamonds are surrounded by a white area,
which is rhombic-elliptical.   This entire area, white and red,
represents a buffalo-scrotum.   The surface adjacent to it is
blue, which denotes haze and smoke.   At the ends of this blue
area are somewhat irregular white trapezoids; and in them, irregular green triangles.   Both are life-symbols.   All the figures
thus far described are enclosed by yellow and red lines, which
denote paths.   Along the two sides of the whole pattern is a
series of convex yellow and concave green figures.   These

denote yellow water and green water respectively. Each pair of them represents a lake. The white rectangles separating these lake-figures represent bare ground.

Fig. 6 of Plate xx shows the design on a particularly large parfleche. This design represents the appearance of the country where the maker of the parfleche lived. The triangles represent the mountains visible there. The red and yellow coloring represents the appearance of their surface. These mountains were said not to be rocky, else their representations would have been colored blue. The green on these triangles, as well as the unpainted hide, represent grass and vegetation. All the green lines are paths. The red and yellow rectangles within the wide stripes along the sides are sticks, pointers, or pins for fastening together the front of the tent. The quadrilateral of green lines enclosing the design represents the ends of the earth (hăneisa^n biitaawu).

Fig. 32 (r$\frac{88}{81}$1). Design on Rawhide Bag. Width of bag, 46 cm.

On the rawhide bag shown in Fig. 32 a diamond in the centre represents a lake. Two short blue lines at its corners are streams of water flowing into the lake. In the centre of this large diamond is a smaller green one, which represents a frog. Black lines radiating from this green rhombus are the frog's legs. Besides the diamond, the central white area, which itself signifies sandy soil, contains two acute triangles. Short black lines in these, corresponding to those denoting frog-legs in the diamond, represent buffalo-tails attached to the ornaments on the tent. The border surrounding this interior ornamental area consists of a pattern of red and blue triangles. The red triangles are tents; the blue, mountains.

The blue lines enclosing this border represent the ocean, or the large body of water which is called by the Arapaho hää͞tetc without being geographically localized or known.

On the back, the enclosing blue lines have the same signification of the ocean. The longitudinal blue lines form trails. Alternating red and blue marks in them represent tracks.

Fig. 33 shows one of a pair of hide bags that are used for coffee, sugar, berries, or other food that must be kept, especially during travels, in a pouch with a small and close opening. For this reason there is no loose flap serving as cover, as in most other bags; but the ends of the pouch are closed with soft skin (so that the whole bag is much like a bellows), and a slit is cut into one of these ends. The two large triangles at the two ends represent tents. The central diamond represents two tents. Between them a white stripe with black dots in it represents a buffalo-path with buffalo-tracks in it. The four red obtuse triangles along the sides are mountains. Small yellow triangles enclosed by them are

Fig. 33 (50/44 a). Design on Rawhide Bag. Width of bag, 44 cm.

tents. The double blue lines surrounding the entire pattern represent mountain-ranges. Small rectangles in this border, colored red and yellow, represent lakes.

On the back, all the stripes of double blue lines are mountain-chains, and the small red and yellow rectangles are again lakes.

Fig. 34, *a*, shows a small square bag. The rectangles with three teeth each are bear's claws (wasixta). The long triangles are mountains. The small acute triangles within

these are caves inhabited by bears. As in the last bag described, the blue enclosing lines are mountains seen in the
distance. On the back, the blue square with its diagonals
represents the bääxôti, or big wheel, one of the Arapaho sacred
tribal objects. It is a wooden hoop with two strings tied
across it. As has been stated before, the square and the
circle are often equivalent in Arapaho symbolism, the circle
being generally regarded as something four-sided, so that the
symbolism here is not so forced as it might appear. On the

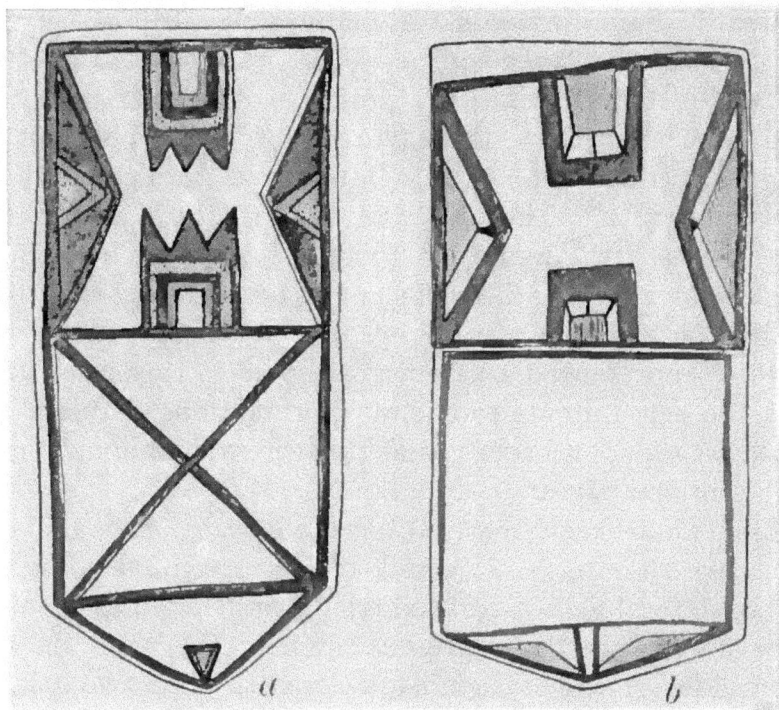

Fig. 34, *a* ($\frac{50}{878}$), *b* ($\frac{50}{1888}$). Designs on Rawhide Bags. Width of
bags, 20 cm., 22 cm.

triangular piece forming the cover-flap, the blue line bordering the edge represents the rainbow, and the small red triangle is the heart.

Fig. 34, *b*, shows a bag of about the same size as the preceding, with much the same pattern and symbolism. The
rectangles represent bear-feet. The triangles are the places
where the bears live, *i. e.*, the mountains. The small black
marks just below the vertices of these triangles are wild

cherries, which the bears eat. On the back, the blue lines at the edge are rivers, along which the cherries grow. On the cover-flap the blue lines have the same signification, while the red segments bordering them are the red banks of the rivers.

Fig. 5, Plate XXI, shows the design on the front of a very small hide bag, probably intended for a little girl to use in picking berries. The design is very similar to the two last described, but the symbolism is different. The triangles, it is true, represent in this case also mountains; and the small squares in them, caves in the mountains. But the two rectangles with the three-toothed ends were said to represent, not bear-feet, as their form would lead one to expect, but steep, high mountains, the narrow white space between them being a deep canyon. The yellow area within the rectangles represents earth. The blue lines at the top and bottom of the design represent "the lowest ground." The back of this bag is not shown in the illustration. It resembles exactly the back of the bag shown in Fig. 34, *a*; but whereas the design in that case represented a ceremonial hoop, in this case it represents the earth, or its four ends or directions (häneisa^n). It should be added, however, that this ceremonial hoop is itself a symbol of the earth.

Three square, rather small bags, with very similar designs, are shown in Figs. 1, 2, and 4 of Plate XXI. In Fig. 1 the two equilateral yellow and red triangles situated at the middle of the sides of the bag represent the heart. Two diamonds in the middle of the design, each consisting of two triangles, represent the morning star. At both ends of these diamonds are trapezoidal figures, one half red and one half green. These represent the body, also the life-symbol, also tents. The straight lines bordering the design, and trisecting it, are rivers. On the cover the small red triangle is again the heart. The line following the edge of the cover is a mountain.

Fig. 2, Plate XXI, shows a medicine-bag. As in most medicine-bags, whether square or cylindrical, the rawhide is not white, but brown. All the triangles, whatever their shape, represent mountains. The uncolored stripes trisecting the design are paths. The dark-green stripes enclosing the design

1

2

3

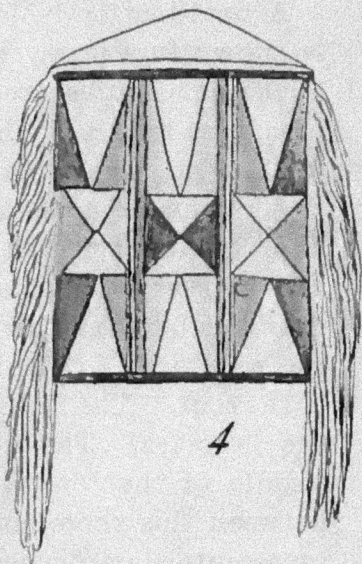

4

5

DESIGNS ON RAWHIDE BAGS.

are rivers.   The unpainted portion of the pattern represents ground.   On the cover, red triangles represent mountains.

Fig. 4, Plate xxi, shows another square medicine-bag made of browned rawhide.   All the equilateral triangles are tents; the right-angled ones, mountains.   The lines trisecting the design are buffalo-paths.   The whole pattern represents the sky.   This bag has a fringe along each side, which is not generally found on any objects made of rawhide except cylindrical medicine-cases.

These last three bags are all colored only with red, yellow, and dark green.   In pattern they agree closely, without being identical or copied one from another.

A food-bag or bellows-shaped pouch, opening at the end, is shown in Fig. 3, Plate xxi.   The familiar three-toothed triangular figures are bear-claws.   The wide stripes are all mountain-ranges.   The small blue and yellow bars contained in these stripes are dark and yellow rocks on the mountains.

A rawhide bag is shown in Fig. 1 of Plate xxii and Fig. 35.   The triangles and segments of circles represent hills. The two large triangles, yellow in the centre, are tents.   The rhombus between them represents the interior of a tent.   The green, which is outside, represents the beds along the walls of the tent.   The red is the ground.   The blue is ashes around the fireplace.   The yellow in the centre is the fire in the middle of the tent.   The red, yellow, and green rectangle between this rhombus and the opening of the bag (Fig. 35) represents a parfleche.   The yellow and blue squares at the corners of the bag represent bags of soft hide, used to hold clothing, etc.

On the back of the bag (Fig. 35) the entire rectangular design represents a shelter or brush-hut of branches, the parallel stripes being sun-rays falling through interstices in the foliage.   The small white rectangle, containing a red equilateral triangle and enclosed by green lines, is the body, the red triangle being the heart.

On the triangular flap of hide serving as cover, the four low segments of circles, colored yellow and green, represent hills. The rest of the design, which can be described as a red and blue triangle with a white rectangle set up on its point, represents a red hill, with a road going up and down it (*i. e.*, over it).

The bag as a whole represents a turtle, loose strips of green cloth hanging from the corners being legs.

The bag shown in Fig. 2 of Plate xxii is much browned by age. The figure in the middle of the bag was said to represent a pattern painted on buffalo-robes and called biinäbi′t. This robe-design, like all other designs in Arapaho art, is not altogether fixed and constant. One form of it occurs on a buffalo-calf blanket which has been described elsewhere.[1] Other forms of it are more conventionalized. The biinäbi′t design is considered sacred among the Arapaho. It is said to have come from the Apaches.

Fig. 35 (₁⁹⁰₈₃). Design on Rawhide Bag. Width of bag, 36 cm.

The bag shown in Fig. 3, Plate xxii, has an unusually vari-colored appearance, because the four paints upon it are distributed in small areas. All the isosceles triangles represent tents. The smallest and lowest of the triangles enclosed in each are considered as doors. The three-pronged black figures represent the poles projecting above the tent. The diamond in the middle of the whole design, having at-

[1] Bulletin of American Museum of Natural History, 1900, p. 85.

1

3

2

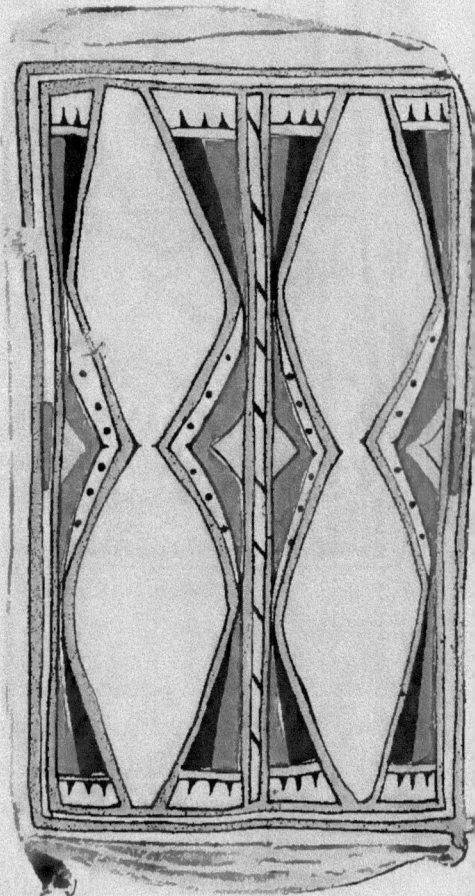

4

PAINTED BAGS.

tached to it two of these figures, is regarded as representing
two tents. Inside this diamond, two red lines represent the
crossing of paths ; the yellow represents the sun ; and the
green, the sky. Both at the top and at the bottom of the front
surface of the bag is a red rectangle containing a blue one,
which in turn encloses a yellow one. This entire rectangular
figure represents a path. At each end of this figure is a blue
right-angled triangle, representing, on account of its color,
grass or vegetation. A similar yellow triangle adjacent to
each of these represents wood or sticks. The red lines separating these blue and yellow triangles represent trails. The
blue lines enclosing the entire design on the front of the bag
are also trails. The white ground-color of the bag represents
sand.

It will be noted that on this bag green denotes the sky; and
blue, grass. Such identification of green and blue occurs in
other instances, but is not usual when both colors are present
on the same object. Ordinarily the same word is used for
" green " and " blue " in Arapaho.

On the back of the bag is a design in blue. It consists of
a rectangle divided into four parts by three lines parallel to
the short sides of the bag. On each of these sections there is
a row of from three to four circular black dots placed parallel
to the short sides of the bag. The blue lines all represent
water; *i. e.*, streams. The dots are horse-tracks. On the
serrated cover-flap, low red and yellow triangles are hills or
mountains; blue lines bisecting them, trails.

Fig. 4 of Plate XXII shows a bag made to hold food, especially coffee or sugar. Formerly it would probably have been
used for berries. The design on this bag, like several others
mentioned, and like the tent-ornament designs, was said by
the owner of the bag to have been first made by the mythical
character, Whirlwind-Woman. All the triangles, whatever
their color, represent hills. The yellow signifies daylight.
The small, black, pointed marks represent monuments of stones
on hill-tops, such as are often left there by those who have
sought the supernatural; they also represent the buffalo-robes
of old men, set up to be prayed to; lastly, they represent

tent-pegs. The series of six black spots, which is repeated four times, denotes that Whirlwind-Woman successively sat down in six places around the bag that she was painting with this design. In a similar manner, a parfleche is sometimes painted by four women sitting on four sides of it, so that the hide does not have to be turned to be painted at all its ends. The ten black diagonal lines in the white stripe that longitudinally bisects the design were the last marks made in process of painting.[1]

On the back of this bag a rectangle formed or enclosed by double green lines represents the whole earth. The lines themselves are also rivers. Alternating red and blue transverse lines, which divide the rectangle into eight parts, are buffalo-paths leading to the river. The red denotes meat of the buffalo, the blue (equivalent to black) represents buffalo-hides.

Fig. 36 (₅₀/₁₅₀). Design on Bag. Width of bag, 47.2 cm.

Fig. 36 shows the two sides of another food-bag. The pattern on the front is longitudinally bisected by a narrow unpainted stripe, which represents a river. Several small black marks in this stripe represent dried meat; i. e., the contents of this bag. The triangles are all mountains. Of the colors, red and yellow signify

---

[1] The black, brown, or dark-blue thin lines with which the colored areas painted on rawhide are usually bordered, are put on after the colored areas, not before. Their purpose seems to be, not to assist the maker in the application of the colors, but to give to the colored areas a sharper outline.

earth; blue, haze or smoke. The decoration on the back consists of two very different halves. One half is painted in blue and yellow; the other seems merely sketched in outline in brown, having an unfinished appearance. It was, however, made thus intentionally. The two halves are also different in design. This lack of symmetry is exceptional. The colored half represents inhabited country; the uncolored, a country that is wild and uninhabited. In the colored half the flat, low, blue triangles are mountains, the pentagonal areas in them being lakes. The six acute triangles are also lakes. The yellow in these triangles represents vegetation in autumn. The blue lines enclosing the design are streams of water.

The uncolored design is enclosed by blue lines representing the sky, and itself represents distant scenery. The triangles are mountains. Small triangles in two of these represent caves; small squares in two of the others are camp-sites. The T-shaped figures on these same triangles represent imaginary figures of persons seen on mountain-tops.

The entire bag also represents a mole. The opening of the bag is the mouth of the mole. Four loose strips of red cloth at the corners of the bag are its legs. Two small painted triangles not shown in the illustration are the ears of the animal.

In the bag illustrated in Fig. 37 the spaces between the figures on the front side are not left white and unpainted, as is generally the case, but are colored yellow. This yellow represents daylight. All the triangles on this side, as well as the diamond in the middle, represent mountains. The interior of the diamond, and the interior of the equilateral triangles touching the diamond, represent caves. Round spots on the four triangles nearest the corners of the bag are rocks.

On the back, blue lines are buffalo-paths, blue diamonds in these are buffalo-wallows. Blue triangles are very high mountains, while yellow triangles were said to be that portion of these mountains which is underground.

A small square bag of hide is shown in Fig. 38. The acute

triangles represent tents. The obtuse triangles are mountains. Of the colors on these latter, the green represents
forests; the red, foot-hills; the blue, rocks; and the white,
sand. The two large white areas represent snow.

On the back, the square formed by the four green lines
along the edges is the whole earth. The two diagonals are
rivers. The crosses are the morning star.

On the triangular flap serving as cover, the two crosses are

Fig. 37 (⁵⁰⁄₅₅₅). Design on Rawhide Bag. Width
of bag, 44 cm.

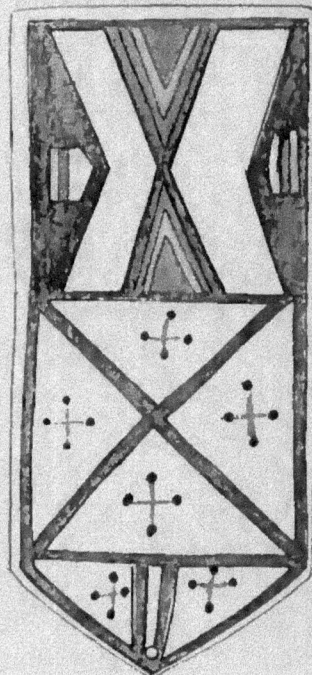

Fig. 38 (⁵⁰⁄₅₅₇). Design on Rawhide Bag. Width of bag, 20 cm.

again the morning star, the two border-lines forming an
angle are the rainbow, a round hole in the hide near the
corner of the cover is the sun, and two vertical lines proceeding from this hole are the rays of the sun.

Fig. 1 of Plate XXIII shows a food-bag. On the front, the
straight lines enclosing the whole design represent roads.

Two low, flat triangles extending along the sides of the bag are mountains; three smaller triangles contained in each represent hills. The unpainted surface of the hide, adjacent to these mountain-designs, represents the open prairie. The diamond in the middle represents the centre of the earth. Red and yellow areas within it represent earth of those colors. At each end of the diamond is a large triangle, which represents a tent. The various colors on this figure of a tent indicate the various colors with which tents are painted or embroidered. The white triangles inside the tent-figure are back-rests or pillows such as are used at the head and foot of beds. The blue in the figure of the tent is smoke. It is said by the Arapaho that when any one in a tent is angry or bad-tempered, the smoke from the fire does not rise, but remains inside; but when all are pleasant and cheerful, the smoke goes straight outside. The blue triangles represent smoke hanging in the tent; the blue line, smoke that is rising to issue from the top of the tent. Underneath these representations of tents are blue and yellow triangles, forming a pattern. The blue here represents ashes that have been taken out of the tent; the yellow is the earth on which the tent stands. A red zigzag line separating the blue and the yellow represents paths.

On the back, the lines or stripes represent sun-rays of various colors. Fine black lines separating stripes of different colors represent the black vegetable fibres sometimes used for embroidery.

The fringe on the bag represents niitcaantetäinani, what we do not know; that is, objects out of our possession, or various things too numerous to mention.

Fig. 2 of Plate XXIII shows a bag used for gathering cherries. It is hung around the neck by a thong attached to it. The design on the front has the following meaning. The rhombus in the middle is the earth as it first appeared after emergence from the original water. The red of the rhombus symbolizes paint; the green, earth; the red bisecting line, the course of the sun. The entire square design is the earth as it is now, after it had been extended, with mountains and soil

DESIGNS ON RAWHIDE BAGS.

and rocks of various colors upon it. These mountains are of course represented by the triangles forming the design. On a small yellow triangle, duplicated for symmetry, are two small black lines; these are the first people.

On the back, a square with its diagonals represents, as in a previous instance, the sacred wheel or hoop. This design also represents a shield, both because the shield resembles the hoop in shape and size, and because the bag is suspended by a string around the neck, like a shield. The line bordering the edge of the cover-flap represents a bow.

The bag shown in Fig. 3 of Plate xxiii has two diamonds in the centre of the design painted on its front. Each of these consists of four smaller diamonds, which represent the navel. Two small triangles adjacent to these diamonds represent small loops of hide wound with porcupine-quills, such as are attached to the ends of pendants on tents, cradles, etc. (touçiikǎ′hääna*). Four larger triangles adjacent to the diamonds are tents. Segments of circles below these are brush-shelters. Four long right-angled triangles at the sides of the design are awl-cases.

On the back of this bag the segments represent, as on the front, shelters. The enclosing lines represent the earth. The transverse stripes are paths. On the cover a vertical row of squares represents wooden buckets or bowls.

In the design on the bag shown in Fig. 4 of Plate xxiii, acute and obtuse isosceles triangles represent, as in most cases, tents and mountains. A blue rhombus in the middle is a lake. Yellow and red areas in the figures of mountains represent lakes. Double blue lines enclosing the whole of the design, as also that on the back, are mountain-ranges. Yellow squares on the back of the bag are lakes, black dots denoting their centres (invisible in the figure); and white squares are ravines. The stripes following the notched edge of the cover also represent mountains.

Fig. 39 shows a bag. On the front, a rectangular area contains two triangles and a rhombus, bordered by green lines. These lines represent water. The red and blue backgrounds of the triangles and rhombus represent clouds of those colors.

In each there is a cross, which is the morning star. This rectangular open area is bordered by a four-colored pattern. Along the long sides of this middle space, triangles that are blue, red, and green are tents; small white triangles at their bases are doors. Yellow areas between the triangles are the ground. In the border at the two ends of the rectangular space, similar figures represent tents and their doors; additional small inverted triangles at the vertices are projecting tent-poles. White areas between these tent-figures are the

 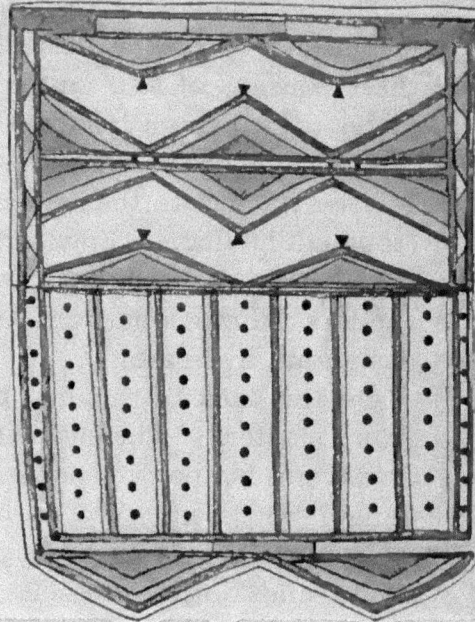

Fig. 39.   Fig. 40.

Figs. 39 (₁₈₃), 40 (₅₅₀). **Designs on Rawhide Bags.** Width of bags, 39.5 cm., 49.4 cm.

ground; and black dots, horse-tracks. Blue lines enclosing this border represent the earth.

Similar lines bordering the back have the same signification. Except for these, the back of the bag is uncolored. Stripes drawn across it in outline are paths. The central one of these stripes, however, is cross-hatched in black. This represents water. On the flap of the bag are three representations of tents with their doors.

Fig. 40 shows a bag painted with red, yellow, and blue.

All the triangular figures are mountains. Small brown inverted triangles at their vertices are imaginary figures that are seen on mountain-tops and look like persons. The long white stripe bisecting the design is a path through a valley between the mountains; and four brown squares in this path are camp-sites. At the two ends of the design, small red triangles are tents. Along the two sides of the design, red, yellow, and blue bands in one line are tent-pins. The two central triangles, together forming a diamond, are also the eye.

On the back, stripes are paths, and rows of black dots are strings of buffalo travelling toward the mountains represented by triangles on the flap.

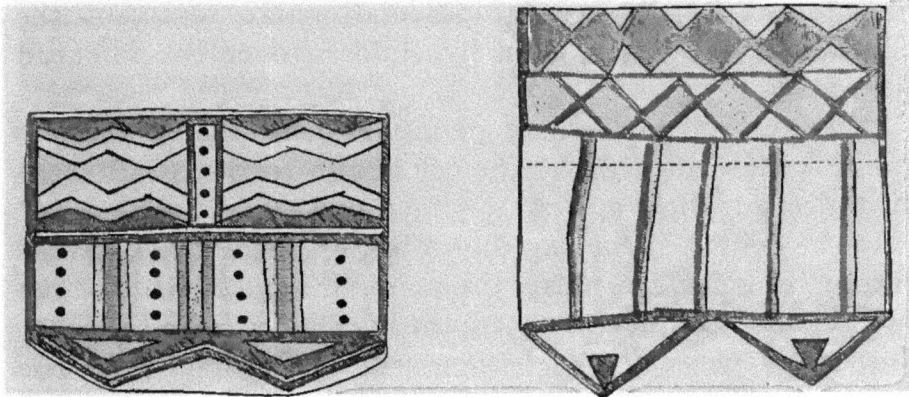

Fig. 41.						Fig. 42.

Figs. 41 ($\frac{50}{1000}$), 42 ($\frac{50}{1018}$). Designs on Rawhide Bags. Width of bags, 32.3 cm., 24.5 cm.

A small narrow bag, used to hold feathers, is shown in Fig. 41. The design on the front is cut into halves by a blue-bordered white stripe, with circular spots in it. The stripe represents the trail of a moving camp; the spots, camp-sites. On each side of this central vertical stripe is the same design. Nearest the edge, blue triangles are mountains. Adjacent to this, a yellow border represents low ground with dried or burned grass. The black lines bounding this yellow border represent dark timber. Adjacent to the yellow is a white zigzag stripe, which is a river. Next to this are two yellow triangles (tents) and a yellow diamond (the eye).

On the back, blue lines framing the entire area are the

earth. Transverse stripes and rows of dots are the various trails and sites of camps on the earth. On the cover, obtuse triangles are mountains.

Fig. 42 shows a small narrow bag like the one just described as a feather-bag. This one was used to hold porcupine-quills, which are generally kept in pouches of gut.

On the front, two rows of irregularly drawn rhombi — one row yellow, and one green — represent strings of german-silver plates formerly worn by the men, hanging from their scalp-locks. The white unpainted triangles adjacent to these rhombi are tents.

On the back, transverse lines represent ropes. On the two flaps serving as a cover, the lines forming angles represent mountains. Small green trapezoidal marks represent the bunches of hair often worn by children over the forehead (itceiçaa^n).

Of the colors on this bag, green represents the earth; red, paint; yellow, daylight. The colors also represent all existing objects of those colors.

In the design on the bag shown in Fig. 1 of Plate xxiv the obtuse triangles are hills; the acute triangles, tents. The two diamonds in the middle are the navel of man and woman. The lines enclosing the design are the camp-circle. The same meaning obtains on the back of the bag. Here transverse stripes are also tent-poles. On the cover, angular figures represent the ears or flaps of the top of the tent; small pointed figures are the wooden pins holding together the front of the tent.

Fig. 2 of Plate xxiv shows another bag. On the front, at each end, are four trapezoids. These represent the "hills" or periods of life. Two at each end are green, and two red and blue. These latter represent red and black paint,— a frequent combination in ceremonials. The white spaces between these trapezoids are lakes. All the triangles in the design are hills and mountains. The white unpainted surface is all water, except the white stripes along the edges and through the middle of the design; these stripes are roads.

On the back, black spots are buffalo-dung. Three trans-

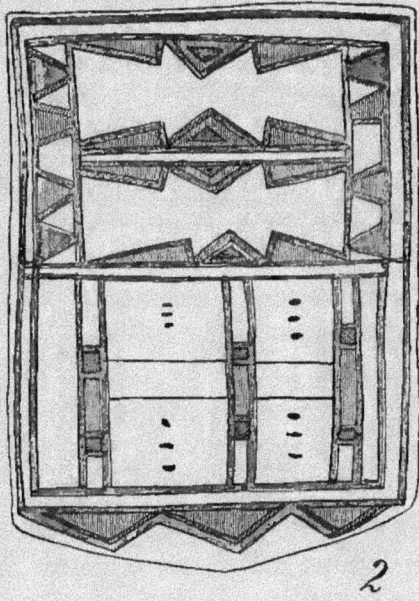

Designs on Rawhide Bags.

verse white stripes with green edges are rivers. Blue squares in them are islands, and red rectangles are red soil or gravel. Four narrow black lines are cracks in the ground. On the flap, triangles represent mountains.

Another bag is shown in Fig. 3 of Plate xxiv. Flat and acute triangles mean, as in so many other cases, mountains and tents. A diamond in the middle is both the navel and a mountain. Dark-green (almost black) lines are creeks; yellow lines, paths.

On the back the unpainted surface represents the earth. Three transverse stripes are paths. Colored marks in these stripes are rocks.

Fig. 4 of Plate xxiv shows a small berrying-bag. Small triangles at the edges of the design on the front are hills. Two very acute isosceles triangles are mountain-peaks. A diamond between them is a round hill. Two lines traversing the design longitudinally are streams. The red and yellow of which they are composed represent two kinds of bushes or trees (red and yellow willow?) growing along the banks. The blue lines enclosing the design are häneā'ⁿkaaⁿ ("as far as the eye can reach," or the horizon, probably equivalent to the earth).

On the back, narrow black lines are paths, and black spots are clouds.

Hide cases that are approximately cylindrical but taper slightly toward the bottom, and are usually somewhat over a foot long, are generally known as "medicine-cases" and "feather-cases," and are used, as their names indicate, to hold small shamanistic and ceremonial objects. They are made of rawhide, which is not, however, white, as it is in ordinary bags and in parfleches, but brown, perhaps from having been smoked. There are in the Arapaho collection of the American Museum of Natural History three flat rectangular rawhide bags that are also brown; but all three of these were used, like the cylindrical cases, to hold medicine or ceremonial objects.

The most frequent painting on the cylindrical medicine-cases is a pattern of inverted tents. There may be either

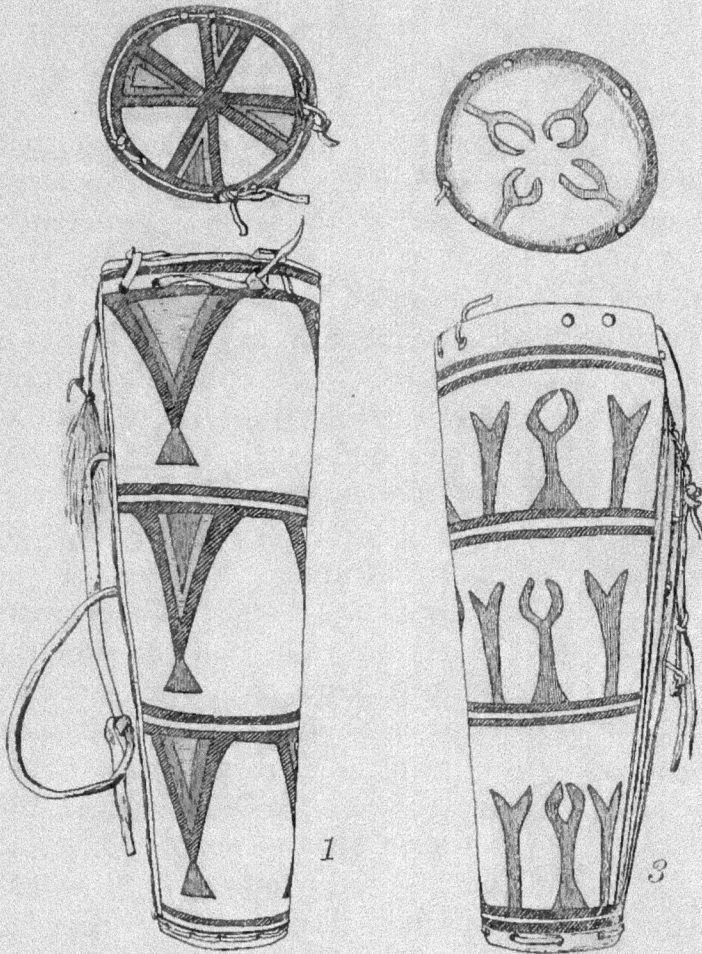

DESIGNS ON MEDICINE-CASES.

two or three rows of tents. These are painted in red, black, and yellow, — the only colors that appear to be used on medicine-cases; sometimes even the yellow is omitted. Fig. 1 of Plate xxv shows such a case. The top cover has a design which may be considered as four tents or as the morning-star cross.

A second kind of design on medicine-cases is shown in Fig. 2 of Plate xxv. The symbolism of this design is elaborate. It has been described before.[1] It represents with some detail the acquisition of supernatural power, especially of control

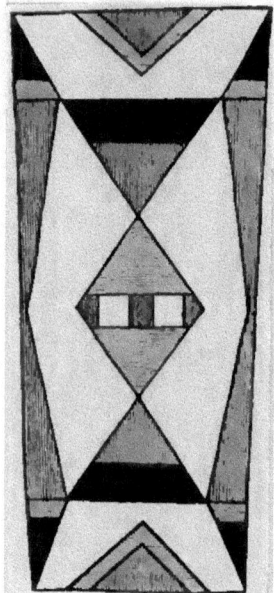

Fig. 43 (⁵⁰/₈₈). Design on a Medicine-case. Length, 50 cm.

of the buffalo, by the owner of the case. Another case, whose design is very similar to the last, is shown in Fig. 3 of Plate xxv. Nothing is known of the significance of this design. The Arapaho declare that the symbolic decoration that occurs on this kind of medicine-case was used (this probably does not mean invented) by a medicine-man who was famous for his power over the buffalo, and by his followers. This medicine-man is said to have died not very long ago. How far the symbolism of these similarly ornamented cases was alike, is not known.

In the Field Columbian Museum in Chicago there is a Kiowa medicine-case whose design is somewhat intermediate between these two kinds of Arapaho designs. This pattern consists of inverted triangles resembling the inverted tents of, Fig. 1 of Plate xxv. At their vertices are wide crescents, causing the entire figures to resemble some of the figures of Fig. 3, Plate xxv.

Fig. 43 shows a third kind of design from a medicine-case. This is painted in red, yellow, and black, on one side or half of the case. The other half of the case is left unpainted, and the top is missing. The triangles (eight in all) represent

---

[1] Bulletin of the American Museum of Natural History, 1900, p. 82; and American Anthropologist, 1901, p. 319.

tents. The two long red areas along the sides of the design are the red of evening. The diamond in the centre is called the navel, and therefore a person. There are three small red figures in this diamond. The one in the very centre represents the person[1] owning the case; the two at the corners of the diamond represent human beings. In general pattern,

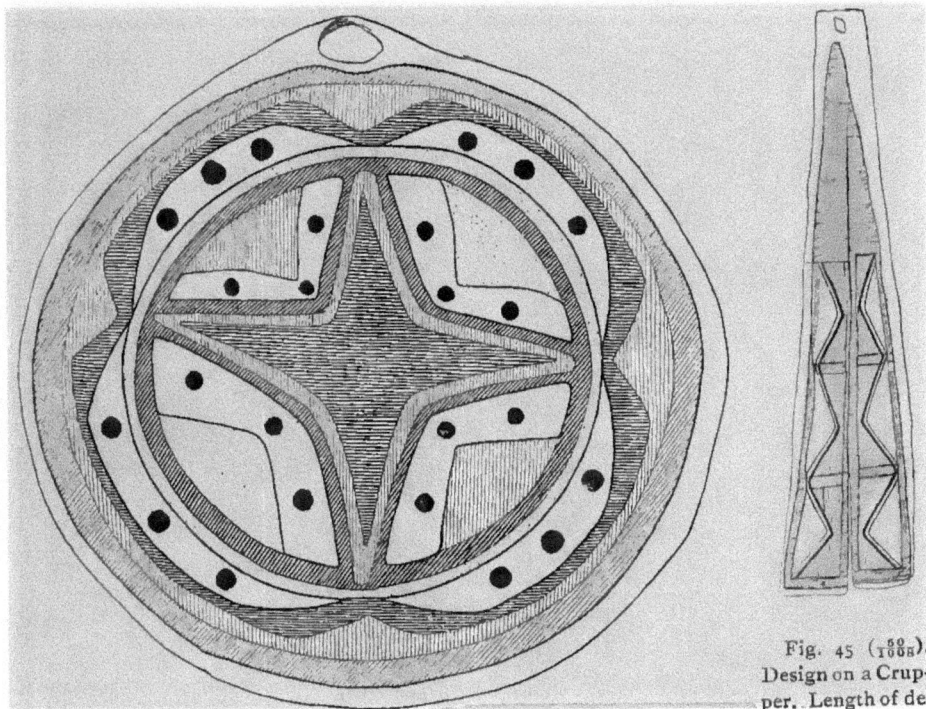

Fig. 44 ($\frac{50}{532}$). Cover of a Shield. Diam., 28 cm.

Fig. 45 ($\frac{60}{1008}$). Design on a Crupper. Length of design, 47 cm.

this cylindrical case resembles the average parfleche more than it does the average medicine-case.

An Arapaho medicine-case with a fourth kind of design is in the Field Columbian Museum of Chicago. The figures on this resemble bear-foot symbols.

A piece of rawhide used to cover a shield is shown in Fig. 44. The large cross or star-shaped figure in the middle represents the morning star. All the triangles on the shield are tents. The circles, both inner and outer, represent the sun. The round black spots represent bullets, evidently those that the shield is intended to stop.

[1] This may possibly mean the spirit-person that owns or inhabits the medicine-case.

The design painted on the rawhide portion of a crupper is shown in Fig. 45. On each half there is a dark-blue zigzag line in the centre, which represents a range of mountains. The red on the inner side of the zigzag line represents the earth. Light-blue [1] stripes dividing the red area into sections, and surrounding the whole design, are rivers. The

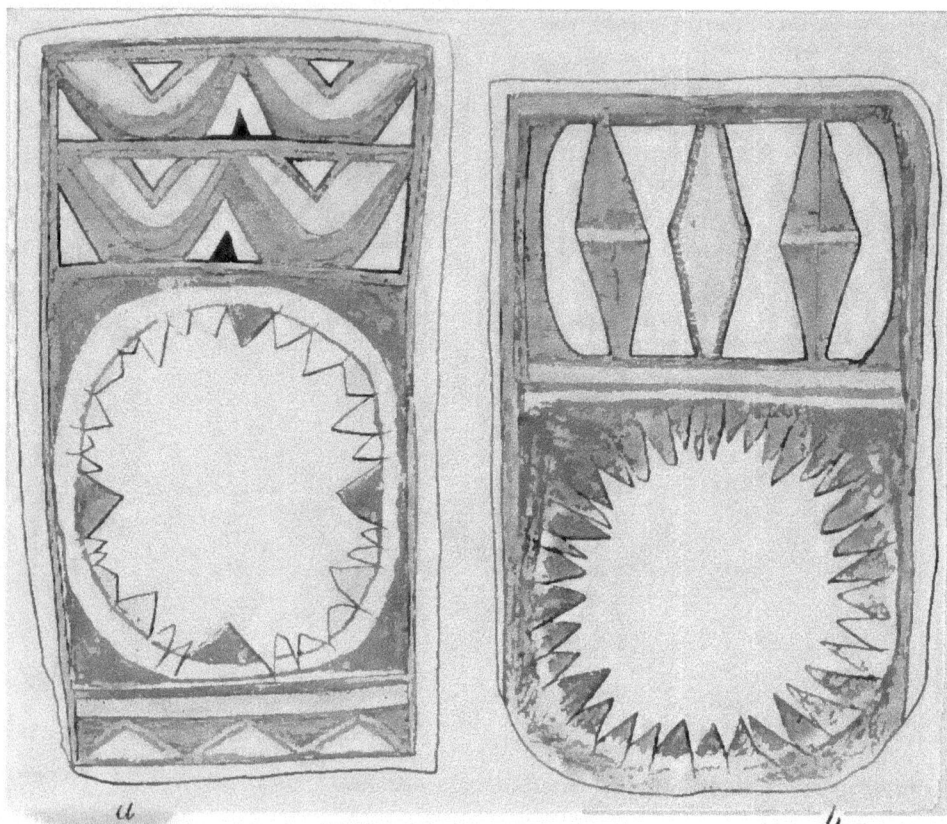

Fig. 46, *a* (⁹⁹⁄₁₅₁), *b* (⁹⁹⁄₁₅₄). Rawhide Hats. Length, about 35 cm.

light-blue color also represents the prairie covered with a certain blue flower (tcänäätänäeinoûû).

Young men sometimes wear a sun-shade that may be described as the brim of a hat without the crown. It consists of a piece of rawhide somewhat over a foot long. Near the back end of this, a circular area about six inches in diameter has a number of radii slit into it. When this part of the

---

[1] The light-blue is represented by horizontal shading.

rawhide is pressed upon the top of the head, the two dozen or more sectors yield, and stand up, forming a circle around the head. Fig. 46 shows two of these hats or sun-shades as they appear seen from above, with the points (sectors) standing nearly upright.

On one such sun-shade, shown in Fig. 46, *a*, a number of differently-colored zigzags (on the front projection or brim of the head-dress) represent tents. Each bend in the zig-zag forms a triangle, and these represent tents. At the opposite end of the sun-shade a row of smaller triangles also represents tents. All the straight lines on the piece of hide represent paths. The pointed projections of hide standing up around the head-opening in a circle represent men dancing. A blue circular line at the base of these projections represents a circle worn in the ground from their dancing.

In another such sun-shade (Fig. 46, *b*,) the circular row of projections was interpreted as signifying the camp-circle of tents.

A summary of the symbolism of the decorative forms that have been described is presented in Plates xxvi–xxxi. The decorative forms of the same symbolic significance are here brought together. Thus all the forms taken by the symbols, for instance, of a man or of a tent, are readily review-able and comparable.

From this summary have been excluded all symbols whose significance depends altogether on their position, like the beads denoting rat's ears in Fig. 21, *g*. In such cases the shape of the symbol itself obviously is often of no consequence. On the plates are shown all the distinct forms of each symbol. Whenever a symbol has been found a number of times with the same form, these occurrences are represented only once in the illustrations.

Inasmuch as the technique of embroidery and that of painting are necessarily quite different, it has seemed best to separate the symbols which are embroidered, whether in beads or in porcupine-quills or in fibres, from those which are painted on rawhide. For the same reason a third separate summary has been made for those symbols that are neither embroidered nor painted, but consist of attachments such as pendants, fringes, strings, loops, or feathers: in short, all the symbols consisting of decorations which are not flat like bead or paint designs, but three-dimensional.

In the list below is also given the total number of occurrences of each symbolic signification, on all the objects that have been described.

A preliminary list of symbols was illustrated in an earlier paper.[1] On that occasion, however, symbols on objects of a religious nature were included in the series, while in the present case such objects have been left for subsequent separate treatment, and the list has been made up from specimens on which the ornamentation is decorative rather than ceremonial or pictographic.

LIST OF SYMBOLS WITH REFERENCE TO PLATES XXVI–XXXI.

OBJECTS REPRESENTED.	EMBROIDERED DESIGNS. Fig. No.	PAINTED DESIGNS. Fig. No.	THREE-DIMENSIONAL DESIGNS. Fig. No.	NUMBER OF OCCURRENCES.
Human Figures.				
Person	1–3	242–246	—	8
Person sitting	4	—	—	1
Person standing	5	—	—	1
Persons dancing in a circle	—	—	430	1
Persons in tent or sweat-house	6	247–248	—	3
First human beings	—	249	—	1
Mythic dwarfs	7	—	—	1
Women	—	250	—	1
Imaginary human figure	—	251–252	—	2
Body and Parts of the Body.				
Body	—	253–254	—	2
Navel	8	255	—	4
Navel-string	9	—	431	2
Heart	—	256	—	4
Heart and lungs	10	—	—	1
Head	11	—	—	1
Matted hair	—	257	432	2

[1] Bulletin of the American Museum of Natural History, XIII, p. 69.

OBJECTS REPRESENTED.	EMBROI-DERED DESIGNS. Fig. No.	PAINTED DESIGNS. Fig. No.	THREE-DIMEN-SIONAL DESIGNS. Fig. No.	NUMBER OF OCCURRENCES.
Eye..........................	12–14	258–260	—	6
Tooth........................	—	—	433	1
Fingers......................	—	—	434	1
Legs.........................	—	—	435	1
Ribs.........................	—	—	436	1
Track........................	15	—	—	2
Animals.				
Buffalo......................	16	261–263	—	4
Wolves......................	17	—	—	1
Coyotes......................	—.	264	—	1
Rats.........................	18	—	—	1
Eagle........................	19–22	—	—	5
Thunder-bird.................	23	—	—	1
Magpie.......................	24	—	—	1
Swallow......................	25	—	—	1
Snake........................	26–27	—	—	4
Lizard.......................	28–30	265	—	4
Turtle.......................	31–34	—	—	4
Frog.........................	35	266	—	2
Fish.........................	36	—	—	1
Bees.........................	37–38	—	—	2
Ants.........................	—	—	437–438	2
Butterfly....................	39–43	—	—	5
Beetle.......................	44	—	—	1
Water-beetle.................	—	267	—	1
Dragon-fly...................	45–47	—	—	3
Cricket......................	48	—	—	1
Spider.......................	49	—	—	1
Crayfish.....................	50	—	—	1
Centipede....................	51–53	—	—	3
Leeches......................	54	—	—	1
Caterpillar..................	55–59	—	—	5
Worms or maggots.............	60–64	—	—	9
Game, variety of animals.....	65	—	—	2
Parts of Animals.				
Bear-foot....................	66–68	268–272	—	9
Bear-ear.....................	—	273–274	—	2
Bear-den.....................	—	275	—	1
Coyote-tracks................	—	276	—	1
Buffalo-eye..................	—	277	—	1
Buffalo-skull................	—	278	—	1
Buffalo-scrotum..............	—	279	—	1
Buffalo-intestine............	69	—	—	1
Buffalo dew-claw.............	—	280	—	1
Buffalo-hoof.................	70–71	—	—	3
Buffalo-track................	72	281–282	—	3

EXPLANATION OF PLATE XXVI.

ARAPAHO SYMBOLISM IN EMBROIDERED DESIGNS.

*** Numbers in parentheses, when accompanied by Roman numerals, refer to plate figures, otherwise to text figures. Where the specimen bearing the symbol is not illustrated, reference to its catalogue number is given.

FIG.
1. Person. (XIV, 7)
2. "   (22)
3. "   (25)
4. Person sitting. (II, 1)
5. Person standing. (II, 1)
6. Persons in tent or sweat-house. (Bull. Am. Mus. Nat. Hist., XIII, p 8.3)
7. Mythic dwarf. (V, 4)
8. Navel. (II, 3)
9. Navel-string. (VIII, 6)
10. Heart and lungs. (IV, 1)
11. Head (14, b)
12. Eye. (II, 2)
13. "   (27)
14. "   (27)
15. Track. (II, 2)
16. Buffalo. (I, 4)
17. Wolves. (XIV, 6)
18. Rats. (VII, 2)
19. Eagle. (XIII, 5)
20. "   (XII, 3)
21. "   (23, b)
22. "   (23, c)
23. Thunder-bird. (Bull. Am. Mus. Nat. Hist. XIII, p. 83)
24. Magpie. (VI, 2)
25. Swallow. (7, b)
26. Snake. (III, 2)
27. "   (XI, 1)
28. Lizard. (III, 1)
29. "   (XI, 6)
30. "   (21, h)
31. Turtle. (II, 5)
32. "   (20, c)
33. "   (XII, 4)
34. "   (XII, 2)
35. Frog. (28)
36. Fish. (III, 4)
37. Bee. (XIV, 5)
38. Bees. (XIV, 5)

FIG.
39. Butterfly. (III, 4)
40. "   (XVII)
41. "   (III, 1)
42. "   (VIII, 3)
43. "   (XII, 6)
44. Beetle. (7, a)
45. Dragon-fly. (IV, 1)
46. "   (25)
47. "   (XII, 6)
48. Cricket. (XII, 1)
49. Spider. (Cat. No. $\frac{50}{888}$)
50. Crayfish. (II, 4)
51. Centipede. (V, 2)
52. "   (Cat. No. $\frac{50}{818}$)
53. "   (XII, 5)
54. Leech. (X, 2).
55. Caterpillar. (IV, 1)
56. "   (II, 1)
57. "   (21, d)
58. "   (XVII)
59. "   (XII, 2)
60. Worms or maggots. (Cat. No. $\frac{50}{888}$)
61. Worm. (I, 3)
62. "   (21, h)
63. "   (25)
64. Worms. (21, h)
65. Game, variety of animals. (V, 5)
66. Bear-foot. (24, a)
67. "   (27)
68. "   (26)
69. Buffalo-intestine. (5, e)
70. Buffalo-hoof. (II, 2)
71. "   (XIV, 7)
72. Buffalo-track. (I, 7)
73. Buffalo-path. (31)
74. "   (XIII, 4)
75. Buffalo-wallow (XIII, 4)
76. Buffalo-horns. (5, f)
77. Mythic cave of the buffalo. (Cat. No. $\frac{50}{818}$)

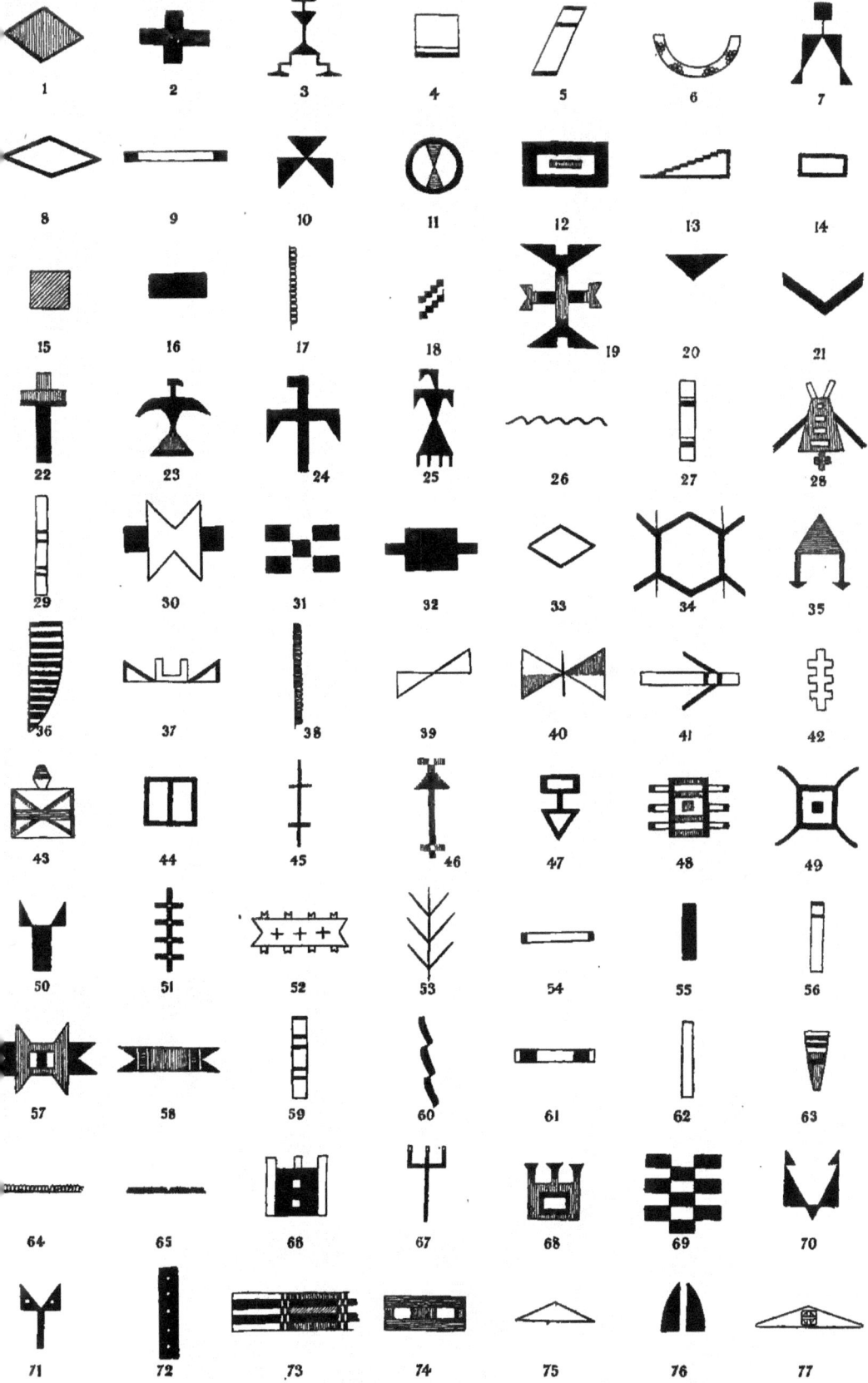

EXPLANATION OF PLATE XXVII.

ARAPAHO SYMBOLISM IN EMBROIDERED DESIGNS.

∗*∗ Numbers in parentheses, when accompanied by Roman numerals, refer to plate figures, otherwise to text figures. Where the specimen bearing the symbol is not illustrated, reference to its catalogue number is given.

FIG.
78. Cattle-track. (XIII, 5)
79.   "   (XIII, 5)
80. Horse-ears. (III, 1)
81. Horse-track. (V, 4)
82. Elk-leg. (XV, 2)
83. Elk-hoof. (V, 2)
84. Deer-hoof. (V. 2)
85. Rabbit-tracks. (II, 5)
86. Beaver-rib. (20, a)
87. Scales on Beaver-tail. (XI, 2)
88. Beaver dam and huts. (20, a)
89. Turtle-claw. (XII, 4)
90. Turtle-egg. (XII, 4)
91. Snake skin-markings. (5, f)
92. Horned-toad skin-markings. (III, 4)
93. Joints and stomach of frog. (20, c)
94. Markings of lizard. (20, b)
95. Bee-hole. (XIV, 5)
96. Ant-hills. (24, c)
97.   "   (V, 5)
98. Ant-hill. (XVII)
99. Ant-path. (24, c)
100. Dragonfly-wing. (XII, 6)
101. Spider-web. (Cat. No. $\frac{50}{338}$)
102. Centipede-tracks. (XII, 5)
103. Worm-hole. (21, h)
104. Tree. (XIII, 3)
105. Trees on mountain. (24, b)
106.   "   "   (II, 1)
107.   "   "   "   (5, b)
108. Leaf of "Yellow-herb" (27)
109. Willow-leaf. (XVII)
110. Mushrooms. (21, e)
111. Cactus. (V, 5)
112. Mountain. (6)
113.   "   (Bull. Am. Mus. Nat. Hist., XIII, p. 83)
114. Mountain. (25)

FIG.
115. Mountain. (XI, 6)
116.   "   (XIV, 6)
117.   "   (24, a)
118.   "   (XIII, 6)
119. Mountains. (23, a)
120.   "   (II, 1)
121.   "   (XI, 5)
122. Mountain. (XIV, 2)
123. Snow-covered mountain. (Bull. Am. Mus. Nat. Hist., XIII, p. 83)
124. Snow-covered mountain. (XII, 3)
125. Valley or canyon. (XIV, 2)
126. The Earth. (Cat. No. $\frac{50}{843}$)
127.   "   "   (XIII, 5)
128.   "   "   (24, c)
129. Dirt, clay. (24, c)
130. Rocks. (24, b)
131.   "   (II, 1)
132.   "   (25)
133.   "   (8)
134.   "   (II, 1)
135.   "   (24, c)
136.   "   (X, 1)
137.   "   (21, f)
138.   "   (23, b)
139.   "   (23, b)
140. Path. (I, 4)
141.   "   (XV, 2)
142.   "   (XVI)
143. Crossing paths. (XII, 3)
144. Holes in a path. (XIV, 5)
145.   "   "   "   (II, 1)
146. Path going over a hill. (I, 3)
147. River. (V, 1)
148.   "   (24, b)
149.   "   (IV, 2)
150. River with islands. (XIV, 2)
151. River. (XIV, 2)
152. Spring. (24, b)
153. Lake. (Bull. Am. Mus. Nat. Hist., XIII, p 83)
154. Lake. (II, 3)

ARAPAHO SYMBOLISM.

EXPLANATION OF PLATE XXVIII.

ARAPAHO SYMBOLISM IN EMBROIDERED DESIGNS.

** Numbers in parentheses, when accompanied by Roman numerals, refer to plate figures, otherwise to text figures. Where the specimen bearing the symbol is not illustrated, reference to its catalogue number is given.

FIG.
155. Lake. (XIII, 6)
156. Scum. (28)
157. Sun. (XIII, 2)
158. Sunrise. (I, 3)
159. Sun-rays. (XIII, 2)
160. Star. (IV, 2)
161. " (III, 1)
162. " (IV, 1)
163. " (Cat. No. ⁵⁰⁄₈₁₂)
164. " (6, a)
165. " (7, b)
166. " (XII, 1)
167. " (VIII, 3)
168. Morning star. (8)
169. " " (V, 3)
170. " " (VII, 1)
171. " " (15)
172. " " (27)
173. " " (XIV, 1)
174. " " (VII, 3)
175. " " (24, b)
176. " " (1, 8)
177. " " (6, a)
178. " " (21, c)
179. Morning star at the horizon. (6, a)
180. Morning star with rays. (1, 8)
181. Constellation. (6, a)
182. Milky way. (6, b)
183. Cloud. (27)
184. " (II, 4)
185. " (Cat. No. ⁵⁰⁄₈₁₂)
186. Lightning. (III, 5)
187. " (Bull. Am. Mus. Nat. Hist., XIII, p. 83)
188. Rainbow. (20, d)
189. Rain. (Bull. Am. Mus. Nat. Hist., XIII, p. 83)
190. Tent. (IX, 2)
191. " (15)
192. " (XI, 2)

FIG.
193. Tent. (XIII, 2)
194. " (V, 2)
195. " (XIII, 4)
196. " (21, a)
197. " (XIV, 8)
198. " (21, b)
199. " (V, 3)
200. Camp-circle. (15)
201. " (27)
202. " (30)
203. Boundary of habitation. (V, 4)
204. Brush-hut. (15)
205. " (V, 5)
206. Pole of sweat-house. (III, 2)
207. Covering of sweat-house. (III, 2)
208. House. (XV, 1)
209. Fence. (25)
210. Rock monuments. (23, a)
211. " " (15)
212. Soft bag. (VIII, 5)
213. Box. (XIII, 5)
214. Knife-case. (22)
215. Sinew. (VIII, 6)
216. Rack for saddlery. (8)
217. " " " (II, 1)
218. Rack for meat. (23, c)
219. Rope. (8)
220. Saddle-blanket. (8)
221. Man's stirrup. (8)
222. Woman's stirrup. (8)
223. Lance. (Cat. No. ⁵⁰⁄₁₀₀₈)
224. Bow. (1, 4)
225. Arrow. (XIV, 4)
226. Arrow-point. (XVIII, 5)
227. " (XI, 2)
228. " (XI, 2)
229. " (1, 4)
230. " (XIV, 3)
231. " (II, 3)

ARAPAHO SYMBOLISM.

EXPLANATION OF PLATE XXIX.

ARAPAHO SYMBOLISM IN EMBROIDERED AND PAINTED DESIGNS.

*** Numbers in parentheses, when accompanied by Roman numerals, refer to plate figures, otherwise to text figures. Where the specimen bearing the symbol is not illustrated, reference to its catalogue number is given.

FIG.
232. Arrow-point. (XIII, 5)
233. Pipe. (XII, 2)
234. " (5, f)
235. Gambling-counters. (20, d)
236. Female dress. (VIII, 5)
237. Hiiteni (life, prosperity). (Cat. No. $\frac{50}{842}$)
238. Hiiteni (life, prosperity). (V, 2)
239. Hiiteni (life, prosperity). (II, 5)
240. Hiiteni (life, prosperity). (5, b)
241. Thought. (22)
242. Person. (XXV, 2)
243. " (XXV, 2)
244. " (43)
245. " (43)
246. " (43)
247. Persons in tent or sweat-house. (XX, 2)
248. Persons in tent or sweat-house. (XVIII, 3)
249. First human beings. (XXIII, 2)
250. Woman. (XIX, 1)
251. Imaginary human figure (36)
252. Imaginary human figure (40)
253. Body. (XXI, 1)
254. " (35)
255. Navel. (XX, 4)
256. Heart. (35)
257. Matted hair. (42)
258. Eye. (XX, 4)
259. " (41)
260. " (40)
261. Buffalo. (Bull. Am. Mus. Nat. Hist., XIII, p. 85)
262. Buffalo. (XXV, 2)
263. " (40)
264. Coyotes. (XIX, 2)
265. Lizard. (XX, 5)
266. Frog. (32)
267. Water-beetle. (XVIII, 3)
268. Bear-foot. (XVIII, 5)

FIG.
269. Bear-foot. (XIX, 2)
270. " (34, a)
271. " (34, b)
272. " (XIX, 5)
273. Bear-ear. (XX, 2)
274. " (XX, 2)
275. Bear-den. (34, a)
276. Coyote-tracks. (XIX, 1)
277. Buffalo-eye. (XX, 2)
278. Buffalo-skull. (XXV, 2)
279. Buffalo-scrotum. (XX, 5)
280. Buffalo dew-claw. (XX, 2)
281. Buffalo-track. (XX, 3)
282. " (33)
283. Buffalo-path. (XXI, 4)
284. Buffalo-wallow. (37)
285. Buffalo-dung. (XXIV, 2)
286. Mythic cave of the buffalo. (Cat. No. $\frac{50}{842}$)
287. Mythic cave of the buffalo. (XX, 1)
288. Mythic cave of the buffalo. (XIX, 4)
289. Abundance of buffalo. (Bull. Am. Mus. Nat. Hist., XIII, p. 85)
290. Horse-tracks. (39)
291. Wild-cherry. (34, b)
292. Fibrous water-plant. (XXIII, 1)
293. Mountain. (XX, 4)
294. " (38)
295. " (35)
296. " (XVIII, 4)
297. " (XX, 1)
298. " (XXIII, 2)
299. " (XXI, 4)
300. " (XXV, 2)
301. " (XXIV, 3)
302. Mountains. (32)
303. " (33)
304. " (XXIV, 2)
305. " (XX, 2)
306. " (37)
307. " (XXIII, 4)
308. Mountain-peak. (XXIV, 4)

ARAPAHO SYMBOLISM.

EXPLANATION OF PLATE XXX.

ARAPAHO SYMBOLISM IN PAINTED DESIGNS.

*** Numbers in parentheses, when accompanied by Roman numerals, refer to plate figures, otherwise to text figures. Where the specimen bearing the symbol is not illustrated, reference to its catalogue number is given.

FIG.

309. Mountain-peak. (XXI, 5)
310. Cave. (36)
311. " (XXI, 5)
312. Valley or Canyon. (XVIII, 4)
313. " " " (XXI, 5)
314. " " " (XXIII, 4)
315. Meadow. (Cat. No. $\frac{50}{055}$)
316. The earth. (XXV, 2)
317. " " (XIX, 6)
318. " " (XXII, 4)
319. Ends of the earth. (XIX, 1)
320. The earth at its first emergence. (XXIII, 2)
321. Cracks in the ground. (XXIV, 2)
322. Rock. (37)
323. " (XXI, 3)
324. " (XXIV, 3)
325. Path. (XXIV, 4)
326. " (XXII, 3)
327. " (XXII, 3)
328. " (XXIV, 3)
329. " (XXIII, 3)
330. Crossing paths. (XXII, 3)
331. Path with tracks. (XX, 2)
332. " " " (32)
333. Path going over a hill. (35)
334. Circle worn by dancing. (46, a)
335. River. (XXII, 4)
336. " (38)
337. " (XXIV, 3)
338. " (39)
339. " (32)
340. River with islands. (XXIV, 2)
341. River with islands. (XIX, 2)
342. Lake. (32)
343. " (XX, 2)
344. " (XX, 5)
345. " (XXIV, 2)

FIG.

346. Lake (XXIII, 4)
347. " (XXIII, 4)
348. " (36)
349. " (36)
350. Ocean. (32)
351. Sun. (44)
352. " (XXV, 2)
353. Sun-rays. (XXIII, 1)
354. " (35)
355. Star. (44)
356. Morning star. (XXI, 1)
357. " " (39)
358. " " (38)
359. Sky. (36)
360. Cloud. (XXIV, 4)
361. Rainbow. (38)
362. Flame. (XIX, 4)
363. Smoke. (XXIII, 1)
364. Tent. (XXV, 1)
365. " (42)
366. " (43)
367. " (43)
368. " (XVIII, 4)
369. " (33)
370. " (46, a)
371. " (XIX, 1)
372. " (Cat. No. $\frac{50}{055}$)
373. " (XXII, 3)
374. " (39)
375. " (XIX, 6)
376. " (XIX, 6)
377. " (XX, 4)
378. " (XX, 1)
379. " (XX, 3)
380. Tent-door. (XXIV, 1)
381. Tent-pin. (XX, 6)
382. " (XIX, 1)
383. " (XXIV, 1)
384. " (XVIII, 4)
385. Loop for tent-pins. (XXIII, 3)

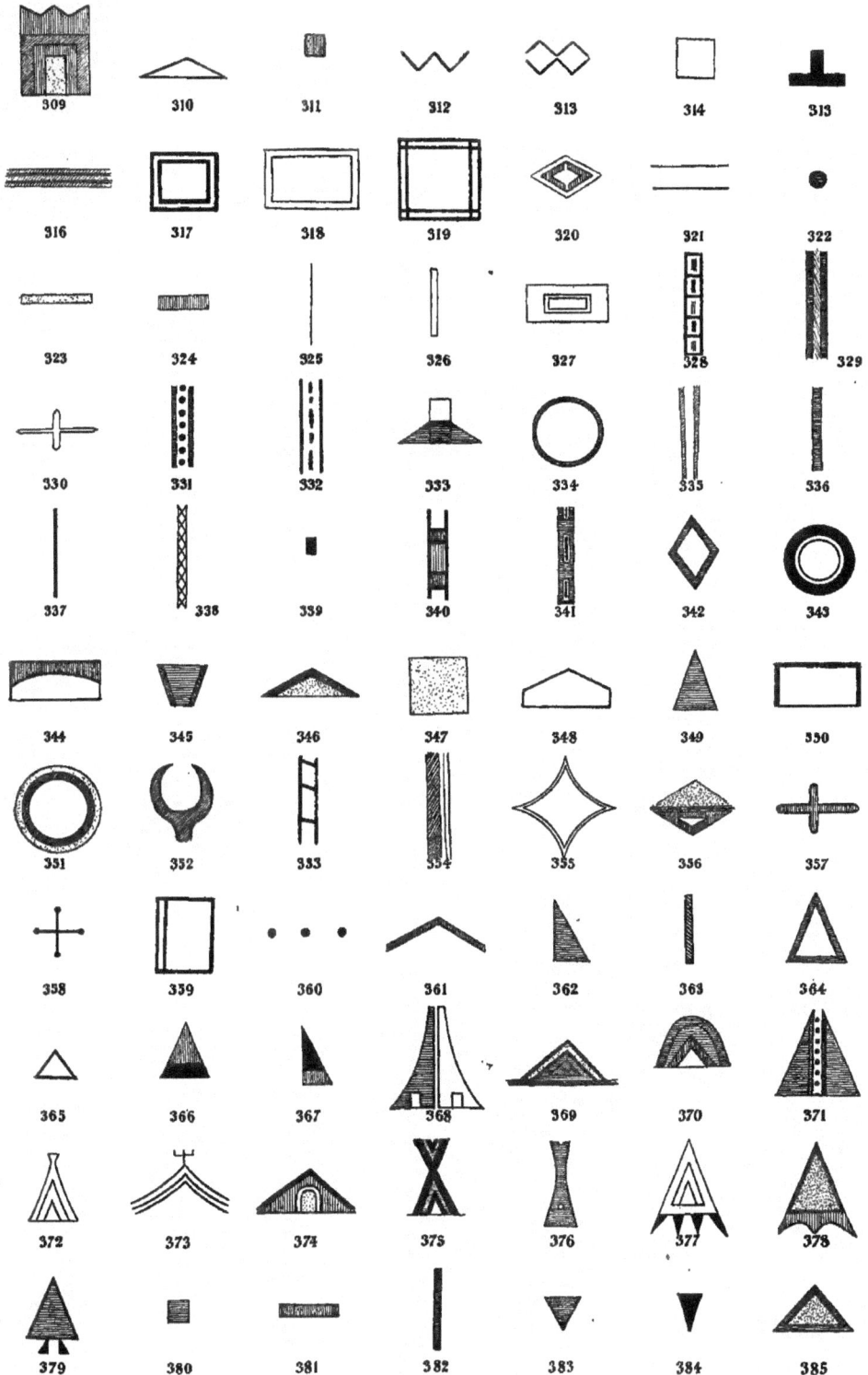

ARAPAHO SYMBOLISM.

EXPLANATION OF PLATE XXXI.

ARAPAHO SYMBOLISM IN PAINTED AND THREE-DIMENSIONAL DESIGNS.

⁎ Numbers in parentheses, when accompanied by Roman numerals, refer to plate figures, otherwise to text figures. Where the specimen bearing the symbol is not illustrated, reference to its catalogue number is given.

FIG.
386. Tent-poles. (XXIV, 1)
387. Tent-flaps. (XXIV, 1)
388. Tent-pendant. (32)
389. Interior of tent. (35)
390. Tent-site. (XIX, 6)
391. Camp-site. (41)
392.   "   (36)
393.   "   (XIX, 1)
394. Camp-circle. (XVIII, 2)
395. Brush-hut. (XXIII, 3)
396.   "   (35)
397. Sweat-house. (XVIII, 3)
398.   "   (XXV, 2)
399. American tent. (46, b)
400. Rock monument. (XX, 4)
401. Bed. (XIX, 3)
402.   "   (XXIII, 1)
403. Parfleche. (35)
404. Soft bag. (35)
405. Bucket or vessel. (XXIII, 3)
406. Medicine-case. (XXV, 2)
407. Awl-case. (XXIII, 3)
408. Paint-stick. (XVIII, 3)
409. Rope. (XVIII, 3)
410.   "   (42)
411. Bow. (XXIII, 2)
412. Bullets. (44)
413. Ceremonial wheel. (34, a)
414. Ceremonially used robe. (XX, 4)
415. Robe design. (XXII, 2)
416. Metal hair-ornaments. (42)
417. Hiiteni (life, prosperity). (XVIII, 3)
418. Hiiteni (life, prosperity). (XX, 5)
419. Hiiteni (life, prosperity). (XXI, 1)
420. Hiiteni (life, prosperity) (Bull. Am. Mus. Nat. Hist., XIII, p. 85)
421. Hiiteni (life, prosperity). (XVIII, 5)

FIG.
422. Hiiteni (life, prosperity). (XX, 4)
423. Contents (of bag). (36)
424. Centre. (XXIII, 1)
425.   "   (XVIII, 2)
426.   "   (XXIII, 4)
427. Stops (in a course). (Cat. No. 50⁄225)
428. The four hills (periods) of life. (XXIV, 2)
429. Supernatural instruction. (XXV, 2)
430. Persons dancing in a circle. (46, a)
431. Navel-strings. (VIII, 5)
432. Hair. (14, b)
433. Tooth. (VIII, 5)
434. Fingers. (7, c)
435. Legs. (14, b)
436. Ribs. (14, b)
437. Ants. (7, a)
438.   "   (24, c)
439. Burrs in buffalo-hair. (30)
440. Snake-rattle. (5, f)
441. Snake-tongue. (5, f)
442. Paths. (27)
443. Rivers. (XIII, 4)
444. Sun. (7, c)
445. Sun-dog. (VI, 3)
446. Stars. (7, c)
447. Star. (XI, 1)
448. Tent-pin. (14, b)
449. Loop for tent-pins. (14, b)
450. Tent-pendants. (14, b)
451.   "   (XVI)
452. Camp-circle. (46, b)
453. Dry meat. (XVI)
454. Ear-pendant. (XIV, 8)
455. Coffee. (XIV, 6)
456. The many things unknown. (XXIII, 1)
457. Property possessed. (7, c)
458. Desire of accomplishment. (VI, 1)

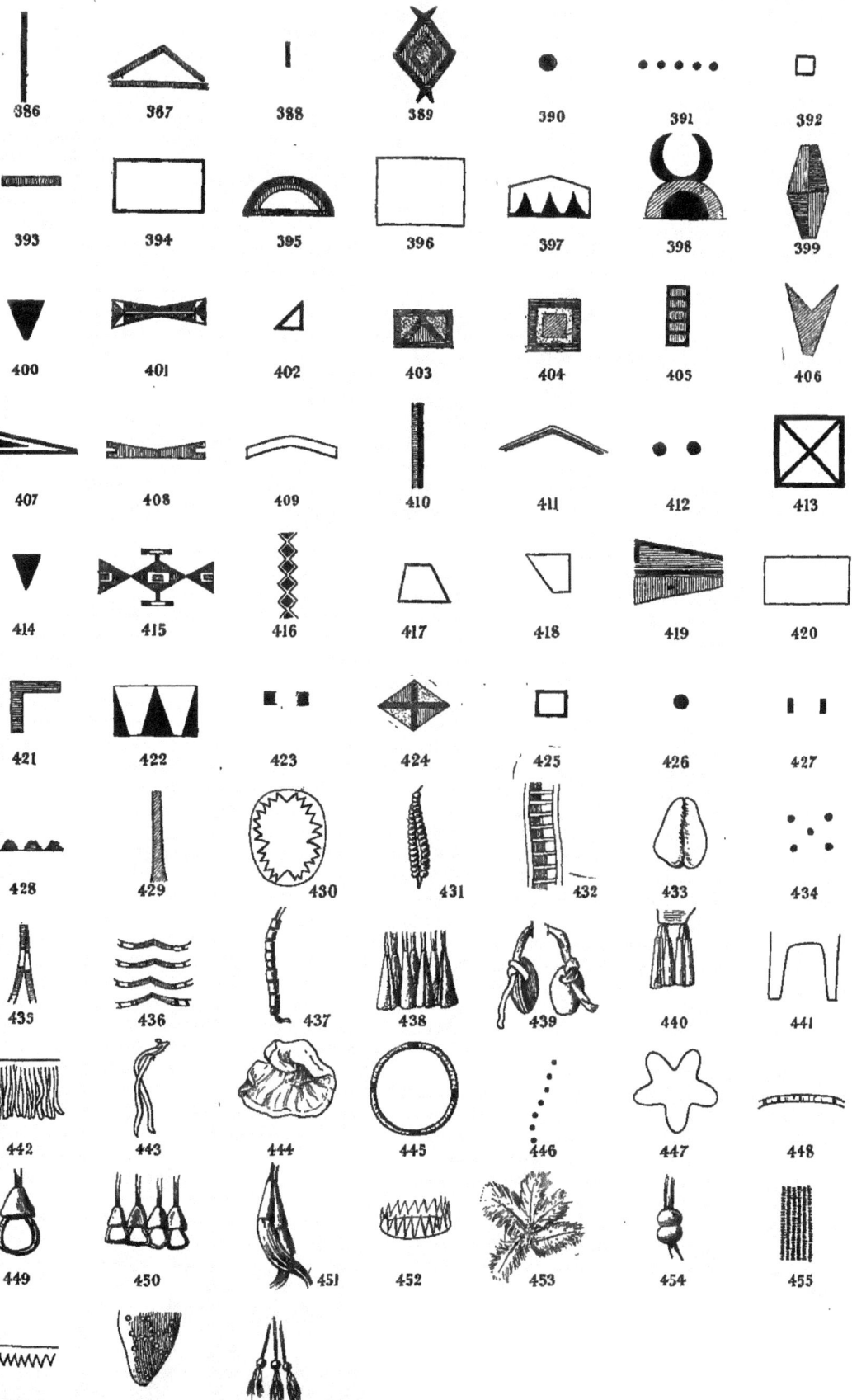

386

387

388

389

390

391

392

393

394

395

396

397

398

399

400

401

402

403

404

405

406

407

408

409

410

411

412

413

414

415

416

417

418

419

420

421

422

423

424

425

426

427

428

429

430

431

432

433

434

435

436

437

438

439

440

441

442

443

444

445

446

447

448

449

450

451

452

453

454

455

OBJECTS REPRESENTED.	EMBROIDERED DESIGNS. Fig. No.	PAINTED DESIGNS. Fig. No.	THREE-DIMENSIONAL DESIGNS. Fig. No.	NUMBER OF OCCURRENCES.
Buffalo-path..........................	73-74	283	—	5
Buffalo-wallow......................	75	284	—	2
Buffalo-horns.......................	76	—	—	1
Burrs in buffalo-hair...............	—	—	439	1
Buffalo-dung........................	—	285	—	1
Mythic cave of the buffalo.........	77	286-288	—	4
Abundance of buffalo..............	—	289	—	1
Cattle-track........................	78-79	—	—	2
Horse-ears.........................	80	—	—	1
Horse-tracks.......................	81	290	—	3
Elk-leg.............................	82	—	—	1
Elk-hoof............................	83	—	—	1
Deer-hoof..........................	84	—	—	1
Rabbit-tracks.......................	85	—	—	1
Beaver-rib..........................	86	—	—	1
Scales on beaver-tail..............	87	—	—	1
Beaver dam and huts.............	88	—	—	1
Turtle-claw.........................	89	—	—	1
Turtle-eggs........................	90	—	—	1
Snake-rattle........................	—	—	440	1
Snake-tongue.......................	—	—	441	1
Snake skin-markings..............	91	—	—	1
Horned-toad skin-markings......	92	—	—	1
Joints and stomach of frog........	93	—	—	1
Markings of lizard................	94	—	—	1
Bee-holes..........................	95	—	—	1
Ant-hills...........................	96-98	—	—	3
Ant-paths..........................	99	—	—	1
Dragonfly-wing	100	—	—	1
Spider-web.........................	101	—	—	1
Centipede-tracks...................	102	—	—	1
Worm-holes........................	103	—	—	1

Plants.

Tree................................	104	—	—	1
Trees on mountain.................	105-107	—	—	3
Leaf of "Yellow-herb"............	108	—	—	1
Willow-leaf........................	109	—	—	1
Wild-cherry........................	—	291	—	1
Mushrooms........................	110	—	—	1
Cactus..............................	111	—	—	1
Fibrous water-plant...............	—	292	—	1

Earth.

Mountains, hills, and ranges......	112-122	293-307	—	71
Mountain-peak.....................	—	308-309	—	3
Snow-covered mountain..........	123-124	—	—	2
Cave...............................	—	310-311	—	3

OBJECTS REPRESENTED.	EMBROIDERED DESIGNS. Fig. No.	PAINTED DESIGNS. Fig. No.	THREE-DIMENSIONAL DESIGNS. Fig. No.	NUMBER OF OCCURRENCES.
Valley or canyon	125	312–314	—	5
Meadow	—	315	—	1
The earth	126–128	316–318	—	16
Ends of the earth	—	319	—	4
Visible world	—	—	—	1
The earth at its first emergence	—	320	—	1
Cracks in the ground	—	321	—	1
Dirt, clay	129	—	—	1
Rocks	130–139	322–324	—	20
Path	140–142	325–329	442	39
Crossing paths	143	330	—	2
Path with tracks	—	331–332	—	2
Holes in a path	144–145	—	—	2
Path going over a hill	146	333	—	3
Circle worn by dancing	—	334	—	1

Water.

Rivers or streams	147–149, 151	335–339	443	33
River with islands	150	340–341	—	3
Spring	152	—	—	3
Lake	153–155	342–349	—	14
Scum	156	—	—	1
Ocean	—	350	—	1

Heavens, Light, Fire

Sun	157	351–352	444	5
Sunrise	158	—	—	1
Sun-rays	159	353–354	—	4
Course of the sun	—	—	—	1
Sun-dog	—	—	445	1
Star	160–167	355	446–447	13
Morning star	168–178	356–358	—	25
Morning star at the horizon	179	—	—	1
Morning star with rays	180	—	—	1
Constellation	181	—	—	1
Milky way	182	—	—	1
Sky	—	359	—	3
Cloud	183–185	360	—	4
Lightning	186–187	—	—	3
Rainbow	188	361	—	3
Rain	189	—	—	1
Flame	—	362	—	1
Smoke	—	363	—	1

Manufactured Articles.

Tents	190–199	364–379	—	55
Tent-door	—	380	—	1
Tent-pins	—	381–384	448	6

Objects represented.	Embroidered Designs. Fig. No.	Painted Designs. Fig. No.	Three-Dimensional Designs. Fig. No.	Number of Occurrences.
Loops for tent-pins	—	385	449	2
Tent-poles	—	386	—	1
Tent-flaps	—	387	—	1
Tent-pendants of rattles	—	—	450–451	2
Tent-pendants of buffalo-tails	—	388	—	1
Spaces between tent-poles	—	—	—	1
Interior of tent	—	389	—	1
Tent-site	—	390	—	1
Camp-site	—	391–393	—	4
Camp-circle	200–202	394	452	8
Boundary of habitation	203	—	—	1
Brush-hut	204–205	395–396	—	5
Sweat-house	—	397–398	—	2
Poles of sweat-house	206	—	—	1
Covering of sweat-house	207	—	—	1
House	208	—	—	1
American tent	—	399	—	1
Fence	209	—	—	1
Rock monuments	210–211	400	—	4
Bed	—	401–402	—	2
Triangular head-rest	—	—	—	1
Parfleche	—	403	—	1
Soft bag	212	404	—	2
Box	213	—	—	1
Bucket or vessel	—	405	—	1
Medicine-case	—	406	—	1
Knife-case	214	—	—	1
Awl-case	—	407	—	1
Sinew	215	—	—	1
Rack for saddlery	216–217	—	—	2
Rack for meat	218	—	—	1
Paint-stick	—	408	—	1
Rope	219	409–410	—	4
Saddle-blanket	220	—	—	1
Man's stirrup	221	—	—	1
Woman's stirrup	222	—	—	1
Lance	223	—	—	1
Bow	224	411	—	2
Arrow	225	—	—	1
Arrow-point	226–232	—	—	8
Bullets	—	412	—	1
Pipe	233–234	—	—	2
Ceremonial wheel	—	413	—	2
Gambling-counters	235	—	—	1
Female dress	236	—	—	1
Ceremonially used robe	—	414	—	1
Robe design	—	415	—	1
Metal hair-ornaments	—	416	—	1
Dry meat	—	—	453	1

Objects represented.	Embroidered Designs. Fig. No.	Painted Designs. Fig. No.	Three-Dimensional Designs. Fig. No.	Number of Occurrences.
Ear-pendant..................	—	—	454	1
Coffee......................	—	—	455	1
Abstract Ideas.				
Hiiteni (life, prosperity).........	237–240	417–422	—	14
The many things unknown.......	—	—	456	1
Property possessed.............	—	—	457	1
Contents (of bag)..............	—	423	—	1
Centre.......................	—	424–426	—	3
Stops (in a course).............	—	427	—	1
Direction whence..............	—	—	—	1
Direction whither..............	—	—	—	1
The four hills (periods) of life.....	—	428	—	1
Desire of accomplishment........	—	—	458	1
Supernatural instruction........	—	429	—	1
Thought.....................	241	—	—	1

Although the technique of embroidering and of painting, and the appearance of the objects made in these two styles, are quite different, yet a comparison of the two series of symbols (Figs. 1–241 with Figs. 242–429) shows that the individual symbols of the same meaning are generally considerably alike, whether they are embroidered or painted. The embroidered symbols, while often very simple, sometimes reach greater elaborateness and realism than any of the painted ones. Painting is of course capable of much further development in these directions than is beadwork, but the decorative painting of the Plains Indians is more conventionalized and less realistic than their embroidery.

It is apparent that there is much individuality in the interpretation given to the decorative designs employed by the Arapaho. One person attaches a certain significance to the ornaments on an article belonging to him; another person may possess an article ornamented in a similar fashion, and interpret the ornamentation entirely differently. Even the identical symbol may have many different significations to the various owners of different objects. For instance, on the

objects that have been described in this paper, the rhomboid
or diamond-shaped symbol can be found with the following
ten significations: the navel, a person, an eye, a lake, a star,
life or abundance (hiiteni), a turtle, a buffalo-wallow, a hill,
the interior of a tent. All of these meanings, except the first
two, are totally unrelated. If the significance of the decoration on a larger number of specimens had been obtained, it
is probable that the known number of meanings attached to
this symbol would be still larger. What makes the variability of this system of decorative symbolism appear still
more plainly is the fact that nearly all of these ten significations have also been found attached to very different symbols. Thus a person is denoted, on other specimens that have
been described, by a small rectangle, triangle, square, or
cross, by a dot, by a line, as well as by rudely realistic designs. The eye is represented by a rectangle, and again by a
nearly triangular figure. A lake is represented on different
specimens by a square, a trapezoid, a triangle, a pentagon,
a circle, or other figures. A star is often represented by a
cross; the life-symbol by a trapezoid, hills by triangles.
In fact, of these ten significations, that of the navel is the
only one that was found several times and always represented
by the same symbol.

It thus appears that there is no fixed system of symbolism
in Arapaho decorative art. Any interpretation of a figure is
personal. Often the interpretation is arbitrary. Much depends upon what might be called symbolic context. In a
decoration which symbolizes buffalo-hunting, a stripe naturally represents a bow; on a parfleche whose decoration represents such parts of the landscape as mountains, rocks, earth,
and tents, an identical stripe would naturally have the
signification of a river or of a path; but whether a path or
a river, would depend on the fancy of the maker of the parfleche. On another man's parfleche such a stripe may represent a rope; on still another, red paint or the blue sky, because
the maker of this particular article thought of the color of
the stripe before he did of its shape. Naturally one person
cannot guess what the decorations on another person's par-

fleche or moccasin or pouch signify. Usually an Indian refuses to interpret the ornamentation on an article belonging
to some one else, on the ground that he does not know; but
he may give a tentative or possible interpretation.

Where such a wide variability exists, and where every individual has a right to his opinion, as it were, it follows that
it is impossible to declare any one interpretation of a given
ornamental design as correct or as incorrect. Even the
maker or possessor of an article can give only his personal
intention or the signification which he individually prefers.
Since the decorative symbolism on his article is not intended
as a means of communication, he is satisfied to follow his own
fancy in private; and if any one else chose to attach a different meaning to his ornamental designs, he would probably
make no objection. He might criticise the other for his pre-
sumption, but he could not well prove him incorrect.

Naturally there is great difference in the degree of interest
shown in the symbolism of decoration by different individuals.
One person thinks about the significance of his designs,
another chiefly of their appearance. The former will probably give a coherent interpretation of his designs if he is
questioned; the symbols of the latter will have their most
common conventional meaning, without much reference to
each other. Young people especially are likely to think and
care little about designs that they make or see. On the other
hand, a person interested in symbolism sometimes has two or
three interpretations for one symbol or for a design. Such
double sets of significations given by one person are generally
not hesitating or doubtful, but apt and happy, as well as
elaborate and coherent; the reason being that the maker of
the design has planned it with more than the usual amount
of attention to its meaning, or has subsequently studied it
with interest. One must not be misled on this point by
analogy with the pictorial, undecorative, unceremonial art of
our civilization. The Indian, in embroidering a moccasin or
painting a parfleche, never dreams of making a picture that
can be recognized by every one at sight.

It is probable that, among the hundred and fifty and more

specimens whose symbolism has been described, there are some whose owners were not their makers, and had never given a thought to the significance of their decorations previous to the occasion on which they explained these decorations at the request of the author. That this should not have happened, can hardly be expected; but in all such cases, these persons undoubtedly fell back upon the common conventional symbolism that is current in the tribe. This is shown by the fact that all the decorative symbolism that was learned runs along certain lines. For instance, tents are very frequently represented; but in only one single case was a house, such as the Indians now largely live in, represented by the decorations. Hence there seems to be a conventional system of symbolism, a fairly distinct and characteristic tribal manner of viewing and thinking about decoration. What this way of thought is among the Arapaho, it has been the purpose of the preceding pages to show by bringing together as large a mass of individual cases of decorative symbolism as possible. That here and there an interpretation may be poor, even from the Indian's standpoint, or another untrustworthy, is of little moment. As has been said, no interpretation of a design can be considered really right or wrong. If the explanations of decorated objects, taken all together, illustrate one method of thinking, and are evidences of one system of symbolism, the purpose of their presentation will have been achieved.

The lack of desire or attempt to represent realistically in art which is in any degree decorative, and the accompanying lack of absolute or fixed meaning of designs, are not new and unparalleled phenomena. On the northwest coast of America, Dr. F. Boas has told the author, an Indian is often unable to state what a carving or painting represents, unless he has made or is using the object. This is really a more remarkable case than among the Arapaho, for the art of the North Pacific coast is far more realistic than that of the Plains Indians. While highly conventionalized and always decorative, it remains sufficiently realistic to enable a white man to see in nearly every case that a representation of something is intended (which in the case of Arapaho art, if he had no knowledge of the subject, he would probably not suspect); and with a little practice the student can often recognize, without the Indian's help, the particular animal or object represented.

In northwestern California the situation is analogous. Here the principal art is basketry. The number of names of basket-patterns is small, and they are known to most of the women. The patterns on many baskets will be given the same names by every member of the tribe. On other baskets, the design will be differently called by two persons. It is then usually to be seen that the design is of a form more or less intermediate between two patterns, and that both persons who gave differing names for it were right: each had as much reason as the other. Moreover, both the names given in such a case are generally taken from the limited list of standard and well-known pattern-names of the tribe. So in this part of the continent, also, there is a conventional system of decorative symbolism; and, though this system is much more narrow and rigid than that of the Arapaho, there is a similar variability of interpretation among individuals.

Corresponding to individual variability of symbolism in Arapaho art, is the almost infinite variation of the decoration. Narrow as are the technique and scope of this art, almost every piece of work is different from all others. There seems to be no attempt at accurate imitation, no absolute copying. An Arapaho woman may make a moccasin resembling one that she has seen and liked, but it is very seldom that she tries to actually duplicate it. Of common objects, the writer does not remember to have seen two that were exactly identical, or intended to be identical. Two classes of articles, however, do not fall under this rule. These are, first, certain ceremonial objects, which naturally are made alike, as far as is possible, for ceremony is the abdication of personal choice and freedom; secondly, objects which are decorated with a more or less fixed tribal decoration. These objects are tents, robes, bedding, and cradles. It has been shown, however, that at times there is some variation even in the decorations of these objects. This distinctly tribal ornamentation forms a class quite apart from the more personal ordinary ornamentation. For instance, the seven sacred work-bags that have been mentioned, and the ceremonies connected with them, are used only in the making of the "tribal" ornaments.

This endless variety and absence of direct copying are common in American Indian art. Dr. Boas has seen only very few pieces of art of the North Pacific coast that were duplicates. In California the author has found that, unless baskets are made for sale, a basket is rarely reproduced exactly by the same woman, and just as rarely by another. The same seems to be true of the pottery of the Southwest. Everywhere each piece is made independently, though always under the influence of the tribal style.

Conventionality of decoration has been referred to repeatedly in descriptions of specimens. It can often be followed out into minute detail. A glance at Plates I, xx, xxI, and Figs. 5, 23–28, 32–34, will show to what extent it obtains.

The conventionality of symbolism which has been mentioned appears most clearly in the frequency of certain classes of objects in the symbolism, and the almost total absence of others. The scope of this symbolism may be briefly described as follows.

Plants are very rare in representation; human beings are not abundant; while animals, in comparison with these two classes, are numerous. Of plants, trees are most frequently represented, flowers not at all. Of animals, the larger mammals are rare. Only the buffalo and wolves and coyotes have been found, and these generally represented in a very simple manner, as by dots or small rectangles. Deer, elk, horses, and dogs are not represented. Almost all the animal representations are of small animals,— the reptiles, fish, rats, and especially insects and invertebrates in considerable variety. It may be remembered that paint-pouches, navel-amulets, knife-cases, and other articles which are representative in their entirety, generally represent small animals. Of parts of the body, of man, the navel is the most frequent in symbolism; of animals, the foot or track. Of the total number of symbols, animal representations, however, form only a minor part. Of natural objects, mountains and hills, singly and in ranges, are very frequent. Rocks, earth, vegetation, ravines, and the world are also found often. Representations of water are less frequent than the preceding; but rivers, creeks, lakes, and springs are all not rare. Of celestial objects, the sun, moon, clouds, sky (except as denoted by color alone), rainbow, and milky way are all represented infrequently. Stars, and especially the morning star, whose name and symbol is the cross, one of the simplest and most obvious geometric figures, are exceedingly abundant. Paths are common symbols. Of objects of human use or manufacture, tents are most frequently represented. Of symbols of abstract ideas, the hiiteni, which seems to signify life and abundance, is the most common.

The symbolism of colors irrespective of forms is generally the following. Red represents most commonly blood, man, paint, earth, sunset, or rocks. Yellow denotes sunlight or day, or earth. Green usually symbolizes vegetation. Blue represents the sky; haze, mist, fog, or smoke; distant mountains; rocks; and night. White is the normal background; when it has any signification, it denotes snow, sand, earth, or water. Black and brown rarely have any color significance; they are practically not used in Arapaho decorative art except to give sharpness of outline to colored areas, and occasionally in very minute figures. Water does not seem to be associated very strongly with any color. Clouds are as rarely symbolized by color as by forms.

The symbolic decoration that has been described is of course far from pictography. A pictograph serves as a means of record or communication, and is normally not decorative; while this art is too decorative to allow of being read. Yet there is considerable similarity in the symbols used in both systems. Moreover, the significance of a piece of decoration is at times as extended and coherent as that of a pictograph.

There is a class of ceremonial objects, used especially in the modern ghost-dance and related ceremonies, whose form and decoration are not fixed and prescribed, but depend upon the taste and desire of their owner. Many of these objects are nearly pictographs, yet are made with a considerable attempt at ornamentation: they may, as a class, be described as decorative — but not geometrically decorative — and highly symbolic. Usually these objects are painted or carved in outline, with free lines. Ceremonial articles of this class are not described in the present chapter, but are mentioned here because they reveal a form of art that is midway between symbolic decoration and picture-writing.

Another variety of symbolism that is found chiefly in connection with ceremonial objects, but which it may be well to refer to here, attaches signification to various parts or appendages of such objects. For instance, feathers sometimes denote spirits, or again clouds, or wind, and hence breath and life. Fur, hoofs, sticks, strings, bells, pendants, fringes, etc., are often symbolic in this way.

In closing this discussion of Arapaho decorative symbolism, it is desired to state that the closeness of connection between this symbolism and the religious life of the Indians cannot well be overestimated by a white man. Apart from the existence of a great amount of decorative symbolism on ceremonial objects not described in this chapter, it should be borne in mind that the making of what have been called tribal ornaments is regularly accompanied by religious ceremonies; that some styles of patterns found on tent-ornaments and parfleches are very old and sacred because originating from mythic beings; that a considerable number of objects are decorated according to dreams or visions; and, finally, that all symbolism, even when decorative and unconnected with any ceremony, tends to be to the Indian a matter of a serious and religious nature.

NOTE.

After p. 9 had been printed, I secured the missing terms of relationship in the Arapaho dialect.

father's brother	neisa′naⁿ
mother's sister	ne′inaⁿ
son of brother of a man } son of sister of a woman }	ne′ih′äⁿ
daughter of brother of a man } daughter of sister of a woman }	nata′ne

It will be seen from these terms that the Arapaho system is identical with that of the Gros Ventres.

UNIVERSITY OF CALIFORNIA PUBLICATIONS

IN

AMERICAN ARCHAEOLOGY AND ETHNOLOGY

Vol. 12, No. 3, pp. 71-138   June 28, 1916

ARAPAHO DIALECTS

BY

A. L. KROEBER

CONTENTS

PART I—DIALECTS OF THE ARAPAHO GROUP

PART II—SKETCH OF ARAPAHO PROPER

PART III—NOTES ON GROS VENTRE

The investigations upon which this essay is based were carried on, in 1899, 1900, and 1901, through the generosity of Mrs. Morris K. Jesup, and under the direction of the Trustees and officers of the American Museum of Natural History, to whose courtesy the writer expresses his indebtedness.

PART I

DIALECTS OF THE ARAPAHO GROUP

THE DIALECTS

According to the latest authority, Dr. Truman Michelson,[1] the languages of the great Algonkin family fall into four primary, substantially co-ordinate, but very unequal groups. Three of these are Blackfoot, Cheyenne, and Arapaho. The fourth, or Eastern-Central, comprises all the other dialects of the family. The Blackfoot, Cheyenne, and Arapaho were buffalo hunters in the open plains. The other tribes with scarcely an exception were timber people. It is erroneous, however, to look for an exact repetition of this primary cultural cleavage in the linguistic organization of the family. The Blackfoot, Cheyenne, and Arapaho tongues are as distinct from one another as from the remaining languages. This fact had indeed been asserted, in so far as the imperfect evidence permitted opinion, before Dr. Michelson's exact comparative studies, and has long rendered very improbable, at least as regards the Blackfoot and the Arapaho, the prevailing assumption, which is still largely current, that all the Plains Algonkin tribes are recent offshoots from the main body of the stock in the wooded region. It cannot be emphasized too strongly that wherever these tribes may originally have lived, they were not, for a long time past, close relatives and perhaps not even neighbors of the Cree, Ojibwa, or any other known Algonkin division. The recent brilliant discovery of Dr. E. Sapir that the far-away Yurok and Wiyot languages on the Pacific Coast of California are Algonkin proves that the history of this great assembly of tongues cannot be deduced by any off-hand inference from recent habits of life or distribution of the Indian tribes involved. The writer believes that the Arapaho have been separated from the Central and Eastern Algonkins for more than a thousand years.

The Arapaho recognize five former divisions of their people. As placed by them in order from south to north, these were the Nā^{n}waθinähā'na^n or South-?-people, the Hā^{n}anaxawūne'na^n or Rock-people, the Hinana'e'ina^n or Arapaho proper, the Bāsa^{n}wūne'na^n or Wood-

---

[1] Science, xxxv, 675, 1912, and Bureau of American Ethnology, Twenty-eighth Annual Report, Washington, 221–290, 1912.

house-people, and the Hitōune'naⁿ or Begging-people. The last are the tribe that calls itself Ha'ā'ninin and has long been known as Atsina or Gros Ventre of the Prairie. The Arapaho proper have for a considerable time been divided into a northern and a southern branch. As the language of these two halves scarcely differs even dialectically, the distinction, however important historically, may be disregarded in the present connection.[2] The three other tribes have long since coalesced with the Arapaho. The Bāsaⁿwūnena, whose dialect was very similar to that of the Hinana'ĕinaⁿ, are still to be found among them in some numbers, though without any identity as a separate group. A very few people remembering something of the Nāⁿwaθinähānaⁿ dialect were living in 1899. From one of these was obtained the brief vocabulary given below. This dialect is more divergent from Arapaho proper than either Bāsaⁿwūnenaⁿ or Gros Ventre, and, at least superficially, shows some resemblance to Cheyenne. No one was found who remembered the speech of the Hāⁿanaxawūnenaⁿ, which is said by the Arapaho to have been the most different from their own. One of their submerged dialects, probably this Hāⁿanaxawūnenaⁿ tongue, some Arapaho declare to have been intermediate between their own speech and Blackfoot. The statement is here made only on Indian authority. It is not impossible that some specimens of this speech may yet be recoverable by careful search among the Arapaho.

A brief comparative vocabulary of the four dialects on which material could be obtained is appended. This is unfortunately badly selected, and the phonetic perception and rendering are no doubt inadequate even for Arapaho and Gros Ventre, which the author had ampler opportunity to hear. Further, the words in the two other dialects were obtained from people who no longer habitually used them, perhaps had never done so. Still, the lists contain new information, which may never be duplicated, and are therefore given with all their imperfections.

---

[2] Mr. James Mooney (Bur. Am. Ethn. Ann. Rep., XIV, 954, 1896, and Bur. Am. Ethn., Bull. 30, 73, 1907), gives the five Arapaho subdivisions differently, apparently through identifying the Nāⁿwaθinähāna with the Naⁿwuinenaⁿ, the southern half of the Arapaho proper. He therefore virtually omits the former and exalts the southern branch of the Arapaho into a distinct division. Politically this may be correct for recent centuries, but the existence of a markedly separate Nāⁿwaθinähānaⁿ dialect, as discussed below, necessitates the recognition of this people, instead of the southern Arapaho proper, as one of the five divisions, from the point of view of language and earlier history. The only alternative is to assume the specimens of speech obtained as Nāⁿwaθinähānaⁿ to be not Nāⁿwaθinähānaⁿ, but Hāⁿanaxawūnenaⁿ, a proceeding which would reconcile all conflicting statements, but which would be arbitrary.

COMPARATIVE VOCABULARY

English	Arapaho Hinana'eina^n	Southern People[1] Nä^nwaθinähänä^n	Wood-lodge People[2] Bäsa^nwŭnena^n	Gros Ventre Ha'äninin
1	tcăseix	teä^ncilaha'[3]	nänīsetci	tcăθeity
2	nīsi	nīsähä'	nänīsehi'	nīθä
3	nåsa^n	nahaha'	nänåsei	nåθä'
4	yein^i	niabaha'	yänånei	yäni
5	yäθan^i	niotanähä'	yanaθanī'	yätani
6	nīta^ntax^u	neixθioti	nīteätax	neityä^ntos
7	nīsa^ntax^u	nīciota^n	nīsa^ntax	nīθä^ntos
8	nåsa^ntax^u	nexiotähähä^n	nänåsä^ntax^weit	nåθä^ntos
9	θi'^a	cioxtähähä^n	ciotaxahei	ä^nhäbetä^ntos
10	bätätax^u	maxtoxtahähä^n	båtcätoxe	betä^ntos
man	hinen^i	hiten	hini	hineni
woman	hisei	hihi'i	hisäna^n	hiθä
child	teia^n	hakutsa'anähä[4]	teia^nnihi'	teia^nnä
white man	nih'ä^nθa^n	matsōhuθa	ni'ä^ns[5]	nix'ä^nt
father	neisana^n	hiθextīn	hīsanänin*	nīθina^n
mother	neina^n	häictīn	neinah*	neina^n
elder brother	nåsähä'	nixtsia^n	nih'sa*	nåθähä'
son	neihä^n'	neictä'	neihä'*	neihä'
daughter	natane	naxtänähä	natänä*	natan
grandfather	näbäcibä	(h)amacīm	näbäcibähä'*	näbeseip
grandmother	neibähä^n	(h)ihi'im	neibähä^n*	niip
grandchild	neici	ni'icitähä^n		niisä
eye	bäcīsä	masixsan	hicīsä	besōθ
nose	beic	maic	hiθeä	beicä
mouth	bäti	matīn	hitcinä	betyī'
tooth	beitciθ	meitcixta	hinītcic	bītsit^i
tongue	beiθan		hinīθan	biitani
ear	wanatana'		hinatana'	wanotan
neck	bäsona^n		hisa^n	waθana
belly	wanot	moxta^n, monoxta^n	hinot*	wanot^e
hand	bätcet		hitcet	båtyetyi
foot	wa'a^nθ^i	mo'oxts	hi'ä^nc	wa'a^nts
house	nīna^n	mī'in	nīna^n, nī'in*	nīn, nīn^an
house	ha'ä^nwu	hä'axamunθ	ha'ä^nwu*	
bow	bätä	ma'axta	bätä*	bät
arrow	hoθ^i	hot	hoci*	hotsi
sun, luminary	hīcīs	hīcihiä^n	hīcīs*	hīsös
star	haθa'a^n		haθa'aha'a^n	hatou
water	nete^i	nete	netsi*	nets, nits
river	nīteiye	tīte	nīteiye*	nītsä^n
stone	haha'anä^nkä^n	haxta^n	haha'anä^nkä^n	axa'änä^ntyä^n
earth	bīta'ä^nwu	mixta'amu	bīta'awu	bīta'awu
fire	icitä^n	ih'citä^n	hixt, ih'tä^n*	isötä^n
wood	bäc^i, bäx-	ma'	bäci,* bäx	bis
metal	beitciθei	mähi'itsitä	beitciθei*	beitsit
road	ba'a^n	mihia^n	ba'ah*	
tree, cottonwood	hahä^nt^i	hoxtoxt	hahätci*	hahä^ntina^n (pl.)
grass, medicine	waxu'	maxsou	waxu',* waxuina^n (pl.)	wasiina^n (pl.)
horse	hiwaxuhä^nx-äbi (pl.)	masoutihem	hiwaxuahäθa,* hiwaxuh^nxcb (pl.)	hiwas'hä^nθ
dog	heθ-äbi (pl.)	hatam	häθä,* häθabiha^n (pl.)	hote
buffalo bull	hanä^ntcä^n	hitä^nmō^n	hänä^ntcä*	hänä^ntyei
buffalo (herd)	hīθeina^n		hīcinan	hītä^nnan
deer	bihi'i	mixtihi	bihi'i*	bihi'i
antelope	nisitcä^n, na^nsitcä^n	teasitca^n	nictcä*	na^nsity
elk	hīwax^u	himaxsout	hiwax^u*	hiwasö^n
mountain sheep	hotä'	hoxtähä^n	hotä'*	hote

English	Arapaho Hinana'einaⁿ	Southern People[1] Nāⁿwaθinähä́naⁿ	Wood-lodge People[2] Bǎsaⁿwŭnenaⁿ	Gros Ventre Ha'āninin
beaver	häbäc	hamaha'	häbäc*	häbes
rabbit	naⁿkᵘ	mäⁿkut	naⁿkᵘ*	naⁿtse
bear	woxᵘ	mahom	woxⁿ,* waxuinaⁿ (pl.)	was
wolf	häⁿxei		häⁿxĕ*	häⁿθei
skunk	xouhu	saoθ	xouhu*	θouu
eagle, bird	ni'ihi	tcäsei	ni'ix	ni'ihi
crow	hou	hahäha'	hou	ouu
magpie	wa'uei	mouxtiäⁿ		wouxei
turtle	bä'änaⁿ	ma'änaⁿhäⁿ	bä'än*	bä'änou
supernatural	nänäbä'änaⁿ, bätǎnaⁿ	nǎnamätit	tanänäbä'änaⁿ	bǎtä-
large	bänǎsaⁿ	mänacie	bänǎsaⁿ	bǎsöu
white	naⁿk-	wanätsiäⁿ	naⁿk-*	nanäⁿtsa
black	wa'otäⁿ	moxtsiäⁿ	wa'otäⁿ*	wa'otäⁿyaⁿ
red	bǎ-	maoxtaheini		baxa'aⁿ
yellow	nīhaⁿyaⁿ	hītianie	nīhaⁿyaⁿ*	nīhaⁿyaⁿ

NOTES ON VOCABULARY

[1] From Tall Bear.

[2] Unmarked words from the wife of Row-of-Lodges; starred words from Tall-Bear.

[3] An l was recorded, but seems doubtful, as the Arapaho ordinarily are unable to pronounce this sound. The word for "rain" in the same dialect was, however, recorded both as häⁿsivaxta and häⁿsilaxta.

[4] "Small." Evidently contains the diminutive suffix, as does the Bǎsaⁿwŭnenaⁿ form.

[5] The manuscript record may be read either with final s or θ.

Additional Words—Arapaho Proper

young man	hanaxa'aha	mountain	häⁿ'ǎni'
young woman	hīteiyaⁿ	night	bīkaⁿ
old woman	bätäbi(ä)	moon	bikōsīs
old	bähä'ei, behi'i	sky, cloud	hanaⁿ'
human being	hinenitäⁿ	thunder	baxa'aⁿ
ghost	θīkᵘ	fog	bä'änaⁿ
head	hakuhäⁿ	creek	kaha'aⁿwu
hair	beiθe'ä	snow	hī
throat	beitaⁿ	tent pole	hakäⁿx
bone	hixu	robe	hou
heart	bätäⁿ	awl	bei
arm	bǎnec	dress	bīxŭti
elbow	bätic	bed	häⁿ
sinew	haotäⁿ	boat	θiwu
milk, breast-water	bäθenetc[l]	meat	haseinou
penis	haθäⁿ	pipe	= rib
testicle	bäθǎs	tobacco	cīsäⁿwaⁿ
vagina	hähätc	corn	beckatänaⁿ
tail	bätihi'i	fruits	bīnaⁿ
rib	hītcaⁿ	bush	bīc
liver	hic	coyote	kaⁿ'aⁿ
kidney	hitīθiθ	buffalo cow	bii
blood	bǎ	fly	noubäⁿ
excrement	bǎ, bi-hiθ	louse	bätei
shadow	bätäθaⁿ	worm	bīsäⁿ, hīsaⁿnaⁿ
shaman	bätǎt	fish	nawat

Some of the more readily noted correspondences in sound between Arapaho and the other Algonkin languages, and within the Arapaho dialects, will now be given. There is no pretense that these observations are complete. The material used in the comparisons is familiar to students of the subject in the works of Baraga, Jones, Lacombe, Hayden, Rand, Petter, besides many others whose efforts have not been drawn upon. For this reason the Indian forms of the words referred to in English have not been given. The few who may follow up the present suggestions can verify them with ease, and will be at least as familiar with the material as the writer. The following abbreviations have been used to designate groups, languages, and lialects:

E-C	Eastern-Central Algonkin
Mi	Micmac
F	Fox
O	Ojibwa
Cr	Cree
Ch	Cheyenne
Bl	Blackfoot
A	Arapaho group of dialects
Ar	Arapaho proper
GV	Gros Ventre
B	Bäsa^{n}wünena^n
N	Nä^{n}waθinähäna^n

Of the symbols used, c is š or sh as customary in American philology, θ is the same as English surd th, x is a surd fricative approximately in k position, ä is a as of "bad" in American English, ä^n and a^n are nasalized vowels, ö is somewhat as in German, but probably unrounded, and ' is the glottal stop.

EXTERNAL PHONETIC CORRESPONDENCES OF THE GROUP

K

Assuming the Eastern-Central group of dialects, in which are included the great majority of those belonging to the family, to be most representative of the original or former condition of Algonkin, it is clear that original k is but rarely retained in the Arapaho division. It appears most commonly as s or h, or is entirely lost or represented only by a glottal stop.

k>k: wolf. Ch, Bl, A.
k>t: black, E-C, k; Ch, xt; A, t.
k>tc: metal. Ch, k; Bl, ks; A, tc.
k>s: neck, nose, eye, woman, antelope, one. Ch shows k, x, ts. GV usually has θ for s.
k>h, x: beaver, deer, bone, bear, sun, skunk. E-C has k or sk; Bl, usually

k; Ch is variable.

k > ',—: bow, turtle, red, star, eagle, foot, nine. E-C again shows sk as well as k, also kw. Ch usually agrees with Arapaho, while Bl oftener retains k, but is variable.

T

Algonkin dental stops seem to be of two kinds. One appears with but little variation as t in all dialects, including Arapaho. The other varies between t, d, n, and l in the Eastern-Central group, is t in Cheyenne as in Gros Ventre and Nānwaθinähānaⁿ, but θ in Arapaho proper and Bāsaⁿwūnenaⁿ.

t > t: bow, heart, fire, night, daughter, buffalo bull, ten, reflexive suffix. Bl has some inclination toward ts or st, N toward xt.

t, d, n, l > θ: tongue, tooth, foot, star, metal, dog, five. Mi, t, d, l; O, d, n; Bl, tʔ, kʔ; Ch, Na, GV, t; Ar, Bä, θ.

t > tc: pipe, mouth, six. E-C, t; Bl, —; Ch, ʔ; Bä, GV, tc; Ar, t, tc.

P

Original labial stops begin to be lost or altered as soon as the Eastern-Central division is left behind, and seem to have disappeared entirely from the Arapaho group.[3]

p, b > k: rabbit, white, sit, sleep. E-C, p, b; Bl, p, k; Ch, k, x; Ar, Na, Bä, k; GV, ts. These are the principal occurrences of k in Arapaho that the author can account for by any phonetic rule.

p, b > tc: tooth, water, night. E-C, p, b; Bl, Ch, p w; A, tc.

N

N usually recurs unchanged in all Algonkin groups, though in some stems the sound varies between n and y. There may be two distinct original sounds involved.

n > n: bone, man, daughter, turtle, one, two, three, six, sing, water, fish, drink. In the last three stems m sporadically supplants n.

n, y > n, y: tongue, mouth, neck, wolf, four, five, sleep. All dialects except Mi and O have y in some of these stems. F and Na show ny.

M

M of original Algonkin seems to be retained quite regularly in Eastern-Central, in Blackfoot, in Cheyenne, and in the Nānwaθinähānaⁿ dialect of Arapaho. In the three other Arapaho dialects it is entirely lacking, and replaced by b and w. As between these two

---

[3] E. Sapir, American Anthropologist, n. s., xv, 538, 1913.

sounds, the rule is that b occurs before the front vowels i, e, ä, än, and w before the back vowels u, o, a, an.[4] This is a consistent phonetic law of Arapaho; even within the dialect the same stem changes from b to w if the vowel becomes a back one. Compare Ar neibähän, my grandmother, and hiniiwahan, his grandmother. It is also illustrative that in trying to say the English word "buffalo," the Gros Ventre, whose idiom follows the same law, speak waθanou instead of baθanou. All Arapaho labial sounds seem to be derived from original m.

m>b (i): eat, defecate, give, dog, deer, earth.
m>b (e): metal.
m>b (ä, än): blood, red, bow, wood, turtle, beaver, ten, drink.
m>w (a, an, o): bear, fish, grass, black.

In a few words m changes to n in Arapaho. In these Cheyenne has n also.

m>n: eagle, house.

W

A more remarkable change is that of original w to Arapaho n. This probably represents the transition w>m>n.

w>n: buffalo herd, antelope, rabbit, white; perhaps also ear. Ar, Bä, GV, regularly n; Na, sometimes m; Ch, Bl, E-C, w.

S

Eastern-Central s, like t, sometimes recurs in Arapaho, sometimes becomes θ. There is thus the possibility that eastern s, with which c (sh) has been included, represents two sounds originally distinct.

s>s: sun, fire, wind, rain, tobacco, two, three. Bl, Ch, and Na show —, h, or x frequently. GV alone has θ sometimes: tobacco, two, three.
s>θ: hair, nine, eat, defecate. E-C, s, tc, dj; Ch, Na, s; Ar (and Bä?), θ.
s>h: stone, yellow. A dialects have h, except Na t. Perhaps allied to the change k>s, h.

VOWELS

The vowels of Arapaho also evince fairly regular correspondences with those of other dialects, though the cause of their most marked peculiarity, the frequent nasalization of ä and a, is not clear to the writer. Counting än and an for the present with ä and a, four principal equivalences are noticeable.

---

4 bā'an, road, and baha'an, thunder, are exceptions noted in simple stem words.

	Mi	F	Cr, O	Bl	Ch	Na	Ar, Bä, GV
Type 1	i	i	i	i	i	i	i
Type 2	*var.*	ä, e	i	(i)	(i)	a	ä, e
Type 3	a, o, u	a	a	a, o	o	a	a
Type 4	*var.*	a	a	*var.*	o, u	o, u	u

It is evident that there is a special similarity between Fox and the Arapaho group, at least under the orthographies that have been employed; that Nān waθinähãnaⁿ leans towards Cheyenne; that the latter favors a sound usually written o,[5] and Blackfoot the vowel i.

Type 1—i>i: nose, eye, tooth, sun, fire, water, eat, defecate, give, two, reflexive suffix. GV alone several times has ö, which in most its occurrences in that dialect seems to replace Ar i.

Subtype 1*a*—i, e>i: woman, pipe, six. F, e; Cr, O, Bl, Ch, i, e, a; A i, sometimes ei.

Type 2—i, ä>ä: heart, bow, wood, dog, beaver, turtle, red, drink, two, three, four, ten. Mi, ?; F, ä; Cr, O, i; Bl, Ch, i often, but not always; Na, ä, oftener a; Ar, Bä, GV, ä.

Subtype 2*a*—i, e>e: hand, man, water, metal. Mi,?; F, e; Cr, O, i; Bl, i; Ch, a back vowel; Na, e, ä; Ar, Bä, GV, e.

Type 3—a>a: daughter, wolf, buffalo, rabbit, turtle, fish, star, stone, pipe, yellow, jump, sleep. Mi, back vowels, possibly only variant orthographies for a; F, Cr, O, a; Bl, a or o; Ch, o; A, a, aⁿ. GV occasionally shows ou.

Subtype 3*a*—Same, except Bl i, A sometimes ä: tongue, neck, beaver, dog, five, ten.

Subtype 3*b*—Same, except Ar, and sometimes other A dialects, open o for a: neck, bear, black, sit.

Type 4—a>u: bone, bear, skunk, rabbit, grass.

INTERNAL PHONETIC CORRESPONDENCES OF THE GROUP

BASAⁿWUNENAⁿ

Within the Arapaho group, Bãsaⁿwũnenaⁿ differs little from the principal dialect. S or c sometimes appears for θ, as in tooth, foot, white man. This is not a reversion to original s which Arapaho θ at times represents, but a further specialization, since Arapaho θ in these words stands for original t. On the other hand, Arapaho s, or c, becomes θ in Bãsaⁿwũnenaⁿ in the word for nose, and x in fire and wood. In other stems Arapaho θ, s, and c recur unchanged in Bãsaⁿwũnenaⁿ. T occasionally appears as tc: tree, mouth, six, ten.

All the Bãsaⁿwũnenaⁿ body-part terms obtained from both informants begin with the possessive prefix of the third person hi-, instead of the indefinite wa-, bä-, of Arapaho, which elsewhere in the family is represented by ma-, mi.

---

[5] Petter, Mem. Am. Anthr. Ass., I, 448, 1907, denies that Cheyenne properly possesses the vowels i and u.

GROS VENTRE

Gros Ventre presents greater changes.

Ar x>GV s: grass, elk, bear, eight, ten. GV evidently clings to the older sound which Ar has altered.

Ar x>GV θ: wolf, skunk. GV apparently has specialized.

Ar θ>GV t: tongue, white man, dog, buffalo, buffalo herd, star, metal, five, "nephew" (when not called "son"), father-in-law, son-in-law, brother or sister-in-law of opposite sex.[6] Comparison shows Gros Ventre to be the more conservative, as the Ar sound stands for original t.

Ar θ>GV ts, tc: foot.

Ar t>GV tc, ty: mouth, hand, six. Bä shows a similar tendency. In many other words, on the other hand, such as ear, belly, fire, mountain sheep, black, eight, ten, both Ar and GV have t.

Ar s, c>GV θ: eye, neck, woman, tobacco, two, three, seven, eight, father, older brother, "niece" (when not called "daughter"), daughter-in-law, wife.[6] In some of these words Ar s represents original s or h, in others original k. In other instances Ar s of both origins remains s in GV.

Ar tc was usually heard as either ts, or ty, nearly ky, in Gros Ventre.

Ar k>GV ts: rabbit, white.

Ar i>GV ö: eye, sun, fire.

NAⁿWUθINAHANAⁿ

Nāⁿwuθinähänaⁿ not only departs farthest from Arapaho proper but stands nearest of the known Arapaho dialects to Cheyenne and Eastern-Central. It presents enough peculiarities, however, to be more than a mere transition.

Nāⁿwuθinähänaⁿ agrees with Cheyenne in retaining m which Arapaho has converted to b and w; in fact the dialectic pronunciation of "Washington" was given as moⁿcten. It agrees with Cheyenne and Ojibwa in having w, or b, in certain words which possess n in Arapaho. Like these two dialects, it shows n as the initial of the words for four and five, where Arapaho has y. In all these points it departs from the Arapaho group of dialects in the direction of the Central and Cheyenne groups.

As regards s and h sounds, correspondences of all three types, s>h, x>s, s>s, are found between Arapaho and Nāⁿwuθinähänaⁿ. Arapaho x is probably an h with partial stricture rather than a true palatal fricative. In place of it Nāⁿwuθinähänaⁿ sometimes has s, sometimes a sound written xs. In "bear" h equals x.

Arapaho θ was usually rendered by t, once or twice by s and ts, in the Nāⁿwuθinähänaⁿ words obtained. Three words in this dialect

---

[6] Bull. Am. Mus. Nat. Hist., XVIII, 9, 1902.

were recorded with θ, but the sound does not agree regularly with any Arapaho sound in tnese cases, and must be considered doubtful.

Arapaho ä was sometimes rendered by ä in Nā^{n}wuθinähäna^n, sometimes by a. Ei becomes e.

The x or h so frequently written before t, ts, and s in Nā^{n}wuθinähäna^n causes the suspicion that the informant was exaggerating a real or imaginary greater degree of aspiration, either of vowels or of consonants, than he believed Arapaho to possess. It seems somewhat doubtful whether full xt, xts, and xs were really spoken. Cheyenne, however, shows a similar parasitic x or h before t, as well as before k. Yurok also has xk, and Fox 'k.

PART II

SKETCH OF ARAPAHO PROPER

Phonetic Elements

It is fourteen years since the writer has heard Arapaho or Gros Ventre. At that time his understanding of the nature and formation of spoken sounds was vague. Some experience with and much interest in the two languages have, however, left many distinct motor impressions of words; and a comparison of variant orthographies makes other points clear which inability of interpretation rendered baffling at the time. The following notes may therefore still have some value.

Arapaho vowels are:

u, ū, open.
o, very open, often confused with a^n; long, ou.
a^n, $\bar{a}^n$, nasalized, possibly spoken with the tongue slightly more raised than in the following.
a, ā.
A, less clear than a, was often written, but not regularly, and has been omitted from the present orthography.
ä, ā̈, as in American English "bad."
$\ddot{a}^n$, $\bar{\ddot{a}}^n$, nasalized.
e, very open, sometimes resembling ä; long, ei.
i, ī, open.

Gros Ventre adds to these a mixed vowel ö, sometimes heard as almost o, sometimes as ü. This is a derivative from i. Arapaho ei was sometimes heard with an approach to the quality of öi.

The extreme openness of most of these vowels, as well as the presence of ä, are conspicuous resemblances to the phonetics of Yurok, now that Dr. Sapir has shown the connection.

Long vowels are more or less doubled. See text III, note 1.

Final vowels, unless long or accented, are surd or whispered. The nature of surd vowels was not understood by the author at the time his notes were recorded; they were therefore sometimes omitted, sometimes written as sonant, sometimes indicated by small superior characters. So far as it could be restored with what seemed reasonable safety, the latter orthography has been employed in this paper. The writer is strongly of the impression that no word in Arapaho really ends in a consonant, a final surd or sonant vowel being always present;

but proof or disproof of this belief must be left to future investigators. Gros Ventre may furnish an exception in the case of final surd n; but this sound seems to owe its quality to the surdness of the preceding vowel. In Gros Ventre, also, the surdness of final vowels seems more complete than in Arapaho.

Vowels followed by a glottal stop (') show usually, perhaps always in distinct speech, an echo. Nähä and nähää, this, were written indiscriminately for nähä'ä, perhaps more exactly nähä'ᵃ. The orthography nähä' should be sufficient.

Arapaho consonants:

k, t, and tc (English ch) are probably sonant during part of the explosion, as in so many Indian languages. The g mentioned by Dr. Michelson was not observed. When final, these stops seem to be entirely surd, and their explosion takes on a vowel color.

In Gros Ventre, tc is replaced by two sounds: ts, the general equivalent of Arapaho tc, and ty, which often stands for Arapaho t. The two are however not as different in articulation and sound as the orthographies might indicate. Ty seems to be a very posterior t; it is sometimes heard as ky, and the Arapaho so render it in trying to reproduce Gros Ventre.

b is a full sonant, as would be indicated by its origin from m, and by its alternation, both in Arapaho and Gros Ventre, with w.

w, y, and n need no discussion. Gros Ventre surd n has been mentioned in connection with the surd vowels.

s and c (sh) are difficult to distinguish. They were very much confounded by the writer, though he is inclined to consider them two sounds.

x and h were also much confused. It seems that x is really an h with considerable stricture, and that h is fainter than in English, so that h and ' might have been better orthographies. If this is the case, the nature of the two sounds is the same as in Yana, Mohave, and other Californian languages.[7] In Gros Ventre initial h is particularly faint, and was often not heard. Final h or x, that is, h followed by a surd vowel, is strong in both languages.

θ is a surd dental fricative like English th in thin.

Vocalic changes are illustrated throughout the grammatical and textual material presented below, but are very complex. Changes proceed from stem to suffix, from suffix to stem, and from stem to prefix; they are sometimes in the direction of assimilation, at other times of contrast. Consonant alterations, especially between b and w, follow the vowel changes. Here again the similarity of process to Yurok is marked.

Consonantal changes are also somewhat obscure, but it is of note that in part at least they follow the interdialectic equivalences between Arapaho and Gros Ventre.

---

[7] Present series of publications, x, 62, 1911.

Composition

The intricate subject of word composition is too little plain in
Arapaho to allow of more than a listing of some of the principal
forms which word compounding has been observed to take. These
comprise nouns containing two or more elements used also as independent words, a few words containing elements occurring only as
"prefixes," and a larger number ending in elements which are always
"suffixes." Verbs consisting of two verb stems, or of a verbal and
an adverbial stem, are more conveniently considered in connection
with the subsequent section treating of the structure of the verb.

A. NOUNS COMPOUNDED OF TWO SEPARATE WORDS

Noun and noun, the first determining the second:

hāⁿ-n-isei, "Bed-Woman"
heθa-bic, dog bush
heθa-w-aⁿwu, dog lodge
hi-tce'äox-aⁿwu, club lodge, club dance
bīsäⁿ-n-oxⁿ-inaⁿ, worm weeds
waxn-sei-naⁿ, bear, women
nītcīhe-hinen, Kiowa (nītciye, river)
nih'äⁿθ-ousei, white-man woman, American woman
cīcīyē-n-axu, snake weed, snake medicine

Verb with a noun as its object, which can also be used as a separate,
independent substantive:

wan-isei-nä-hiθi, they go after women, burrs
notī-sei-n-äⁿt¹, looks for a wife
hi-netci-bī-niθ¹, the giver of water, he who owns the waters

It will be seen that the noun comes before as well as after the
verbal element. It is not certain how far these examples are to be
interpreted as being verbs or as being nouns. Hence the term "incorporation" is avoided for them.

Noun with following verb or adjective stem, the former determining the latter, but the entire word being nominal. It will be seen that
the majority of the forms are proper names. Compare the verbal
suffix -ni.

ha'äti-n-ahaⁿkäⁿ, "Lime Crazy"
wax-tcīyei, "Bear Creeping" (cīcī, creep)
wax-kukatäni, "Bear Spotted (Is)"
häⁿxä-ba'äni, "Wolf Red (Is)"
hisei-waotäⁿni, "Woman Black (Is)"
icitäⁿ-kūθaⁿ, fire drill

Verb, adjective, or adverb preceding and determining a noun:

h-axänθ-inenina^n, funny men, name of a band (axän^t-ēhi, laughable)
na^{n}wu-nenitäna^n, south people
hawah-a^{n}wū, many houses, town
ha^{n}wä^n-ū-n-anaxa'ahä, praying young man
häbät-äθ, large dog (heθ)
häbät-ä^{n}xe, large knife (wä^{n}xe)
häbäθ-inen^i, large man
häbäθ-ī-waxū, large bear (wox^n)
hätcax-ä^{n}xe, small knife
hätcäc-inen^i, small man
kaha'ū-cī-nin, half a day
haseihi-n-axucītana^n, sacrifice (sun dance) paintings
niha^n-n-ouha^n, yellow buffalo calves (wou)
waotä^n-n-ou, black crow (hou)
kä^{n}ku-na^{n}tinei, "One-eyed Sioux" (ka^{n}kou-iya^n, patch on)
ka^{n}kuiy-äθäbi, scabby dogs
hä^{n}t-etc^i, large water, ocean (netc^i, water)
cītci-nä-waxu, lasting weed (cīcītci, stretch)
tcäyataw^n-inenitä^n, untrue person, spirit
θawaθ-inenitä^n, real person, human being

B. NOUNS AND VERBS FORMED WITH PREFIXES

wot-i-, in fire, into fire.

woti-tan-ēhi, fire-starter
wot^i-tanä-tanä-na^n, they burn it
hä^{n}ix-woti-θ-a^n, they put him in the fire
wotī-ka^{n}hu-na^n, they ran into the fire
woti-tanä^n, added wood to the blaze

sä'ä-, sä'i-, flat.

sä'ä-bäxa^n, flat wood, boards
sä'ei-tca'a^n, "flat" (straight tubular) pipe
sä'ä-hiθi, flat ones, bedbugs
tah^n-sä'i-ci, after she lay
sä'ä-beitciθä, flat metal, spade
sä'i-ce-θäna^n, roof
sä'ä-sana^n, sliced meat
hä^{n}ix-sä'ä-se'esī, then cut them into slices
sä'i-θi-xa-h-uθen^i, I peg you out flat
sä'i-θi-xa-h-un, the crucified one, Christ
sä'i-ci-w-anaxa'ä, "Lie-abed-long Young-man"

nä-, relating to clothing.

nä-tä^{n}nei, take off moccasins
nä-tatahä^n, take off leggings
nä-θibi, take off clothes
nä-ya^n-un, dress!

kaka-, relating to mental action.

> kaka'-uθetcaⁿ-naⁿ, thoughts
> kako-xa'änätaⁿ, think about it

C. NOUNS AND VERBS FORMED WITH SUFFIXES

-ī-nⁱ, on measures of time. Compare the suffix -inⁱ on the numerals 11 to 19, which is no doubt the same.

> kahaū-cī-ni-n, half a day
> tihi'-sī-ni, yesterday
> tayu-nī-nⁱ, tatayou-nĭ-nⁱ, autumn (tai, cold)
> tcätcī-nⁱ, winter, year
> īsibī-ta-nī-ni, bedtime, time for lying down
> xäⁿtäei-nī-nⁱ, shortly after, sometime later
> tahᵃ-tcäni-bihiyaⁿ-ni, when it was late in the night

-ätīt ⁱ, on names of ceremonial acts. The last part of this suffix is almost certainly an ending denoting the third person.

> tcä'-ätīt ⁱ, welcoming
> tceitaⁿ-h-ätīt ⁱ, ear piercing
> tiaxaⁿ-n-ätīt ⁱ, foot touching, an invitation
> tcätcecī-n-ätīt ⁱ, untying, a redeeming
> tcaoxu-tcäbi-h-ätīt ⁱ, foe-shooting, the settling of a dispute by a game or test

-ahᵃwäⁿt ⁱ, dance. Also seems to contain the ending of the third person.

> hou-n-ahᵃwäⁿt ⁱ, crow dance
> hasaⁿ-n-ahᵃwäⁿt ⁱ, rain dance
> nou-t-ahᵃwäⁿt ⁱ, dancing out of sun dance
> ka'ei-n-ahᵃwäⁿt ⁱ, round dance, ghost dance
> tawa-n-ahᵃwäⁿt ⁱ, cutting dance
> naⁿä-n-ahᵃwäⁿt-anibä, all of you dance around me!

-tanä, burn, do to or with fire.

> woti-tanä-t ⁱ, he makes a fire
> hä-tanä-hei, put the fire out!
> hä-tanä-θ-äⁿt, he extinguishes it
> hä-tanä-kana-θei, drench the fire
> wot ⁱ-tanä-hokani, they burn it

-tcä-na, cook; probably from the same radical as the last.

> hi-tcäna-ät ⁱ, gridiron
> tcäbitäna-tcäna, fried bread
> nī-te-tcänä-θäyei-naⁿ, I maintain the fire constantly

-i-θetca^n, think.

> kaka'-uθetca^n-na^n, thoughts
> wax-^{n}θetca^n, feel sad (wa^{n}sa^n, wa^{n}xeit', bad, ugly)
> hä^n-s-iθetca^n-hoku, she thought
> bi'a^{n}h-ouθetca^n, I truly thought
> hä^{n}nä^n-kaxtaw-ūθetca^n-t', then she thought something was wrong

-θibi, relating to clothing. This and the preceding three elements seem verbal and could with equal propriety be listed among the suffixes or stems of the next section.

> nä-θibi, undress
> tcī-θibi-t', he dressed

-a^{n}wu, water.

> haxecī-n-a^{n}wunetc', muddy water
> tcänätä^n-n-a^{n}wunetc', blue or deep water
> θä^{n}θi-a^{n}wu, high or rough waves
> kaha'-a^{n}wu, creek
> kakuiy-a^{n}wu, sticky liquid, molasses

-(i)yei, tent: nīna^n, nīnan, tent.

> näyei, häyei, hiyei, my, your, her tent
> yeiyi, set up a tent
> sīs-äyei, take down a tent
> n-eiha^{n}wū-uyei, I have no tent

-akac, -akay, tent, house.

> häbät-akay', large tent
> hätcax-akay', small tent
> wa^{n}θei-n-akay, wa^{n}θei-n-akac, an old brown tent
> waotä^{n}na-h-akay-eit', "Black Lodge," his tent is black
> bätäbi-h-akac, old woman's tent
> hī-beitciθei-n-akay-anit', who has the metal tent
> hina-n-akay-a^n, "main" pole, by which tent is raised
> tcīt-akahay-inä^{n}t', enter-tent-song, sung when water is brought into the peyote tent
> heθaw-akay-a-ni, in the dog tent

-äθä', fire.

> bänäs-äθä', a large fire
> hī-bäxutcän-äθä, when the fire became low
> kox-k-aθä-ya^n-na^n, kindlings

-anihi', pet, domestic animal; perhaps contains the diminutive suffix quoted below.

> tcīy-anēhi, furry, shaggy dog
> ta'-anähi-hi', short-legged dog
> n-eiha^{n}wū-t-anihi', I have no horses

-h-ā^{n}x^u, plural -h-ā^{n}xäbi, horse, domestic animal.

n-äbīt-ā^{n}xabei-t^i, steals horses or cattle
noti-n-ā^{n}xäbī, looks for horses
hiwaxu-hā^{n}xäbi, horses (hiwax^u, elk)

-ä'ei, head, hair, neck.   The independent word for "hair" is beiθe'ä, for "his head" hakuhä^n.

ot-ä'ei-hi, comb hair
hä^{n}tit-ä'ei-niθi, beheaded ones
tcä'ä'ei-n-axa'ana^{n}x^u, round-head-ax
tcästc-ä'ei-niθi, scratched head
bäbä'-a'ei-n^i, you are curly haired
na^n-ta^n-h-īcīb-ä'ei-nei-t^i, and when he laid his head down
ka^{n}k-ä'ei-θi, Blackfeet (with erect hair)
kax-ä'ei-sibät^i, fractured his skull
ka^n-xu-hä^{n}ix-täb-ä'ei-kū-θ-äna^n, then again they cut off his head
behic^i-täb-ä'ei-θēhi, all cut off heads
täb-ä'ei-bäs-ī, cut-head-wood, stumps
täb-ä'ei-na^n, cut-head, hornless saddle
tcih-täs-ä'ei-ci, lay your head on!
na^{n}k-a'ei-n, white-neck, starched collar
tah^a-tcih^i-bä-tcīt-ä'ei-xa^n-θi, when they all put their heads in

-i-θä, nose.   The independent word is beic.

täb-īθä-bic, cut-nose-bush, whose fruit appears noseless like a skull

-ēhi, face.

kou-ēhi, swell-face, mosquito
kahan-ehi, hair burnt off
hä'-ni-täbi-eihī-t^i, struck him in the face

-θä^{n}θ-i, fingers, hand.   Independent word, bätcet.

hähīs-θä^{n}θ-ōhu, wash hands

-a^{n}t, leg.   Independent word, wa'a^{n}θ^i.

hawah-ā^{n}t-ät^i, many legs, centipede

-ixta^n, nail, claw, foot.

was-ixta^n, bear claws, bear foot (wox^u, bear)
hä^{n}s-ixtä^n-cīsa^n, "Sore-foot-child"

-ineihi, tail.   Independent word, bätihi'i.

tä^{n}ta^{n}ka-n-ineihi, raccoon (twisted, ringed tail?)
taxa^n-n-ineihi, opossum (smooth tail?)
wa^{n}θeiniθ-ineihi, bat, also Satan (brown, or old, ugly tail?)

-hi'i, -hä', -hähi, diminutive.

> hanaxa'aha, young man, hanaxa'ä-hi'i, boy
> bätäbi(ä), old woman, batäbi-hähi
> teiaⁿ, child, teiaⁿ-n-ähä'
> cīcītci, duck, cīcītce-häⁿ'
> ta'anähi-hi', short-legged dog

VERBS

WORD-FORMING PREFIXES

Among the elements prefixed to verbs, it is clear that those which are essentially word-forming come nearest the stem, while those whose purpose is more strictly relational or grammatical on the whole precede them. As might be expected, no hard and fast line can, however, be drawn between the two classes.

Word-forming prefixes, in turn, are often difficult to separate from independent words. Thus, täs-i- and tcän-i- mean "on" and "under" in verbs; but provided with the locative suffix -i-hi' they are adverbs which stand alone. Just so xou-wu-hu', "straight," and xanou, "immediately," are employed, in the forms xou- and xanou-, as prefixes to verbs. Verbs themselves, like tcäsis, "to begin," and θaⁿku-h, "to follow," are used as prefixes to other verbs.

Apparently related to this last group are such elements as tā'-, tou-, "to stop," and ta, tou, "to strike, tie, or be or come in contact with"; kax-, "through," and kax, "to impact violently"; tcäθ-i-, "away, outdoors," and tcäθ-i, "to depart or elope"; tcäb-i-, "past, alongside," and tcäb-i, "to travel."

It is true that even when these elements are themselves verbs they are not used merely with the personal suffixes, but that second elements such as -hi, -ni, -ku, -xa, -h are added to them. Now these added elements, which are frequent on indubitable verb stems, have all been listed as suffixes. But the possibility is by no means precluded that these "suffixes," whose significance usually is of the vaguest and most general, are themselves the real stem of the verb; in which case the preceding element, which is so much more specific in meaning as usually to carry the principal idea conveyed by the complete word, would after all be a prefix of the adverbial or prepositional type familiar from so many other languages.

For instance, θi- or θei- occurs as the first etymological element of a considerable number of verbs or nouns in all of which the idea of "in" or "on" or "projecting upward" is contained. Thus, θi-ayaⁿ, "a post"; θei-ka-h and θei-wa-n, "to carry on the back." On the other hand, the frequent element -ku is always at the end of words, and often adds little if anything to the meaning of the stem to which it is attached, as in äbīta-ku, "to steal," of which the stem appears without the -ku, but with the same denotation, in äbītä, "to steal," n-äbīt-īhi, "thief," h-äbīt-ā^{n}xabei-ti, "he steals horses." When, however, the prepositional "prefix" θei- and the vague "suffix" -ku are put together they form θei-ku, "to put in." In the same manner the combination of the variant θi- with the suffix -ok^u, apparently an intransitive equivalent of transitive -ku, results in θi-ok^u, "to sit." Which part of θei-ku and θi-ok^u is what in other languages would be called the stem? If the first element is a verb stem, then θei-wa-n, and such parallel forms as tcīθi-n-a^{n}ha-b, "to enter in order to see," are clearly compound or double verbs. If the second element is a verb stem, then äbītä-ku must be a compound of two verbs.

That Arapaho, like Shoshonean and some other American languages, possesses true compound verbs—verbs functioning as such and composed of two verbs—is thus probable. But either θei- or -ku, or both, and with them a large number of other elements, are lost as affixes. And yet the process involved in these cases is not one of mere simple word-compounding, for apparently θei- never occurs without a following element and -ku never without a preceding one. In short, it would seem that the Arapaho verb is frequently, perhaps normally, compounded of elements which themselves either are, or can become, verbal in force.

It is therefore possible that the old terms "polysynthesis" and "holophrasis," which in recent years have been in justifiable disrepute on account of their vagueness and their implication of processes totally foreign to other languages, may, when the Algonkin, and for that matter the Iroquoian and Caddoan languages, are more precisely understood, be rehabilitated with a new and exact meaning. And still extreme caution seems called for in drawing any such inference. "Incorporation" is another linguistic concept which has been reestablished of late years; and yet the justification was brought about only by an abandonment of the very traits which "incorporation" was originally and long believed to denote. Bandied about without standing for anything definite, the term "incorporation" was abused until the very existence of the process was challenged and denied. And when the reality of the process was finally demonstrated the proof resolved itself into the recognition of pronominal incorporation as a familiar and purely grammatical method represented in some degree in most languages, and of nominal incorporation as a form of the equally familiar process of etymological word-compounding, with only the one distinctive feature that in "incorporating" languages noun and verb can be combined to form verbs, whereas in other idioms they combine only into nouns. In short, the concept of incorporation involves only a new application of a widespread and well known linguistic process, not a new and unique process itself. Or it might be said that incorporating idioms differ from non-incorporating ones in degree, not in kind.

In an analogous manner it seems possible that we may ultimately be justified in speaking of Algonkin as truly "holophrastic" or "polysynthetic." But if so, these terms will essentially be only a convenient designation for the linguistic process which allows two verbs to consolidate into a single one.

In fine, the Algonkin verb, so far as Arapaho is representative of it, cannot in any off-hand manner be broken up into the usual elements of "prefix," stem," and "suffix"; and any attempt to apply such a procedure leads quickly to contradictions and inconsistencies that reveal the arbitrariness of the method.

The late Dr. William Jones reached exactly the same conclusion as regards the Fox dialect. He does not separate "prefixes" and "suffixes" from "stems" in the verb, but distinguishes "initial stems," "secondary stems of the first order," and "secondary stems of the second order," making these elements differ from each other not so much in their kind of meaning or in their ability or inability to appear as separate words, as in their mere order or position in the word-compound. This classification is a valuable and important departure from the all too frequent method of forcing new languages to fit old schemes or the categories established in other tongues. That the principles of Algonkin verb formation are in some respects conspicuously different from those of Indo-European Dr. Jones has made very clear; and a realization of this fact is the first requisite to a true understanding of Algonkin structure.

At the same time, while Dr. Jones has cleared away the brush and brought us face to face with the trees, he has not led us out of the forest. This task he would no doubt have achieved, save for his untimely death; but it remains undone. The realization that the Algonkin foot does not fit into the grammatical shoe built around the Indo-European last is, however important, only a first step. The next and necessary one must be the construction of a new type of shoe which upon suitable modification for individual cases will fit both feet. Or, to drop the metaphor, while an application to Algonkin of linguistic categories derived from Indo-European leads to misunderstanding, the construction and use of an entirely novel set of categories for Algonkin is meaningless. The types of structure represented by the two groups of languages obviously have something in common, however different these common principles may in reality be from what superficial acquaintance or a one-sided approach would lead one to suppose. In fact, the determination of what they have in common, involving as it does the recognition of that in which they are different, is an essential purpose of the study of both; for whether our interest lies in the problem of the nature or that of the origin of human speech, a classification is involved. In its widest ultimate aspect philology is concerned not with Algonkin as such nor with Indo-European as such but with all languages. Only when speech in general, its scope and its methods, are better understood will both Algonkin and Indo-European, or for that matter any particular group of languages, be more truly understandable. The real aim of the study of any American tongue, as well as the aim of any deeper research in Indo-European philology, must therefore be the more precise and fundamental determination of their relations to all other languages; and this necessitates concepts and terms which are applicable in common. It is impossible to characterize the wolf in terms of his skeleton, the elephant of his embryology, the whale of his habits, and then to construct a classification which will help to reveal the inherent nature, the development, or the origin of the animal kingdom. True tribute to the memory of Dr. Jones's work will be paid, not by a standing still where his labors were unfortunately broken off when chiefly their negative or destructive side had been completed, but by carrying his efforts and formulations on through a constructive phase to a point, denied to him by time, at which Algonkin will once more appear in a definite relation to human speech as a whole.

What this relation will be the writer does not have knowledge or understanding enough of any Algonkin language to say. But until the science of language is revolutionized by entirely new methods of thinking about it there seem to be only three possible descriptions of the Algonkin verb that have a usable meaning.

The first interpretation is that of the verb as the result of a process of composition similar to that of noun composition, but extended in

Algonkin also to verbs. This essentially is the conclusion of Dr. Jones; and it is also the inference of the present writer. But it cannot be too clearly recognized that even if this explanation is in substance the correct one we do not yet really know anything as to the rules and conditions and limitations of this verb-compounding.

The second interpretation of the Algonkin verb is that of a stem followed by a greater or less number of suffixes. In this case the "initial stem" of Dr. Jones would be the only true stem, his "secondary stems" the suffixes. In support of this explanation is the fact that the initial elements of verbs come nearest to having the power of forming words by themselves, in both Arapaho and Fox; and the statement of Dr. Jones[8] that on the whole initial stems more definitely perform the function of verbs. If this view is correct, the type of Arapaho verb-building would be somewhat analogous to that of Eskimo.

The third possible interpretation is also that of a verb stem with affixes, the word-forming ones, however, being chiefly or wholly prefixes, the stem coming last, except for grammatical endings.

In favor of this last view is the fact that practically all the "secondary stems of the second order" given by Dr. Jones are naturally translated by words which in most other languages are verbs, whereas substantially all his cited "initial stems" and "secondary stems of the first order" can actually be rendered, without much distortion, as adverbs, nouns, auxiliary verbs, or modal particles. It is not certain how far Dr. Jones's examples of each class are fully representative of that class, his lists obviously aiming at well translated instances rather than at fullness; but it is clear that his own presentation of evidence leaves the interpretation of the "secondary stems of the second order" as being true verb stems defined by prefixes, in a position where it cannot be summarily dismissed.

Thus the *"secondary stems of the second order"* listed by Dr. Jones[9] are most simply rendered as follows: egä, dance; tcim (Arapaho tcawou), swim; isä, fly; isähō, jump; ōtä, crawl; usä (Arapaho is-ä, us-ä), walk; gāpā (Arapaho θi-ä^{n}ku), stand; pahō (Arapaho i-ka^n-hu), run; ō, carry on back; hogō, swim, convey by water; pugō, float. *Initial stems* cited[10] are: kī, about; pem(i), past, alongside, incipiently; pyä, hither; pī(t), into; cōsk, straightly, smoothly; sāg(i), projecting, holding; mīk, assiduously; kōg, wetly, with water; kās(ī), by wiping; pas(i), suddenly, hotly; wī, with; tä(wi), painfully; nag(i), stop; pōn(i), cease;

[8] Some Principles of Algonquian Word-formation, American Anthropologist, n. s., VI, 401, 1904.

[9] *Op. cit.*, 394.

[10] P. 388.

wäp(i), begin; kask(i), can, be able; kīc(i), completely; nōtä (pp. 394, 404),
be unable; pag (pp. 393, 403, Arapaho kax-), by striking, with impact. *Secondary stems of the first order*[11] are ä'kw, wood, resisting; nag, hole; tag, color;
nägu, appearance; itä, feel; äne, think; kam, expanse; and the following body
part stems, used objectively or adverbially (in translation) to the verbal element
in the verb complex: cä, ear; kum, nose; tun, mouth; winä, horn; 'kwä, head,
hair, nape; tcä, belly.

Compare also wäp-usä-w³, "he begins to walk" (p. 386) = "incipiently he
walks" (or "he begins in his walk"?); wäpi-pyä-tci-tetep-usä-w³, he begins to
walk approaching in a circle = "incipiently hither circularly he walks" (or
"he begins his hither circular walk"?); pägi-kumä-cin-w³, "he bumped his
nose" (p. 393) = "with impact his nose he struck" (or "he struck his nose
against it"?); täwi-cin-w³, "he fell and hurt himself" (p. 386) = "painfully
he struck" (or "he hurt himself against it, he hurt himself by impact"?);
täwe-'kwä-hō-w³, "he has a headache" (p. 394) = "painfully as to his head
he is" (or "he hurts as to his head"?); pag-ä'kwi-tunä-cin-w³, "he bumps his
mouth" (p. 403) = "with impact against something resisting his mouth he
struck" (or "he struck against something resisting with his mouth so as to be
stopped"?). Translating these Algonkin words as compound verbs gives a
third set of renditions, which are perhaps the truest, but, owing to Indo-
European idiom, almost unintelligible in English: "he begin-walks," "he
begin-hither-around-walks," "he hit-nose-strikes," "he hurt-strikes," "he
hurts-head," "he hit-hard-mouth-strikes."

The posthumous and fuller grammatical sketch of Fox by Dr.
Jones in the Handbook of American Indian Languages[12] gives some
other forms, to which the reviser, Dr. Michelson, has added a hundred
odd further initial stems taken from the Fox Texts of Dr. Jones.
But this increased material does not alter the conclusion which can
be drawn from Dr. Jones's earlier work as here summarized. The
secondary stems of the first order are clearly not the principal stems
of the verb-complexes. The "initial stems" may be verbs. If they
are, the "secondary stems of the second order" are either suffixes or
other verbs compounded with the "initial stems." That they are
suffixes does not seem likely from the character of the examples given.
If their number is substantially limited to those quoted, their suffix
nature might be conceived of; but if their number is indefinitely
large they cannot well be anything but true verb stems. The evidence
of quantity, then, becomes as decisive on this point as that of quality:
and this evidence must be awaited with interest from Dr. Michelson
or some other authority competent to carry on Dr. Jones's analysis.
Meanwhile the strong probability is that if the "initial stems" are
truly verbal in nature the normal Fox verb is a compound binary

---

11 P. 391.

12 Bureau of American Ethnology, Bull. 40, 735–873, 1911.

verb. If, on the other hand, the "initial stems" are essentially adverbial, prepositional, or modal in quality, they deserve only to be ranked as prefixes, even if some of them may have reached this condition by the way of once having been subsidiary verbs; and in that case Fox, and with it no doubt Algonkin in general, possesses verbs that are built up around a kernel of a normal verbal stem or root, as in most languages, and these stems or roots are the "secondary stems of the second order."

The problem has a somewhat different aspect in Fox and Arapaho because Dr. Jones and Dr. Michelson have started their analysis of the verb from the concept of three kinds of stems, while the present treatment proceeds, though with full realization of the difficulties involved, from the more conservative premises of prefix, stem, and suffix. But Arapaho is so obviously Algonkin in its whole plan of expression and word-building that the fundamental problem is undoubtedly identical in the two languages.[13]

One suggestion to future laborers in this field may not be amiss. It is the dropping of the term "secondary stems," at least as applied to those "of the second order." If these "secondary stems" are suffixes, nothing will be gained by denominating them stems. If they are stems, that is, true verbal elements, they are either the real stem of the entire verb or at least one of a pair of stems, and in the latter case probably the ruling and "determined" one of the pair. In that event the designation "secondary" will be misleading. Tentatively the name "final stems," which parallels that of "initial stems" without any implication of primacy or dominance, is proposed.

In short, the undetermined and, in the writer's mind, fundamental problem of Arapaho, Fox, and Algonkin in general is whether these languages say "he enter-looks," "he enters lookingly," or "enteringly he looks." The first solution seems indicated; if it proves fallacious, the third appears more likely to be correct than the second. In either the probable first or third event, however, it can be said that the last element comes nearest to being the principal verb stem of the complex word.

The thorough difficulty of judging this case in the present state of knowledge may be illustrated by the English words "contend,"

---

[13] It is a matter of great satisfaction to the author that since the preceding passages were written, two statements from the pen of Dr. Michelson (Am. Anthrop., n. s., xv, 475, 693, 1913) have been published which evince a very similar realization of the more important aspects of this intricate problem. Dr. Michelson's knowledge of Algonkin is much the greater; that he should have come to nearly the same conclusions is therefore gratifyingly corroborative.

"contest," "conflict," "combat," "compete." If English were as
little understood in its basic structure and history as Algonkin, it
would be a fair inference that "con-" in these words denoted the
verbal idea of "struggle, oppose, fight," and that the second syllables
were adverbially modifying suffixes of this stem. That "-flict" and
"-pete" do not occur independently, and "tend" and "test" when
separate words have an entirely different meaning from their compound forms, would only incline to confirm the conjecture. Obviously
it would require a wealth of accurately understood and exactly ana-
lyzable lexical material before the true nature of the elements of these
words and their strict parallelism to the constituents of "offset,"
"forbid," or "withdraw" became clear. This understanding of
Algonkin we do not yet possess; and therefore, tempting though it
may seem to explain its verb as compounded of two verbal elements,
or of a nominal or adverbial with a verbal element, it is wiser to
proceed with caution. Accordingly, for purposes of presentation, the
old concepts of stem, prefix, and suffix have been retained, subject to
the qualifications discussed, as the categories underlying the following
classification of Arapaho verb elements.

A. Prefixes Used Also as Independent, Separate Words, or Made Into Verbs
by the Addition of an Unspecific, Merely Verbifying Suffix

tcäsis-, begin.

> tcäsis-ina^{n}ei, go off to hunt
> tcesis-ta-ka^{n}hu, begin to flee
> tceθiθ-ouhu, begin to climb

näye-, try.

> tah^a-bä-näyei-θ^i, when all tried
> näyi-kaxk-atī-wa'ou, tried to roll through
> näye-tawa-h-un^i, try to chop it down!

θa^{n}k^u-, following, behind.

> θa^{n}ku-h, θana^{n}ku-h, follow
> θa^{n}ku-na^n-usǎ, come back
> θa^n(k)-ka^{n}outa^n, follow making dust

tā'-, tanā-', tou-, tanou-, stop, cease. The element occurs also as
an independent verb or characteristic first part of the verb in a

number of words which denote contact, impact, or the meeting of an obstacle by a motion.

    tä'-usä, come and stop
    tanä'-usä, stop when going
    kou-tä'-ä^n-bä-, lie abed long (ä^n, bed)
    ha^ntnī-taux-tcä-i-niθi, stopping place
    hä-tou-n-a^nwū-n-eθi, I hold it for you
    tanou-ku-huθi, three first poles erected to hold up the remainder of the tent
    nī-tou-na^n, I strike
    tou-ninät', coup, counting strokes
    tou-ku-hu-ta-ni-na^n, they are tied up for
    tou-ku-hu-i-n-ä^nwū, tying-up house, jail
    tou-tci-hīt', belt
    ta'a-xa-n-eθen', I kick you
    ta^n-ya^n-b-eθen', I bite you
    taa-w-a^nti, taa-b-ä^n, struck him
    ta-wa-hei-na^n, I chop wood
    ha^nt-ta-wa-h-ät', he will cut down the tree
    nītawū-tou, ''Striking First,'' a name

kax- seems to imply violent impact or penetration.   Compare Fox pag-.

    kax-ka'äna^n, it went through
    kax-k-oti-wä^n, rolled through
    kah-ä'ei-si-bä-t', fractured his skull
    kax-aei-t', striking
    kaxa'-axuxa^n, wedge
    kaxa'-ät', there was a fissure
    kax-ouhu, chipped off, shot off
    kaxa'-ä^n-häk^n, shoots him
    kox-k^nθahä^n-na^n, ''breastpins'' of tent
    kox-k-^nθä-ya^n-na^n, kindlings (''through flame starts''?)
    kox-ta-wu-h, touch, do to, copulate

tcäb-i-, passing, past, on, continuing.

    tcäb-ī-hi-t', travels
    tcäb-i-sä, pass on, pass by, be on way, walk, go continually
    tcäb-i-ka^nhu, pass, come by
    tcäb-i-xa^nt', walks
    tcäb-i-xa-h-eθen', I carry you

tcīt-, tcīθ-i-, in, into, entering.

    tcīt-ei, enter, go indoors
    tcīθi-n-a^nha-b, go in to see
    tcīθi-x-teä-hi, run inside, go into
    tcīt-ä-n-a^n, takes him in
    tcīt-awä^nt', dancing in
    tcīt-a^n-bīxūt', undershirt, inner garment
    tcīt-a^nwū, indoors

B. Prefixes Used Also as Independent, Separate Adverbs, or Similar Parts of Speech

h-ixtc-i-, up.

hixtc-äbä, up, above
he-tci'-ixtci-ku-s-i-bä, throw me up
h-ixtc-is, go up

hä$^n\theta$äb-i-, to, reaching to, before, ahead.

hä$^n\theta$äb', toward
hä$^n\theta$äb-i-nou-isä, go there
hä$^n\theta$äb-i-nä-sä, arrive
t-ä$^n\theta$äb-i-nä-usä, when arrives
hä$^n\theta$ä'-ei-sä^n-t', before him
hä$^n\theta$ä'-ei-tä^n, in front
häθaw-unena^n, head men
häθab-äsei, chief woman
häθawä-n-axu, "chief-medicine," a root

tcän-i-, far, down, headlong.

tcän-ihi', under
tcän-isei, give birth to, "drop"
tcän-isi-b-eit', threw him off
tcän-isä, fall off, go down, go far
tcän-i-xouka^n, flew down
tcen-i-ta-ka^{n}hu, flee far
tah^n-tcäni-bihi'iyä^n-ni, when it was far into the night
tcen-a-näbä'ä-t', plunged headlong

täs-, täx-, on, at the top.

täs-ihi', on top of, on, at the top
hä^{n}i-täs-ä-n-ä^n, then he put it on
tä^{n}s-isä^n-θi, mounted (horse)
täx-ohäθi, put hands on
hih'-tä^{n}x-oku-ta-n', which he rode
täsi nīnanä, top of a tent
täsihä^n tca'otä^{n}ya^n, on top of the hill
täsihi' ä^{n}bä, on the bed

ä^{n}xu-, across.

h-ä^{n}x-anä^n, across the stream
ä^{n}xu-n-oti-wa^n, rolled across
h-ä^{n}xu-x-ä^{n}t', the crossing
h-ä^{n}xu-iy-ei-n, sew
tcih'-a^{n}xu-s, come across!

θi-, θei-, on, upon. Perhaps more properly θi'-, θei'-.

    θi-ok^u, sit, live
    θi-a^{n}k^u, stand
    θi-änä, put, place
    θi-a-ya^n, post, monument
    θei-ku-θ, put in
    θei-ka-h-ä^n, carries on the back
    θei-wa-n-ōhu, carrying on the back

häs-, hä^{n}s-i-, hard, very, fast, violently.

    hänä^n, hänou, hard
    hä'nä'ei, hä'nä'ou, fast, very fast
    häsei-yei-hiθe-t^1, very good
    hä^{n}si-i-ka^{n}hu, run hard, swiftly
    häsa'ä^n-t^1, änesa'ä^n, swift
    häsa'a^n-n-oti', ''fast-wheel,'' train
    häseisen^1, wind
    hasa^n-netc^1, rain
    häs-a^{n}ha-b-eti-t^1, looking at oneself
    häs-a^{n}ha-θana^n, sights
    (h)äsi-bä^n, a sore
    hä^{n}s-ixtä^n-cīsa^n, ''Sore-foot-child,'' a name
    äsi-na-ta, hungers for it
    äsi-na-n-ät^1, anger
    äsi-ni-h, to make angry
    t-äs-owa-bi-x-t^1, when he became sick

nou-, na^{n}ä-, naha-, out, around, down.

    na^{n}u-hu', down
    na^{n}ä-hi, go out, come out
    na^{n}ä-sä, walk about
    na^{n}ä-ka^{n}hu, run around
    nou-tä-n-in, bring her out!
    nou-sa-n, drive out
    nou-t-ahawä^{n}t^1, dancing out, a ceremony
    nou-θita^{n}ä^n, went out in file
    nohu-ku-θ, lift up, carry
    na^{n}ä-n-ahawä^{n}t-ani-bä, dance around me!

a^{n}wu-, īna^{n}wu-, hani-, down, falling.

    ha^{n}wu', hanäwu', down
    n-a^{a}wu-hu', south
    n-a^{n}wu-bä'ei, southern berries
    tcih^1-a^{n}wu-inä^n, let it come down!
    tah^a-na^{n}sou-n-a^{n}wu^1-nihi-sä-t^1, while he traveled down-stream
    h-a^{n}wui-nihīhi, down-stream
    t-a^{n}wu-n-īho-a^n, floating down-stream
    īna^{n}wū-sä^n-häk^u, dived, went under water
    h-īna^{n}wū-a^n, it sank
    hani-näa^n, fall
    hani-ku-θa^n, throw down

kou-, kanou-, long, far.

kanaⁿ-aⁿyaⁿ, ''oblong,'' extended
kaⁿäⁿn-ihi', slowly
kanou-ci-bī-θi-hi-naⁿ, I eat a long time
kou-θ-īnät-īt', long life
kou-ta'-aⁿ-bä-, lie abed long
kou-θīhi', some time later
kanou-taⁿtäⁿ, long

xou-, xanou-, straight.

xanou, xaxanou, straightway, immediately
xouwn, xouw-uhu', straight, straight in
xoub-äⁿ, straight
xanoub-i-x-t', straight
tani-xoub-ei, a very straight one
xouwu-xati, take this straight
xanaⁿ-ku-bä, ''straight (across) red,'' name of a design
xouw-usä, go straight

tceib-i, aside, crookedly.

tceib', crooked
tceib-äⁿ, crooked (cf. xoubäⁿ, straight)
tceib-i-s, step aside!
tceib-i-sä-naⁿ, I get out of the way
tceib-i-tcena'äⁿ, jumped aside

tcäθ-i-, away, off.

tcäθi', outdoors
tcäθ-i-äⁿt', he elopes
tceθ-i-kaⁿhu, escape, start off, leave
tceθ-eiaⁿt', goes, departs
tceθ-akouuhu, go farther up
tcäθ-i-θäⁿci-b-eit', blew him away

watäⁿ-, into the camp circle.

watäⁿ-ni', into a camp
watäⁿ-sⁿ, go into the camp circle
watäⁿ-kaⁿhu, go (run?) to camp

ci-, cix-, seciθ-, senix-, into water, in the water.

sec'θ-aⁿwu, at the bank, near the river
hīt' tcih-cīh-kū-θ-i, throw me into the water here!
hänäⁿ-cīh-kū-θ-aⁿt', then he threw him into the water
seniex-tcähit', jumps in the water
näⁿ-tcī-cī-eisäⁿ, come right into the water!
hänäⁿ-nīsaⁿ-cī-eisäⁿ-θi, then both entered the water
waⁿ-cį-e-b, take into the water

nänäb-, north.

> nänäbä', nänäbi', north
> nänäb-isä-t¹, goes north

nīs-bis-, east; nīs-nä-, west.

> nīs-bis-isä, go east
> nīs-nä-isä, go west

naxkᵘ-n-, with, also.

> naxkū-hu', with, together, including, also
> hä ⁿ-bä-naxku-hä ⁿ, you might be included
> nanaxku-ni-hi-tawa, I include it
> naxkū-n-isä, travel with
> haⁿt-naxk-a-tceθ-ei-aⁿt¹, he will go away with him

nä̂s-, hänä̂s-, thus; compare the demonstratives nä-hä', hi-nä.

> nä̂s-īnät-īt¹, thus lived again
> nä̂s-it-ä ⁿt¹, did accordingly
> hänä̂s-iθetcaⁿ-tana-hokⁿ, thought of him thus

tǟbä-, just then, begin to.

> tǟbä, then! lo! just then! being about to, when
> tǟbä-bänä, begin to drink
> tǟbä-tawa-h-ät¹, begins to chop down

kaⁿxᵘ-, kaⁿxä ⁿ-, again, once more.

> kaⁿxⁿ, kaⁿxū, kaⁿxä ⁿi, again, another time, then at last
> kaⁿxä ⁿi-kaθe-n-ä, again lost him
> kaⁿxä ⁿi-naxawⁿ, again was near
> kaⁿ-xä ⁿi-aneθeia-n-ä, once more he struck one down by kicking

hana'utⁱ-, hana'a-, all, completely, enough, sufficiently, until.

> hanaut¹ bītcīxaⁿ tcän-isei, all leaves are falling
> hä ⁿix-hana'uta-ya ⁿ, now was complete
> hana'ut¹-hä ⁿix-yǟθani-sibihei, until he had killed (all) five
> hana'ut¹-haⁿt-īcīte-n-a ⁿ, indeed I will catch it
> hana'ut¹-häh'-naha-'ou, until I killed them all

bǟ-, behi-, behīc-, bäbänei-, all.

> bähīhi', all, everyone, anybody, completely
> bǟ-hi-nihäni-x-t¹, the owner of all
> bǟ-tani-ci-niθi, all have a hole cut
> bǟ-hi-nihaⁿ-you, all are yellow
> bǟ-hi-yeiyaⁿ-unä ⁿ-θi, all have four arrows
> ba-h-äxaⁿ-ät¹, shot all

hä ⁿθei-, all, all who.

> hä ⁿθei, all. See Text I, note 5
> hä ⁿθei-hiθeti-ni, all that were good
> hä ⁿθei-wana-ūneitī-nīθi, all who still lived

C. Prefixes Not Yet Found as Independent Parts of Speech

1. *Apparently Verbal*—

wan-, go to, go for, go after.

hänäⁿ-wan-bī-n-āⁿt¹, then he went to give it to him
wan-i-bī, go to eat
ni-waⁿ-kaⁿhuwa, I went and cut
wan-ote-n, go and gather
wan-i-tcena'aⁿ, go in order to jump
wan-isei-nä-hīθi, burrs, "they who go after women"

näbi-, nawu-, make a motion to, move forward.

näbi-x-tcä-hiθi, made a motion forward
tcena-näbä'-ä-t¹, plunged headlong

nīs-, to, tied to.

nīs-axäyaⁿ, wire fence
nīs-i-äθeiyo, trousers, "tied leggings"
nä-nīs-aⁿku-hu-niθi, the tied ones

na'-, to, arriving.

na'-usä, naⁿ-us, arrive, come to

cīt-, continue.

cīt-isä, journey, go on, keep going

haθa'aⁿ-, truly, surely, indeed, necessarily.

haθa'aⁿ-bīti, indeed I shall be revenged
haθa'aⁿ-häⁿ-t-īcīte-n-aⁿ, surely I shall catch him
haθa'aⁿ-häⁿni'itcei, it must be eatable

2. *Apparently Adverbial, Referring to Manner*—

hinix-, hanux-, very.

hinix-iθeti, very good
hanux-uθeti-n, very good
hīn-tcä-b-īt¹, water-monster ("very-shooter"?)
hinix-hänixt¹, very tall

ni'-, good, well.

ni'-bī-ni, good to eat
ni'-īnaⁿei, good hunting
ni'-bähaⁿ, smell good
ni'-tcei, eatable
ni'-tcäⁿ-t¹, is sweet
ni'-owa-be-hi-naⁿ, I feel well
ni-eh-t¹, is fine-looking

tani-, indeed, very, skillfully.

> tani-xoub-ei, very straight one
> nih'-tani-tcä-īnätī-hok", skillfully he lived again

inā-, fast, more swiftly.

> nih'-inā-sä-t', quickened his pace
> h-inā-nawa, without delay

nani-, näni-, constantly.

> nani-bäni, drink frequently
> neni-nä"ku-t', blind
> nī-neni-s-ei-ka"hu-t', mole ("who constantly runs"?)

īn-i-, aimlessly, randomly, about.

> īn-i-sä, wander, go aimlessly, "bum around"
> īn-i-kuhi, was chased about
> īn-iθ-i-ka"hu, went around
> īn-i-tāθ-ka"hu-h-eit', dragged him along

3. *Apparently Adverbial, Referring to Space—*

tcä-, tci-, back, again, returning.

> tcä'-isā, tci'-isā, tcī-sā, go back
> tcä-yi-ka"hu, run back
> tca"-w-otī-wa", rolled back
> tcä-näih-ā"-t', "again killing," a place

īy-i-, near.

> h-īy-i-sā, come near, approach
> ī-ha"-n, īyi-ha"-n, go after, pursue

a"y-, in front.

> a"y-ei-ka"hu, go ahead

tci-bixā"-, out of the woods, into the open.

> tci-bixā"-u-ka", came running out of the timber

bis'-, up, out.

> hä"ix-bis'-tcena'ā", sprang up

WORD-FORMING SUFFIXES

The etymological "suffixes" of Arapaho verbs are not only less numerous than the "prefixes" but far less concrete and specific, to the degree of being almost grammatical. They comprise transitives, intransitives, causatives and similar derivatives of wide applicability but general meaning.

-ni, to be, to have; verb-forming.

> hihaⁿw-aha'anākäⁿ-ni-n, there are no stones
> hīt-akäⁿxu-i-ni-t', he who has tentpoles
> n-eihaⁿwū-uta-ni-hi, I have no horses
> n-īθe-ti-ni-n, that which is good
> hinana'ei-ni-naⁿ, I am an Arapaho
> inenitä-ni-n', you would be well, living
> bähäei-ähe-ni-t', becomes an old man
> ni'-bī-ni, good to eat
> nätcī-ni, wet (netc', water)
> hi-netci-bī-ni-θ', the water-giver, owner of waters
> nihaⁿ-ni-x-t', is yellow (nihaⁿ-yaⁿ)
> tca'otaya-ni-naⁿ, I am hump-backed
> nänä-ni-naⁿ, I, it is I

-θi, intransitive.

> nä'ä-θi-x-t, resembled (nä'ä-si, thus)
> bī-θi-, eat (bī-n, eat something, bī-θ', food)
> anäⁿ-θi-, be different in appearance

-hi, intransitive.

> h-iθei-hi-näxkⁿ, if you are good
> bihi'i-hi-n, be a deer
> bänī-θi-hi-naⁿ, I eat
> kanäne-hi-naⁿ, I am a coward
> nänäbä-hi-t', what is sacred
> hīθaⁿwu-tai-hi-naⁿ, truly I am cold

-hu, intransitive.

> i-kaⁿ-hu, run
> ta-kaⁿ-hu, flee
> na-kaⁿ-hu, come, bring
> ni-säⁿku-hu-θi, were tied
> nītou-hu-t', shouts
> tcäbixaⁿ-hu-t', flies
> yana-hu-t', pledger, he who vows
> tca'otaya-hu-t', hump backed

-awui-ni, become, begin, be.

> t-īntcäbīt-awui-ni-t[1], he became a water-monster
> ka^{n}nä^n-n-awui-ni-θi, they opened it
> bäni-awui-n[1], spring (bäni-tce, summer)

-owa, feel; bodily condition.

> ni'-owa-be-hi-na^n, I feel sick
> häs-owa-, sick

-si, be in the condition of.

> isi-si, be lying
> bä-tani-si-ni-θi, all have a hole cut
> nằ'ä-si, nằ'ei-si, thus, thus it is
> kah-ä'ei-si-bä-t[1], fractured his head

-bä-n, -wa-n, cause, make, bring about.

> t-aseinou-bä-na^n, I get meat
> axa^n-bä, made laugh
> axa-bä^n, axa-wu, fed them, give me food!
> waxu-bä-, to have medicine
> oti-wa^n, roll (hoti', wheel)

-h, causative.   See the starred forms under the "connective" suffix -h.

-ei, causative.

> hakā^{n}x-ei, make tentpoles
> h-ā^{n}xu-iy-ei-n, sew (ā^{n}xū-, across)
> tcä-tcäb-ei-θi, making pemmican (tceb[1])
> tic-tcībät-ei-t[1], after he made a sweat-house

-xa-h, cause to be in condition of.

> tcäbi-xa-h, make travel; transport (tcäb-i-, passing)
> nä^{n}a-xa-h, bring in (nou-, na^{n}ä-, out)
> tcä'e-xa-h, take back (tcä-, back)
> sä'iθī-xa-h, peg out flat (sä'ä-, flat)
> xouwu-xa-ti, takes it straight (xou-, straight)
> tcä-bi-xa^n-hu-t[1], flies (tcä-b, shoot)
> ni-tanä-xa-hei-na^n, I dig a hole (tana-t[1], hole)
> bä-xa-h, strike

What at first appears to be the stem preceding this suffix is in most cases an element which itself is normally a prefix. Whether the "prefix" tcäbi- or the "suffix" -xa is the true verbal "stem" remains to be determined, as in so many other cases.

-ku-θ, to make a motion leading to the condition or position described in the "stem." This "stem" in turn is often a "prefix" in other words.

> θei-ku-θ, put in (tcīθi-, θei-, in, on)
> nohū-ku-θ, lift, carry (nou-, out)
> tcei-ku-θ, release, let go (tcä-, tci-, back; tcäθ-i-, away)
> hänix-ixtci-ku-θ-än, threw him up (hixtc-, hixtcäbä, up)
> tou-ku-θ, bind
> kankannī-ku-θ-än, he uncovered him
> īθi-ku-θ, seize
> äbita-ku-θ, steal
> bä-kū-tan, "red stand," a head-dress

Probably the same in origin as -ku-θ is an intransitive ending -oku.

> θi-anku, stand (θi-, on, projecting)
> θi-oku, sit, be sitting
> tcän-oku, sit down, seat oneself (tcän-i-, down)
> tänx-oku, ride (täx-, täs-, on)

-ä, to make, bring, cause to be.

> bäs-ä-, carry, bring wood (bäs')
> tcīt-ä-n-an, takes him in

-ta-n, -ta-na, for, to, of, about.

> cī-ta-n, capture for
> ic-ta-n, ici-ta-n, make
> kousa'än-ta-n, attack
> θanwa-ta-n, believe
> cīyi-ta-θ, make disappear for
> änθi-ta-n-ant', tells it to him
> axän-tana-w-ant', makes fun of him
> äheisi-ta-ni, gave to be washed (äheisi-ou, wash one's self)
> hänäs-iθetcan-tana-hoku, thought of him thus
> h-īθi-ku-ta-n-anθi, when they seized them
> isi-bi-ta-ni-ni, bedtime, time for lying
> θähä'i-ta-n, be agreeable (to?)
> kaha'ū-san-ta-b-än, took half of her
> tou-ku-ta-n-än, tied to him
> tou-ku-hu-ta-ni-nan, they are tied up for
> nä-nä(h)ä-ta-n-einan, he killed them for us

-wu-n, to, for, with.

> waθanaha-wu-n, write to
> ata-wu-n, eat up for
> neiänan-wu-n-än, holds it tight for him
> ni-tana-wu-hei-nan, I dig a hole
> kox-ta-wu-h, do to, meddle with

-t^i (-ī-t^i, -ā^n-t^i), forms abstract nouns. This ending seems to be that of the third person subjective.

    bixa^n-θ-et-īt^i, love
    bī-θi-h-īt^i, food, eating
    bäsä-ihä^{n}t-īt^i (ceremonial) touching (by old men)
    hinä-t-īt^i, life
    hinen-tän-īt^i, tribe
    tceita^n-h-ät-īt^i, ''ear-piercing'' ceremony
    tce'-ät-it^i, ''welcoming'' ceremony
    häs-owa-be-h-īt^i, sickness
    änet-īt^i, speech, voice
    waxu-c-it^i, paint, the painting
    ka'ue-h-īt^i, a bleeding
    tou-tci-h-īt^i, belt
    bät-ā^{n}t^i, a dance
    äsina-n-ā^{n}t^i, anger
    h-ā^{n}xū-ā^{n}t^i, a crossing

-ēhi, ōhu, agent, action, instrument, thing for.

    h-äbīt-īhi, thief
    äneti-b-ēhi, speaker
    häbäθ-ēhi, a large one
    kata-ōhu, beadwork (kata-, cover, hide)
    tcawouw-ūhu, swimmer

-ā^n, -y-ā^n, that which.

    θi'a-yā^n, post, monument, goal
    hasei-yā^n, an offering
    bä-θa^{n}to-ā^n, hemorrhage
    bäθi-yā^n, property, clothing
    bänī-yā^n, night, darkness
    bihi'i-yā^n, at night
    kana^n'a^n-yā^n, long, oblong
    niha^n-yā^n, yellow (niha^n-ni-x-t^i, is yellow)
    nihä-yā^n, self (nihä-ni-, to own)

GRAMMATICAL PREFIXES

Grammatical affixes of verbs are prevailingly prefixes, except for most of the pronominal and a few other elements.

k-	interrogative
k-ih'-	
k-aⁿ-	
k-aⁿhei-	
k-aⁿhä-	
k-aⁿhu-	
ī-haⁿwu-	negative
tcī-, tcih-	negative
tcī-bä'-, tcī-bäh-	negative imperative
tcī-	sometimes positive imperative
nī-, nih'-	incompleted action
-īsi-	completed action
nih-īsi-	
hä-n-īsi-	
haⁿt-	future, probably of purpose or intent
haⁿt-ī-	
haⁿt-aⁿn-ī-	
t-	when, after, because
tī-, tih'-	action incomplete
taⁿ-, tahª-	
tīsi-	action complete
tīsīni-	
taⁿhīsi-, taⁿhūsi-	
taⁿhūsīni-	
häⁿ-tī-	optative, "let me"
häⁿ-tih'-	
hih'-	"would that!"
θī-	optative, "let me," "let us"
iθī-	
häⁿ-	meaning not determined
hä-ih-, häⁿ-ix-	'then'[14]
häⁿ-näⁿ-	'then'[14]
nī-	relatively subordinating or noun-making: "he who, which, where"
nih-	
hī-	
nihī-	
hini-	
häⁿ-taⁿ-	where
häⁿ-	while; continuing; "—ing"
häⁿ-tcis-	
naⁿsou-	the same meaning as the last
ti-naⁿsou-	
hawa-tih'-	although

GRAMMATICAL SUFFIXES

-eti	reflexive
-uti	
-hokᵘ	"it is said," quotative
-äxkᵘ	conditional, subordinating
-häxkᵘ	
-näxkᵘ	

---

[14] These two frequent prefixes, whose exact force is not clear, are evidently introductory and appear to contrast with each other. See text III, notes 4, 29.

PRONOMINAL ENDINGS

The pronominal endings of intransitive verbs, including numerals, adjectives, and independent pronouns, are:

I	-na^n
you	-n^i
he	-t^i, or a vowel
we	-na^n
you	-nä^n
they	-θi, or a vowel

These endings are usually added directly to intransitive stems.

bänä-na^n	I drink
n-äneti-na^n	I speak
θioku-t^i	he sits
θia^{n}kŭ-t^i	he stands

The intransitive imperative is the stem.

The intransitive negative with the prefix īha^{n}wu- is formed with prefixed pronominal elements.

I	n-eiha^{n}wu—
you	h-eiha^{n}wu—
he	h-īha^{n}wu—
we	n-eiha^{n}wu—bä (or -hi-bä)
you	h-eiha^{n}wu—bä (or -hi-bä)
they	h-īha^n-wu—na^n (or -hi-na^n)

In these forms -na^n recalls the commonest plural suffix of nouns, -bä is probably the stem for "all," and the vowel change in the third person, as well as the initial prefixes, are suggestive of the possessive prefixes. Perhaps the division should be nei-ha^{n}wu instead of n-eiha^{n}wu.

The transitive conjugation is formed by suffixes. These are:

	Me	You	Him	Us	You	Them	It
I	—	eθen^i	-a^n'	—	-eθenä^n	-ou	-awa^n
You	un^i	—	-a^{n}t^i	-eiä^n	—	-a^{n}tei	-aw^u
He	-eina^n	-ein^i	-a^{n}t^i[15]	-īna^n	-einä^n	-a^{n}t^i	-a'
We	—	-än^i	-ät^i	—	-änä^n	ät^i	-awina^n
You	-eiänä^n	—	-anä^n	-eiänä^n	—	-änä^n	-awinä^n
They	-iθi	-einanī	-a$^n\theta$i[16]	-eina^n	-einä^n	-a$^n\theta$i	-ou

The above forms have been found on most stems. Some verbs, including tcä-b- and kā^{n}ŭ-s, replace the first vowel of the suffix, be it e, ei, ä, or u, by i, except for the inanimate object, the "I-them" form -ou, and perhaps certain other forms of the third person object. Thus, tcä-b-ī-na^n, kā^{n}u-s-iθen^i. Some other verbs, including bäxa-h- and sä'iθīxa-h-, substitute u for e, ei, ä as the first vowel of the suffix

---

[15] Second form: he (B) to him (A): -eit^i.
[16] Second form: they (B) to him (A): eiθ^i.

in the first and second persons object, but contrariwise in the third person object change a to ä, and ou to ei. On the other hand, the stem vowels change according to the suffix in some verbs: nä-nähä', kill, occurs before all persons of the object, animate and inanimate, except the ''A'' form of the third person: nänähä'-eina^n, nänähä-ein^i, nänähä'-eit^i, but nanaha'-a^{n}t^i.

The endings themselves cannot be analyzed in all cases into regularly recurring subjective and objective constituents, although -n^i for the second person singular object, -nä^n second plural subject and object, -ei first plural object, are clear. The impression given by the endings is that the two elements of each occur in a fixed order not so much according as they represent the subject and the object as according to the person denoted. The second person comes last, whether subject or object; between the first and third persons precedence is not so clear.

This is confirmed by the transitive negative conjugation with the prefix -ī-ha^{n}wu-. In this the second person is always prefixed; the first is suffixed as against the second, but prefixed as against the third, while the third is prefixed only when there are two elements of this person. Such a form as hei-ha^{n}wu-bixa^n-θ-eθ also corroborates the inference that -eθ in bixa^n-θ-eθ-en^i is the part that means ''I''.

	Me	You	Him	Us	You	Them	It
I		hei—eθ	nei—a^n		hei—eθebä	nei—a^{n}na'	nei—[17]
You	hei—^{n}		hei—a^n	hei—eiä^n		hei—a^{n}na'	hei—[17]
He	nei—e	hei—e	hī—ä̆	hei—ein	hei—eibä	hī—ä	hii—[17]
We		hei—ä̆	nei—äbä		hei—äbä	nei—äbä	nei—awubä
You	hei—ubä		hei—ä^{n}bä	hei—eiä^{n}bä		hei—ä^{n}bä	hei—awubä
They	nei—ei	hei—ei	hī—äna^n	hei—ein	hei—eibä	hī—äna^n	hī—awū

The transitive imperative forms differ somewhat from the indicative: -un, -in, implies the object of the third instead of the first person. Probably it expresses only the subject of the second person.

bixa^n-x-u	like me!
bixa^n-x-un^i	like him! like them!
hī-s-in^i	fear him!
häseinä-b-in^i	hate him!
bixa^n-t-a^n	like it!
bixa^n-θ-eiä^n	like us!
bixa^n-θ-ä̆	do you (pl.) like him!

The negative imperative, with prefixed tcī-bä-, has the same suffixes. The forms referring to an animate object of the third person are preceded by connective consonants which in the indicative of the same verbs occur before the first and second persons objective.

---

[17] Possibly a final surd ^{n} has escaped notice in these forms.

CONNECTIVE SUFFIXES

The transitive pronominal endings are not added directly to the stem, but are invariably preceded by one of five consonants: b, n, s, θ, h. At first regarded as part of the pronominal suffix, later as a connective characteristic of each verb, these consonants were later seen to correspond to the "instrumentals" of Dr. Jones.[18] Before this, in fact, -h had been recognized as a causative. The four other consonants, on the other hand, do not appear to be significantly instrumental in Arapaho, except in so far as they all occur only on transitive verbs. They certainly do not in most cases refer, except by the remotest implication, to a part of the body or a type or shape of instrument. There are also scarcely any observed instances of one stem appearing, under the same or an altered meaning, with any other than its characteristic consonant.[19] The designation "instrumentals" therefore seems of dubious applicability in Arapaho.[20]

It may be added that a search for a possible phonetic relation between stem and connective consonant gave no results.

Meaning	Verb	Me	You	Him	Us	You	Them	It
see	aⁿha	b[21]	b	w	b	b	w	t
strike	taⁿ	b[21]	b	w	b	b	w	t
hate	äseinä	b[21]	b	w	b	b	w	[t]
shoot	teã	b	b	b	b	b	b	t
tell	ītawū	n	n	n	[n]	[n]	n	t
eat	bī	n	n	n	n	n	n	w
reach	ouxãⁿ-ta	n	n	n	[n]	[n]	n	w
fear	ī	s	s	x	s	s	[x]	t
cut	kãⁿu	s	s	s	s	s	s	x
like	bixaⁿ	θ[22]	θ	θ	θ	θ	θ	t
peg flat	sä'iθī-xa	h	h	h	h	[h]	h	h
strike	bä-xa	h[23]	h	h	h	h	h	h
kill	nä-nähä	'	'	'	'	'	'	t

These connectives or instrumentals change somewhat according to the person of the animate object expressed in the pronominal endings which follow them, and in part according to the stem. Such variations, which are illustrated in the following table, are clearly of a phonetic origin. But a radical change undergone by the consonant

---

[18] Am. Anthrop., n. s., VI, 403, 1904; Bur. Am. Ethn., Bull. 40, 807, 1911.

[19] Except bīī, find, which occurs both as bīī-n and bīī-h; änãⁿka-b, änãⁿka-n, loosen; and cī-n, cī-h, capture.

[20] Compare Michelson, Am. Anthrop., n. s., XV, 476, 693, where substantially the same contention is advanced as regards Fox.

[21] w with subject of second person singular and third plural.

[22] x with subject of second person singular and third plural.

[23] This is the only stem found with the glottal stop.

when the object denoted by the pronominal suffix is inanimate, especially from -w to -t, can scarcely be due to any merely phonetic laws. The author sees in this thorough difference of form when the object is inanimate a further argument against the instrumental nature of these connectives.

CLASSIFIED LIST OF STEMS

A number of transitive verb "stems" follow, arranged according to their "connective" suffixes. This list is followed by one giving the principal ascertained intransitive verbs, which lack connectives.

TRANSITIVE

-b, -w

aⁿha-b	see
änäⁿka-b	loosen (also with -n)
aⁿtanaⁿta-b	buy
äbītä-b	steal
äseinä-b	hate
äyiätä-b	pursue closely
ḫäs-änä-b	think of highly
ka'aⁿ-b	bite
ni-b	marry
tousä-b	bathe
ta-b	strike
taⁿya-b	bite
tähi-b	help
tä-b	cut, break off
teä-b	shoot
waⁿ-ci-e-b	take into water

-n

outäyäⁿ-n	hang up to dry
awūna-ɒ	pity
äⁿina-n	know
īyihaⁿ-n, yïhaⁿ-n	go to, go after, pursue
isa-ɒ	alarm, scare up
icitä-n, ite-n, ätä-n, tä-n	take, catch, seize
nou-tä-n	bring out
tcī-tä-n	take in, bring
bäsä-n	touch
bī-n	eat
bi-ɒ	give
bīi-n, bīi-h	find
koutesa'a-n	chase, drive off
kaⁿäθei-n	cut open belly
kaθe-n	lose grip on
kaⁿkoua-n	envy
kaⁿne-n	open (kaⁿu-s, cut)
kayei-n	pull out, pull off
nouxa-ɒ	meet
nou-sa-n	drive out
nota-n	ask, question (notī-h, seek)
n-īθa-n	go with, come with
nītou-n	breathe in, suck in

cī-n, cī-h   take, capture
cinouhu-n   resemble
tou-n, tanou-n   hold
ta-n   pour
ta'xa-n   kick
wa'awa'a-n   go in, draw in, suck in

With suffix -ta:

ouxā^n-ta-n   reach
ici-ta-n, ic-ta-n   make (n-īci-h, make)
θa^{n}wa-ta-n   believe
kousa'ā^n-ta-n   attack
nä-nähä-ta-n   kill for
cī-ta-n   capture for
touku-ta-n   tie to
tca'ā-ta-n   perceive, notice
tcei-ta-n   visit

With suffixes -wu, -bä:

ata-wu-n   eat up for
isi-bä-n   lay down, go to bed with
θei-wa-n, θei-ka-h   carry on back
tawaha-wou-n   cut tree down for
waθanaha-wu-n   write to
waxu-bä-n   imitate a bear

-s, -x

(n-)ī-s   fear
itä-s, itä-s   meet, reach, arrive at, come to
bä-s   touch
ka^{n}u-s   cut (ct. ka^{n}ne-n, open)
nou-ta^n-s   carry out
tanä-s   pierce, make hole in
tcei-s   give here
wahani-s   unite
waxu-s   paint

-θ

ā^{n}θä^n-θ   rub
ā^{n}θi-θ   narrate
a^{n}kā^n-θ   take home
äneti-θ   speak to
bixa^n-θ   like, love
ka^{n}koutci-θ   scratch
sixahä^n-θ   do thus, show
cīyi-ta-θ   make disappear for

With suffix -ku:

(ī-)tou-ku-θ   bind, tie to
θei-ku-θ   put in
ka^{n}ka^{n}ni-ku-θ   uncover
nohū-ku-θ   lift up, carry
nīsä^n-ku-θ   bind
tcei-ku-θ   release

-h[24]

atä-h   give
-axa-h, -äxä-h   bring, take, carry (in, back, etc.)
*äsini-h   anger, be angry at (äsina-nä-t', anger)
-i-θetca^n-h   think

---

[24] Starred forms show this suffix with an indisputable causative force.

*h-iteaⁿ-h	give pipe to, cause to smoke
iya-h	ignore, not know
bä-xo-h, bä-xa-h	strike
*bäta-h	give medicine to, doctor
bīī-h, bīi-n	find
θouu-h, θäⁿa-h	crush, grind, chew (θaxan, forcibly)
θaⁿku-h	follow
θei-ka-h, θei-wa-n	carry on back
*θiaⁿku-h	make stand
koxtawu-h	do to, meddle with, copulate with
kaⁿkax^uka-h	stab, pierce, sting
kataya-h	cover up
*noti-h	search for, seek (nota-n, ask)
nätäni-h	deceive, trick
n-īci-h, ici-ta-n	make
nicka-h	whip
sä'iθī-xa-h	peg out flat
cī-h, ci-n	capture, take
*tcäbi-xa-h	carry, transport, cause to travel
*tcītei-h	cause to enter, let in
wawa-h	throw over, scatter

INTRANSITIVE

ouhu	climb
ouθ	hang
ot	comb
aⁿku-āⁿ	thaw, be warm
aⁿt-äⁿ	stand
awŭnaⁿ	be closed
äθixtce-hi	shove
anäⁿθi	be different
ätei-ni	make camp, stay over night
ätei-yaka-ni	come to a camp
hiθaⁿbei	be true, right, so
īxane-hi	provide for, favor
īnaⁿ-ei	hunt
inenitä-ni	be well, live
īnikati	play
isi-bi	lie down, go to bed
isi-si	be lying
itou, ätou, ätei-aⁿ	shout, make noise, roar (cf. n-itou-hu)
h-ītou	beg
ītäⁿ-ei	take arms
bäī-ni	be bloody, bleed
bei-tcixu	be red hot
bäbä-ä'ei	be curly haired
bänä, ben¹	drink
bänaⁿθei	smell
bäsäyei	touch
bixou	emerge, rise to surface of water
bīwaⁿ-hu	weep, cry
hähīsi	wash
θīäⁿbä	snore
θibi	have to do with clothing
θīya-hu	cut hair
koxunä	hide, enter a hole
koxahei	dig
ka'-us	drop, fall
ka'uye-	pick fruit
kaⁿout-	make dust
haⁿhei, kohayei	get up, rise, ride
kaⁿkou	patch on
kaxou-hu	chip off

kaxa'a	crack, fissure, dent
kanäne-hi	be a coward
kaⁿäⁿni, kanaⁿäⁿni	be slow
kou, kanou, kanaⁿ	swell (kou-, kanou-, long, far)
kaya'a-hu	fly away
nä-, näyaⁿ	take off (clothing), dress
näⁿθäⁿ	stay
näθkuθei	push
näⁿnou	get ready
näniθe	menstruate
nätcä, netce	die, be dead
nenīnäⁿkᵘ	be blind
nihä-ni	own
nih'äⁿ, nih'ää	sting, hurt, irritate
nībou-hä	use perfume
n-ītou-hu	shout, whistle, breathe (cf. itou)
säse-hi	play, trouble, make noise
säya	chew
cīcītci	stretch
cīyihaⁿti	disappear
tou	strike (tou-ku, bind)
tai	be cold
täye-hi	be ashamed
tcena'äⁿ	jump
tcäni	skin, flay
tcäste	scratch
tcätecti	cut, hurt
tcin	plant, bury
wñaⁿ	rest in water
wäⁿθäⁿ, wanäⁿθäⁿ	abound
waxusī	paint
yana-hu	pledge, vow

In general, transitive stems are used intransitively, or vice versa, so far as their meanings permit, without further change than that produced by the loss or insertion of an "instrumental" connective. The following are the principal observed cases of a more extensive modification.

Transitive	*Intransitive*
akū-hu-, cook	aⁿku-, thaw, be warm
äⁿina-n, know	äⁿin-, know
hīnitä-(t), inhabit	hänitä-, live, stay
isi-bä-n, lay down	isi-bi-, lie down; isi-si-, be lying
ici-ta-n, n-īci-h, do, make	ici-hi-, n-īci-ti-, äci-ta-, do, make
bäsä-n, touch	bäsä-yei-, touch
bīi-n, bīi-h, find	bīi-ti-, bii-hä-, find
bī-n, eat	bī-θi-, eat
notī-h, seek, nota-n, ask	notī-hi-, look, search
naha', nähä', kill	nä'ihei-, näihaⁿ-, kill
ni-b, marry	nī-ni-, marry
tcä-b-, shoot	tca-baⁿ-, shoot
säⁿku-θ, bind	saⁿku-hu-, be tied

Nouns

PLURAL

Arapaho nouns take a plural suffix whether animate or inanimate, this distinction of gender being expressed by the verbs, adjectives, or numerals referring to them and not in the nouns themselves.

The most common plural suffix is -na^n. This has been observed on hic(^{i}), liver; bäseit^i, urine; hā^{n}xēi, wolf; hou, raven; bītei'i, dove; hahā^{n}t^i, cottonwood, tree; kakā^{n}x(^{i}), tent pole; haha'uktā^n, hair braid; haxa'anā^{n}kä^n, stone; haθa^n, penis; hā^{n}kuhā^n, head; nā^{n}tcä^n, chief; hänā^{n}tcä^n, buffalo bull; hinen^i, man; hisei, woman; wa'a, wa'aha, moccasin; kakuiy, tube, gun, whistle; cīsa^{n}wa^n, tobacco; tcībät^i, sweat-house; wana', wrist; hīθeina^n, buffalo; bīsä^n, worm.

With some slight or apparent change of final vowel, this ending occurs also in the following words:

wax^u, grass, herbage, waxuina^n. (contrast waxu', medicine, below)
waxucīt^i, painting, waxucītana^n
hā^{n}kä^{n}x^u, saddle, hā^{n}kä^{n}xuina^n
nic'tceinan^i, buckskin (probably antelope skin), nic'tceinana^n (for nic'-tceinan'na^n?)
bätceot(^{i}), watceot(^{i}), stomach, bätceotana^n
θīk^n, ghost, θeikana^n
θiw^u, bridge, boat, θiwana^n

-a^n, -ha^n (probably really -a$^{n'}$, -ha$^{n'}$) is also common. Before it -ä, -e, change to a; and -x becomes -θ, -c becomes -θ or -x, θ becomes -t.

bätä^n, heart, bätä^{n}ha^n
nicitcä^n, antelope, nicitcaha^n
ni'ihi, eagle, bird, ni'ähiha^n
nītcīye, river, nītcīhaha^n
hōu, robe, houwa^n (ct. hou, raven, above)
ha^{n}kūhu', mouse, ha^{n}kūhuha^n
hãni'i, ant, hãni'iha^n
hanaxa'ähi'i, boy, hanaxa'ähiha^n
hätä^n, sinew, hätaha^n
waxu', medicine, waxūwa^n (ct. wax^u, above)
wou, buffalo calf, wouha^n
tcä'einox, bag, tcä'einaθa^n
ha'uwanux, parfleche case, ha'uwanaθa^n
beic(^{i}), nose, beiθa^n
benec, arm, bänoxa^n
bäs^i, wood, bäxa^n
wa'a$^n\theta^i$, leg, wa'a^{n}ta^n
beitciθ, tooth, beitcita^n
tcaox^u, foe, Comanche, tcaoθa^n

tce'ä^{n}ox^n, club, tomahawk, tce'ä^{n}oθa^n
bītcīe, leaf, bītcīxa^n
tcicihi, night hawk, tciciha^n (*sic*)
hitīθīθ, kidney, hītīθiθa^n (*sic*)

Lengthening or vocalization of the final vowel is fairly frequent:
i>ī; u>ū; ä>ei; a, a^n>ou, au.

hoθ^i, arrow, hoθī
bihi'i, deer, bihi'ī
tca^{n}θani'i, prairie dog, tca^{n}θanī'i
wox^u, bear, woxū
wa'ax^u, nail, wa'axū
netc^i, water, netcī
ni'etc^i, lake, ni'etcī
hä^{n}tetc^i, ocean, hä^{n}tetcī
wāsä^{n}θ(^{i}), arrowpoint, wāsä^{n}θī
häbäs(^{i}), beaver, häbäsī
hiθa^{n}xu, guts, hiθa^{n}xū
kaha'a^{n}wu, creek, kaha'a^{n}wū
hoseina^n, meat, hoseinou
wa^{n}ketc(^{i}), cattle, wa^{n}ketcī ·
hotä', mountain sheep, hotei
bä^{n}cīsä', eye, bä^{n}cīsei
hä^{n}w^u, house, hä^{n}wū
haθa^n', star, haθa'ū (ct. haθa^n, penis, above)
wanatana', ear, wanatana'ū

Apparently formed by a special suffix:

heθ, dog, heθäbī
ka'a^n, coyote, kāxawū
hiwaxuhä^{n}x, horse, hiwaxuhä^{n}xäbi

CASES

An oblique case, usually an objective, was observed on a few nouns.
It seems to be formed by -n^i.

hisei, woman, objective hisei-n(^{i}), compare text III, note 28.

wot nähä' nītcīhe-hinen^i ni'bäbänähäxk^n, this Kiowa was handsome;
hä^{n}ixnouxanē nītcīhe-hineni-n^i, he met a Kiowa.

tuxkanä' bänīnä^{n}t^i nītca-ou-n^i bītcineni-n^i, Tuxkanä' gives a blanket to
Bītcinen^i.

nähä' hinen^i tawä^{n}t^i hi'ihi' haxa'anä^{n}kä^n hinä' hineni-n^i, this man struck
with a stone that man.

A general locative, also serving as an instrumental, is more frequent. It takes the forms -hä', -nä', -bä'; also -i', nⁱ, -ī, -ū, recalling both one type of plural and the objective.

näyei, my tent, näyeihä'
hi'ä$^n\theta^i$, his leg, hi'ä^{n}tä', hi'ä$^n\theta$inⁱ (plural)
bei, awl, beihä'
nītcīye, river, nītcīhä'
haxa'anä^{n}x, ax, haxa'anä$^n\theta$ä'
nīna^n, tent, nīna^{n}nä'
hä^{n}xebⁱ, spring, hä^{n}xebinä'
bä'a^n, road, bä'a^{n}nä'
ha^{n}kūhä^n, head, ha^{n}kūhä^{n}nä'
hakä^{n}x, tent pole, hakä^{n}x^{u}inä'
kakuic, kakuiy, gun, kakuiyanä'
tetcena^n, door, tetcena^{n}nä'
tcäseix, one, tcäseiya^{n}nä', in one spot
wax^u, grass, waxu'unä'
h-ä^n, bed, h-ä^{n}bä'
hoti', wheel, hotībä'
netcⁱ, water, netci
tca'otä^{n}ya^n, hill, tca'otä^{n}nī
hahä^{n}tⁱ, cottonwood tree, hahä^{n}ti', hahä^{n}ti-nⁱ
bīta'ä^{n}wu, earth, bīta'a^{n}wū
wäw^u, ice, wa'awū
heθ-aw-akay-a-ni, in the doghouse

POSSESSION

The personal possessive affixes of nouns are illustrated by the following examples:

Word	Father	Mother	Older brother	Daughter
Vocative	neixa^n	na'a^n		natä
My	neisana^n	neina^n	näsähä'ä	natäne
Your (s.)	heisana^n	heiha^n	häsähä'ä	hatäne
His	hinīsanä^n(nⁱ)	hīnanⁱ	hīsaha'a^n	hitäna^n
Our (incl.)	heisanäninⁱ	heinäninⁱ	häsähä'ehinⁱ	hatanihinⁱ
Our (excl.)		neinänina^n	näsähä'ähina^n	
Your (pl.)		heinänina^n		
Their	hinīsanänina^n	hinaninina^n		hitanehina^n
Somebody's	beisana^n	beina^n	bäsähä'ä	

Word	Grandfather	Son	Sons	Robe
Vocative	näbäcīwa^n	ne'i		(hou)
My	näbäcībähä	neih'ä^n	neih'a^{n}ha^n	natou
Your (s.)	häbäcībähä	heih'ä^n	heih'a^{n}ha^n	hatou
His	hibäcīwaha^n	hī'a^n	hī'a^{n}ha^n	hitouwu
Our (incl.)	häbäcībei-hinⁱ	heih'ehinⁱ		
Our (excl.)				
Your (pl.)				
Their	hibäcībähäina^n			
Somebody's				

Word	Robes	Penis	Dog	Tent
Vocative	(houwaⁿ)	(haθaⁿ)	(heθ)	(nīnaⁿ)
My	natouwaⁿ	neiθaⁿ	netäθäbĭbi	näyei
Your (s.)	hatouwaⁿ	heiθaⁿ	hetäθäbĭbi	häyei
His		hinīθaⁿ	hitäθäbĭwu	hiyei
Our (incl.)	hatouwunⁿⁿ		hetäθäbĭbinⁱ	häyeihinⁱ
Our (excl.)				näyeihinaⁿ
Your (pl.)				häyeihinaⁿ
Their	hitouwunaⁿ		hitäθäbĭbinaⁿ	hiyeihinaⁿ
Somebody's		bäθaⁿ		

Some of the above forms under "our," "your," and "their" may really denote plural instead of singular nouns. The "vocative" in the terms of relationship is the term of direct address: "father!" In the other words given, the corresponding form in parentheses is the nominative.

Several nouns show a suffix with labial consonant in all three persons. This perhaps denotes acquirement of possession.

nat-ahäⁿtī-bi, my tree
hit-ahäⁿtī-wu, his tree
net-äθäbī-bi, my dog
na-nouhuhä-bi, my kit-fox
nä-näⁿtcäⁿ-waⁿ, my chiefs
nä-teiaⁿni-waⁿ, my children

PRONOUNS

The demonstratives, which are alike for singular and plural, animate and inanimate, are:

nähä', nuhu'	this
hinä'	that, visible, or near the person spoken to
hinī	that, invisible, or of reference only

Compare: nä'äsi, thus, nä'eisi, nä'äsaⁿ, it is thus, resembles, nänähisou, alike, nä'aθixtⁱ, he resembles.

Interrogatives:

häⁿnä'	who
häⁿyou	what
häⁿtaⁿ, täⁿti, täⁿteihaⁿ	where
häⁿtaxⁿ	whenever
tou	when
tousaⁿ	why, what kind
tahou, tahoutaxⁿ	how many
touθouhu'	for how much, at what price

A real personal pronoun does not exist. Independent words translatable by English pronouns occur only in answer to questions, or

occasionally for tautological emphasis. They are verbs formed from
a demonstrative stem.

nänä-ni-na[n]	it is I, "I"
nänä-ni-t[i]	it is he, 'he"
nänä-häxk[u]	it must be he, "he"

Compare:

hineni-ni-na[n]	it is a man that I am, "I am a man"
hisei-ni-na[n]	I am a woman
hahä[n]kä[n]-ni-na[n]	I am a fool, I am crazy

The "independent possessive pronouns" are also verbal sentences,
with a possessive prefix and a subjective suffix of the third person.

mine	neinis'tä[n]t[i] ("he is mine")
yours	heinis'tä[n]tī
his	hīnis'tä[n]t[i]
ours	neinis'tä[n]tībina[n]
yours	heinis'tä[n]tīnina[n]
theirs	hinis'tä[n]tīnina[n]

ADVERBS

-ihi', -uhu', is the commonest ending of independent words of
adverbial or prepositional force. Without the suffix, several of the
stems occur as prefixes of verbs.

teän-ihi', under (teän-i-)
täs-ihi', on (täs-i-, täx-)
ka[n]ä[n]-n-ihi', slowly (kou-)
xou-w-uhu', straight (xou-)
bä-h-ihi', all (bä-)
nä[n]-ūhu', out from the river or valley (nou-)
hanawu-n-ihi', ha[n]wui-nih-īhi', down-stream
n-ä[n]wū-hu', south
hawahō-uhu', many times
hi'-ihi', hu'-uhu', with, on account of
hiθa[n]w-ūhu', really, truly (hiθa[n]bei-, to be so)
θei-n-ihi', θeinei-si, inside
kouθ-īhi', some time later
kox-θ-īhi', over, beyond (kax-, violently, through)
ka[n]-kaxuθ-ihi', over a hill
kanaw-ūhu', meanwhile, at the same time
kanax-uhu', obstinately, unduly
nih-īhi', along, during
tou-θo-uhu', at what price (tou, what)
kä[n]kä[n]θ-īhi', homeward

-bä, -bi, -wu, is another ending of adverbs, whose stems in some
cases also serve as prefixes of verbs.

hixte-ä-bä, up, above (hixte-i-)
hä[n]θä-b[i], toward (hä[n]θä-, hä[n]θä-bi-)
nänä-bä, nänä-bi, north
nä[n]tä-bä, at the rear of the tent, opposite the door

-ä^{n}wu refers to the ground:

bīta'ä^{n}wu, earth
hiθä^{n}wu, on the prairie
hiθawä^{n}wu, under ground
naxutä^{n}wu, above ground

-ou:

hän-ä^n, hard, hän-ou, very hard
hä'nä'-ei, fast, hä'nä'ou, very fast
nå'äsi, thus, nänähis-ou, alike
hä-nä', who, hä^n-y-ou, what

NUMERALS

The Arapaho numerals given in the vocabulary are those used in counting, and mean "— times." The cardinals used in sentences are formed like verbs with the prononinal endings -i-θ^i, animate, and -ei, -i-i, inanimate. They occur either with a prefix hä- or with prefixed reduplication. In this reduplication initial y of the stem turns to n. The relationship of these two sounds has been mentioned before. The stem of the cardinal numeral "one" is the same as that of "two," nīs, but has the corresponding singular suffixes -ix-t^i and -e-t^i. In the ordinal and the forms for "six," the stem for "one" appears in what may be its original form, nīt. The stems for "nine" and "ten" are used without reduplication or the prefix hä-. The ordinals are formed, with reduplication, by the suffix -awā. This is sometimes further enlarged by the ending -na' when inanimate, and when animate has the ending -t^i. Numeral classifiers have not yet been observed, except -ä^{n}nä, which is employed when camps, towns, herds, or portions are referred to, and which may be a locative or collective: yäneiy-ä^{n}nä^n-na^n, four bands.

	Counting	*Cardinal*	*Cardinal*	*Ordinal*
1	teǎseix	hä-nīsi-xt^i (an.)	nä-nīsi-xt^i	nä-nīt-awā-t^i
		hä-nīs-et^i (inan.)	nä-nīs-et^i	nä-nīt-awā-(na')
2	nīs^i	hä-nīsi-θ^i (an.)	nä-nīsi-θ^i	nä-nīsi-awā-t^i
		hä-nīs-ei (inan.)	nä-nīs-ei	nä-nīsi-awā-(na')
3	nǎsa^n, nǎsax	hä-näi-θ^i	nä-näi-θ^i	nä-nǎsi-awā-t^i
4	yein^i	hä-yeini-θ^i	yä-neini-θ^i	yä-neini-awā-t^i
5	yäθan^i	hä-yäθani-θ^i	ya-nǎθani-θ^i	ya-nǎθani-awā-t^i
6	nīt-a^n-tax^u	hä-nīt-a^n-taxu-θ^i	nä-nīt-a^n-taxu-θ^i	nä-nīt-a^n-taxu-awā-t^i
7	nīs-a^n-tax^u	hä-nīs-a^n-taxu-θ^i	nä-nīs-a^{n}taxu-θ^i	nä-nīs-a^n-taxu-awā-t^i
8	nǎs-a^n-tax^u	hä-nǎs-a^n-taxu-θ^i	nä-nǎs-a^n-taxu-θ^i	nä-nǎs-a^n-taxu-awā-t^i
9	θi'^{a}	θi'a-taxu-θ^i		θi'a-taxu-awā-t^i
10	bätä-tax^u	bätä-taxu-θ^i		bätä-taxu-awā-t^i

The numerals from 11 to 19 are formed from those for 1 to 9 by the suffix -ini, which occurs also on words denoting measures of time; the tens by the ending -a^n', -a', or u', with change of preceding consonant.

1	tcãseix	11	tcãseini		
4	yein^i	14	yeinīni	40	yeiyu'
5	yãθan^i	15	yãθanīni	50	yãθaya'
7	nīsa^{n}tax^u	17	nīsa^{n}tax^{u}ini	70	nīsa^{n}tasa^n'
8	nãsa^{n}tax^u	18	nãsa^{n}tax^{u}ini	80	nãsa^{n}tasa'

Other forms: nīta^n, first, before; nīsa^{n}ouhu', nisaha'a, both; tcä^{n}xa^n, another one; tcãseix, one, inanimate; tcãsä', one, animate.

The suffix -tax^u, in 6 to 10, appears to be found also in tahoutax^u, how many, and hä^{n}tax^u, whenever.

TEXTS

Only enough textual material is presented here to illustrate some of the leading structural and phonetic features that have been outlined. Several hundred pages of Arapaho texts were secured by the writer. But the foregoing description is, after all, not more than a sketch of part of the salient traits of the language; and any analysis making a pretense at even approximate completeness was impossible, without a study so thorough-going that it would have crowded into the background indefinitely other work which was a nearer duty. With the possible exception of Eskimo, Algonkin, as represented by Arapaho and Yurok, is far the most difficult form of speech encountered by the writer at first hand. How much remains to be done in Arapaho before the language is really understood is revealed by the notes that have been added to the appended texts. The purpose of these notes is elucidation; but whoever consults them will not need the advice that for nearly every point explained there is a problem raised, and several that are not even touched on. For these reasons the entire body of texts recorded has been put in the possession of the Bureau of American Ethnology, in the hope that under the hand of Dr. Michelson or some other investigator better fitted by capacity or long occupation with Algonkin than the writer, their publication will ultimately result in greater usefulness than could be attained now.

TEXT I—A PRAYER[1]

hä^n-heisanā'nin[i2]   nänītäne'ina^{n3} na-h^{a}bäcībē'hin[i4]   häθē'i[5]
Ha! our father,   hear us,   and grandfather.   All

naha'ä^{n}sē'hi'it   nanaxkunihi'ita'wa^{n6} hīci'[7]   nī'ha^{n}ya^n
the shining ones   I also mention,   day   yellow,

häse'isen[i8]   hī'i'θeti   nä'yeitci   i'i'θetin[9]   bita'a^n'wu   ū'θetin[9]
wind   good,   timber   good,   earth   good.

tcäsäe'hi   hä$^n\theta$itcä'θtin[i10]   hiθa^n'wä^{n}wu[11]   naxutä^n'wu[11]
Animal   listen   under the ground!   above the ground

tcäsäe'ihi   nätci[12]   tcesäehe'iha^{n13} tcībäh'tcähä'θtī[14]
animal,   in water   animals,   all listen!

hätcīyawa^{n}ni'na^{n15} ha^{n}twani'bīnī[16]   hä^{n}tihi'iθē'hi[17]
Your food-remnants   we will go to eat.   May they be good!

hä^{n}tihitcihikä^n'tä^{n18} ha^{n}waθa'w^u hīnäitī't[19]   hä^{n}tihiawa^{n}ho'ua^n
May there be long   breath   life!   May increase

hinä^{n}tänī't[19]   teia^{n}nä''[20]   hänätciha^{n}ye'it[21]   hisē'hihi[22]
the people,   children   of all ages,   girl

naha-hana'xa'ähixi[22]   nax'-hine'n   hänätcixa^{n}yē'it   hi'sei
and boy   and man   of all ages,   woman,

bäh^{ä}e'ihähin[23]   hänätcixa^{n}ye'in   bätäbi'   ha^{n}tnīnioxanē'iä^{n}nou[24]
old man,   of all ages,   old woman.   It shall give us strength

bī'ciwa^{n25} ha^{n}neika^n'huθi[26]   hīcī'c   hä^n'θä^n nēixä^n'[27]
the food   while runs   the sun.   Oh that!   my father!

tcixtcä'ä'θtī[28]   näbä'cīwa^{n27} nä^{n}nihi'iθa''a^{n29} kakau'θetca^{n30}
listen,   my grandfather!   for what I ask,   thoughts,

bätä^n'[31]   bixa$^n\theta$etī't[32]   hanaw^{ui}nätī't   ha^{n}tnīnīθixanäbeθen[33]
heart,   love,   happiness!   We will eat you.

Notes

[1] Bull. Am. Mus. Nat. Hist., XVIII, 315, 1907.

[2] 1st pers. pl. inclusive: neisana^n, my father.

[3] -n-, connective; -eina^n, he—me or they—us: thou—us is -eiä^n.

[4] na^n' or nah^a is "and"; the -h^a- may be part of this or part of the possessive elements hä—h-in[1], our; näbäcibä, my grandfather.

[5] Also a prefix of verbs.

[6] na-, for na^n' or nah^a, and; -naxku-n-, with, a prefix of verbs; nih[1]-, incomplete action; ita, stem; -w-, connective; -a^n, I—him.

[7] Cf. hicic, sun, below.

[8] Cf. häsa'a^{n}t[1], swift, and the prefix of verbs häs-, swiftly, violently, very, hard.

[9] These two words were heard as parts of the preceding ones, to the final vowels of which their initial vowels are assimilated.

[10] hä$^n\theta$i- apparently equals hä^{n}tī-, optative; -in[1], transitive imperative.

[11] -ä^{n}wu, an ending of adverbs referring to the ground.

[12] Locative of nete[1], water.

[13] -ha^n, plural; -ēhi, -ehei, may be -ēhi, denoting the agent, -ēhi, face, or -hi'i, -hähi, diminutive.

[14] tcī-, imperative, regular in the negative, occasional in the positive; -bäh'-, all; tcähäθ-t-ī, compare tcäθ-t-, note 10, is or contains the stem.

[15] "Crumbs." Plural, with 2nd pers. possessive.

[16] ha^{n}t-, purposive future; wan-i-, go to do; bī, eat; -n-, connective.

[17] hä^{n}tih'-, optative or precative (cf. note 10), -ih' probably denoting incompletion of action; iθe appears to be the stem meaning good, cf. above, note 9; -hi, intransitive.

[18] hä^{n}tih'-, as in last word; -tcihi-, possibly tcī-, imperative, and n-ih'-, incomplete action; kä^n-t-ä^n suggests the "prefix" kou-, kanou-, long, far.

[19] Cf. hinen', man, hinenitä^n, person, hinana'ei, Arapaho, hīteni, life symbol; -īt', no doubt containing the pronominal ending of the 3rd pers., recurs below on abstract nouns.

[20] Plural (?) of teia^n, child. The form has the appearance of a locative.

[21] Unanalyzed, except for the abstract ending, cf. note 19.

[22] hisei, woman; -hi'i, -hä', -hähi, etc., diminutive; hanaxa'aha, young man.

[23] bähä'ei, behi'i, old, with perhaps the diminutive suffix. Compare the stems for old woman, in the second word following, and for grandfather, as in note 4. The ending of the next word changes from -t to -n, evidently to agree with the unexplained -n of the present noun.

[24] ha^{n}tnī-, or ha^{n}t-, ha^{n}ta^{n}ni-, purposive future; -ni-, perhaps ni'-, good; -oxa-, the stem, cf. axa-wu, give me food, -axa-h-, to bring, take, carry; -n- appears to be the connective, in spite of the -h- of -axa-h; -eiä^{n}nou then would be the pronominal ending, not fully clear, though -eiä^n is thou—us.

[25] Unknown derivation from bī-, eat.

[26] hä^n-, while, continuing; -ne-, for nī-, nih'-, incomplete action; i-ka^n, stem, to move, especially to run, usually with the intransitive suffix -hu.

[27] "Vocative," 1st pers. possessive, regularly a shortened form in terms of relationship.

[28] Imperative: cf. notes 10 and 14.

[29] nä^n-, perhaps my; nih-, nihi-, nī-, hī-, that which, he who, where.

[30] -iθetca^n-h-, to think; kaka-xa'änäta^n, thought, think.

[31] Indefinitive possessive prefix b-ä-, b-ei-, w-a-.

[32] bixa^n-θ-eθen', I love you; for -īt see note 19.

[33] ha^{n}tnī-, one form of future of intent; -nīθixanä-, unanalyzed; -b-, connective; -eθen, I—you.

TEXT II—AN ADVENTURE[1]

bihi'i	hä^{n}ixīna^{n}ei[2]	hitaxa^{n}hok[3]	wotix	touciniehin
"Deer"	now went hunting.	He came to	accidentally	one who was pretty

hisein[4]	behic'nic'tcä^n[5]	hinaninouyuyaxkan	xanou[6]
woman.	All antelope	was her clothing.	Straightway

hä^{n}ixtcetcīθänä^n	taha^{n}ahawä^{n}t[7]	hisein[4]	hä^{n}ixäneitaxawūinä^n[8]
then he wanted to court her	when he saw	the woman.	Then she motioned for him to approach.

wa^{n}hei	ha^{n}tibīä^nθeθen	hä^nθa^{n}hok[3]	bihi'i	nah'nihäya^n
"Well,	let me love you,"	said to her	"Deer."	"And yourself

häcita^{n}nani	hä^nθeihok[3]	hänäiyiha^{n}t[10]	tä^{n}bä[11]
please."	she said to him.	Then he went to her.	Just

ha^{n}tnītena^{n}hok[12]	hīna^{n}nanax	hä^{n}ixwosätouhin[13]	tcesteätcena'ä^n
he will be about to touch her,	to his surprise	then she cried (like a deer),	suddenly jumped,

tcätcebitä'eixa^n[15]	hä^{n}i'bīniha^{n}habä[16]	bihi'i	bihi'i	hä^{n}ixtäyē
ran off looking back.	Then he saw she was	a deer.	"Deer"	then was ashamed

ha^{n}wo-nih'ot-bīä'ä^{n}t[17]	hä^{n}nätcätckä^{n}hut[18]	taxtäyēhit[19]
at being deceived in loving.	Then he returned	ashamed.

häⁿixxãⁿtä'einin	bihi'i	ta'bihi'ihinãⁿtin²⁰	näyēθaⁿnäⁿ
Now later	"Deer"	became like a deer.	In the camp-circle

häⁿixinikuhinäⁿ²¹   bihi'i   wãⁿti   bihi'i   wãⁿti   bihi'i

then was chased   "Deer"   like   a deer.   Like   a deer

nīθetouhäk²²   wãⁿti   bihi'i   tcätcena'aⁿ¹⁴   wãⁿti   bihi'i

he cried,   like   a deer   he jumped,   like   a deer

hähnãⁿkuhnähäkᵘ	häbähiyeihanãⁿtäkᵘ²³	tīcītänät²⁴
he fled on the prairie;	all pursued.	When he was caught,

häⁿixnänaⁿniθaⁿkuaⁿ   bihi'i   häⁿixtatinãⁿ   häⁿixbähäneiänäⁿ²⁵

then his eyes looked different.   "Deer"   now had his mouth open.   Then all held him.

hãⁿnī   häⁿixtcīnīnⁱ   bihi'ihīn²⁶   nã'ãθīcīhitⁱ   bihi'i

At last   then he ceased   being a deer.   For this he is named   "Deer."

Notes

[1] Bull. Am. Mus. Nat. Hist., XVIII, 20, 1902.

[2] For häⁿix-, see note 29 to following text; inaⁿ, hunt; -ei, causative, here: go to.

[3] -hokⁿ, it is said, they say. Cf. Michelson, Bur. Am. Ethn. Ann. Rept., XXVIII, 237, 1912.

[4] An apparent instance of the objective or oblique case: hisei, woman.

[5] bä-, behi'i-, behici-, bäbänei-, all, completely; naⁿsitcäⁿ, nisitcäⁿ, antelope.

[6] Also a "prefix" of verbs.

[7] tahⁿ-, when; n-aⁿha-w, see; -äⁿtⁱ, he—him.

[8] Cf. h-itaxaⁿ in the third word of this text; with this "stem" compare itä-s, itä-s, reach, meet. For häⁿix-, see note 2: -wūinäⁿ, from -wu-n, to, for, with, or more probably from -awui-ni, become, begin, and -n-, connective, -äⁿ, -aⁿ, he—him (a form different from those given above in the table of transitive pronominal endings, and no less common; but their relation is not yet clear).

[9] For haⁿt-ī-bixaⁿ-θ-eθenⁱ, I will love you.

[10] hänä-⹀häⁿnäⁿ-, which see in note 29 to next text; iyihaⁿt suggests the analysis iyi-h-äⁿtⁱ, but the form otherwise found is stem iyihaⁿ with connective -n-.

[11] Also a prefix, but here heard as a separate word.

[12] haⁿt-nī-; ite-n, take; -hokⁿ, see note 3.

[13] häⁿix-; wos-,?; ätou, itou, cry, make a noise, shout; -hi, intransitive; -n,?

[14] Cf. tceesis-, begin; tcä-, again, back, or perhaps reduplication here, "jumped about"; tcena'äⁿ, jump.

[15] Cf. tcä-, backward, again; tceib-i-, aside, crooked; the stem seems to be the same verb of motion as in the word referred to in note 8.

[16] häⁿix-, as ante; bīni-h-, possibly from bīi-n, bīi-h, find; aⁿha-b-äⁿ, he sees him.

[17] Perhaps from bixaⁿ-θ, to love.

[18] häⁿnäⁿ-, as above; tcä-, back, again; -tc-,?; i-kaⁿ-hu, run, travel; -tⁱ, he.

[19] tahⁿ-, when, because; täye, be ashamed, as in the preceding sentence; -hi, intransitive; -tⁱ, he.

[20] ta'-, for tahⁿ- (?); bihi'i, deer; -hi-näⁿti-n, compare nī-waxū-näⁿtⁱ, she who turned into a bear, and the independent word wãⁿti in the next sentence.

[21] häⁿix-; īn-i-, about, aimlessly, at random; -ku-hi-näⁿ, possibly from -ku-θ, make a motion to, transitive, and -hi, intransitive.

[22] ni-θ-,?; etou, for itou or ätou, shout; -häk, for -häxkⁿ, conditional, subordinating.

[23] hä-,(?); bäh-, all, as in note 5; iyeiha-n-, for īyihaⁿ-n, pursue; ãⁿtäkⁿ, uncertain, but evidently contains the "conditional," as the word in note 22.

[24] tīc-i-, when; ite-n, catch; -ät, for -äⁿtⁱ, equals -äⁿtⁱ, he—him.

[25] Again the prefix "all," as in notes 5 and 23.

[26] Perhaps the intransitive verbifying suffix -hi.

TEXT III—TANGLED HAIR[1]

hinen   hä[n]nīxā[n]tihok[u2]   nä[n]hä[n]īna[n]eihok[u3]   hä[n]eita[n]wūna[n]hok[u]
A man   lived alone.   He went to hunt.   He told her

hīnīni   ha[n]ta[n]nīna[n]ēiti[3]   ha[n]na[n]ya[n]   tcībä[n]ta[n]ka[n]ha[n]wunä[n4]
his wife, when he was about to go to hunt: "Mind!   do not look at him

ha[n]tanītä[n]seini[5]   na[n]nä[n]tēiti[6]   hīna[n]hä[n]teineiti[6]   hīha[n]wuxuwa[n7]
when he comes to you   a powerful one   with tangled hair   who is hard to satisfy abou[t]

a[n]tītci   hä[n]īnä[n]ya[n]   ha[n]ta[n]nītä[n]sä'[8]   na[n]   tcībä[n]yei θä[n]eini
plates.   He will make a noise   when he will come   and   do not look there

hītä[n]seinihinä[n]ku[8]   hä[n]īnä[n]ya[n]   hota[n]nītoutca[n]na[n]θi[9]   ha[n]na[n]ya[n]
where he comes.   He will make a noise;   he will shout;   mind!

tcībä[n]neia[n]ha[n]wunä[n4]   na[n]nä[n]teiti   hä[n]bä[n]tcītcītei[10]   hä[n]yeiä[n]'ä[n11]
do not look at him   the powerful one,   he might enter   your tent,"

hä[n]θa[n]hoku[12]   hīnīnin[13]   ta[n]tcä[n]θeia[n]t[i14]   na[n]nä[n]tcä[n]θicīna[n]eihoku[15]
he said to her   his wife   when he went away.   And he went to hunt

tīcīnīhiθa[n]ti[16]   .   hīnīnī   na[n]nä[n]na[n]θa[n]hoku   tīna[n]eiti[17]
after he had told   his wife;   he left her   to hunt.

na[n]hä[n]nä[n]eitä[n]seiniθi[5]   hīnīni   hīna[n]ha[n]teineiniθi[18]
And then he came to   his wife,   he whose hair was tangled.

na[n]hä[n]tcīta[n]ka[n]ha[n]wa[n]hoku[4]   na[n]nä[n]tcä[n]īsä[n]ya[n]ka[n]nei[19]
And she did not look at him.   And he went back

ta[n]tcīneia[n]ha[n]wa[n]ti[4]   hä[n]tcä[n]īsä[n]ya[n]ka[n]ī[19]   hä[n]tīsä[n]nīθi[20]   nuhu
when she did not look at him,   he went back to   where he had come from,   that

hina[n]ha[n]teinihiniθi[18]   ta[n]θa[n]nīheiti   nuhu   tä[n]bä[n]tītä[n]seiti[5]
one with the tangled hair,   he failed   that one   on first coming

nuu   a[n]ha[n]kä[n]neineiθi[21]   hä[n]yawūtä[n]seiθi[5]   nītcīta[n]ka[n]ha[n]wa[n]hoku[4]
that   demented one,   whenever he came to   her who did not look at him.

na[n]yä[n]neinīa[n]wa[n]nī[22]   hä[n]ta[n]nä[n]hoku[23]   ha[n]tcä[n]ci   beihä[n]'ä[n11]
But the fourth time   she made a hole   by means of   an awl

ha[n]xūti   nīna[n]nä[11]   ta[n]hīnä[n]tcä[n]θeia[n]niθ[i14]   hī'ihi'   beihä'ä[11]
at the left of the door   in the tent,   when he tnrned back,   with   an awl,

ta[n]hūhīθiwa[n]ha[n]wa[n]ti[4, 24]   θihä[n]ī θä[n]hīθi[25]   hä[n]häku
as she looked through,   "Let me see him!"   s[h]e said.

hä[n]nä[n]eiwa[n]ha[n]wa[n]ti[4]   hīhīθī'i   nuu   ä[n]ta[n]na[n]tīhīni   ha[n]xūtī
Then she looked out   through   that   hole   at the left of the door

hīθi'i   ha'heitc   hä[n]θeihoku[12]   nä[n]īnä[n]sa[n]ya[n]kani
through.   "Here!"   he said to her   as he turned back.

ta[n]tcīteia[n]neiti[10]   hä[n]θeihoku   ta[n]nīä[n]cinä[n]na[n26]   nä[n]tcīa[n]xa[n]wu[27]
When he came in   he said to her: "I am hungry,   give me to eat,

hänθa^{n}hoku^{12} nuhu'   hīseini^{28} hänä^{n}a^{n}tītcīheiti^{29} ha^{n}einä^{n30}
he said to her   that   woman.   Then she gave him for a plate   a clay one.

hīha^{n}wnänīsou'u^{31} na^{n}tītcīta^{n}na^{n32} hänä^{n}a^{n}titcīheiti^{29}
"It is not the kind   I use for plates."   Then she gave him for a plate

bäcīna^{n30} hīha^{n}wnä^{n}īsou'u   na^{n}tītcīta^{n}na^n hähä^{n}ku
a wooden one.   "It is not the kind   I use for plates,"   he said.

hä^{n}nä^{n}a^{n}tītcīheiti   ka^{n}ka^{n}ha^{n}wa^{n}ti   ka^{n}xu   hä^{n}īnä^{n}eihīti
Then she gave him for a plate   a war-bonnet.   Again   he said the same.

hä^{n}nä^{n}a^{n}tītcīheiti   hībīxūta^{n}nīni^{33} ta^{n}na^{n}nä^n'   hä^nθa^{n}hoku
Then she gave him for a plate   her dress.   "Very nearly!"   he said to her.

na^{n}hä^{n}nä^{n}a^{n}tītcīheiti   hīwä^{n}nīna^{n33} ta^{n}na^{n}nä^n'   hä^nθa^{n}hoku
And then she gave him for a plate   her moccasins.   "Very nearly!"   he said to her.

ka^{n}xu   hä^{n}nä^{n}īcībīniθi^{34} ha^nθiθeineihi'i^{35} nä^{n}nä^n'   hä^nθa^{n}hoku
Again   then she lay down   flat on her back.   "That is it"   he said to her.

na^{n}ta^{n}ha^{n}ta^{n}wa^{n}nīθi^{37} hä^{n}nä^{n}ikä^nθeineit^{i38} wa^{n}hä^{n}īnīsei^{39}
And when he had eaten   then he slit her open.   She was pregnant with twins,

nīsa^{n}u'^{39} ha^{n}na^n'ä^{n}hīa^{n40} nīsa^{n}na^{n39} hä^{n}nä^{n}ī'ītä^{n}na^{n}ti^{41}
both   were boys,   the twins.   Then he took them;

tcä^{n}xa^{n42} nuu   ha^{n}na^n'ä^{n}hīa^{n40} hä^{n}nä^{n}īwa^{n}cieiwa^{n}ti^{43}
one   that   boy   then he put in the water

ha^{n}xäbeinä'^{11} na^n tcä^{n}xa^n a^{n}hä^{n}īθeikūθä^{n44} θä^{n}ya^{n}ka^{n}xu'
in the spring,   and   one   he threw under   the right side of the door

nīna^{n}nä^{n11} hä^{n}nä^{n}na^nθītcä^nθia^{n}ti^{45} tīcθeikūθa^{n}ti^{46} teīīyanä^n'
at the tent.   Then he went away   after he had placed   the children.

hä^{n}īnä^{n}kei   nä-hīnä^{n}ni^{48} hä^{n}einīci'iä^{49} hīnīni
He returned,   this man,   he called   his wife,

hä^{n}ītcä^{n}tiθīni   ta^{n}nīcīa^{n}ti^{49} hinīni   na^n xa^{n}xa^{n}nōu^{50}
she did not answer,   when he called her,   his wife.   And   straightway

hä^{n}īä^{n}ini^{51} ta^{n}nä^{n}eineiθi^{52} ta^{n}tcä^{n}tiθeiniθi^{52}
he knew   that she was dead   when she did not answer.

hä^{n}nä^{n}tcīθīna^{n}ha^{n}wa^{n}ti^{53} ha^{n}hä^{n}eikä^nθeini^{54} neitcīnīhīθa^{n}na^{n}ou^{55}
Then he went in to see.   She was slit open.   "I told you,"

hä^nθa^{n}hoku   hä^{n}nä^{n}ībīwa^{n}huti^{56} hä^{n}nä^{n}na^nθina^{n}hit^i
he said to her.   Then he cried.   Then he went off.

Notes

[1] Field Columbian Museum Publications, Anthrop. Series, v, 378, 1903. The informant spoke with elaborate slowness and distinct syllabification. To this are due the numerous nasalized vowels, which, as Dr. Michelson says, tend to disappear in rapid speech. The slow utterance of the present informant may have caused nasalization to be heard where it was not organic. Dr. Michelson nasalizes o and perhaps other vowels; the author noted only a^n and ä^n, though a^n was sometimes confused with o. Arapaho long vowels were usually heard

and written as geminated or doubled, particularly from this informant. As the writer in studying other languages has, however, found this apperception to be largely an individual peculiarity, such double vowels have in this paper been represented by single letters with the macron, except long e and o, which are represented, as heard, by ei and ou. The tendency to double crest long vowels seems nevertheless actually to be fairly marked in Arapaho, although the slight importance of the trait at best, and the cumbersomeness of its appearance in print, probably make its orthographical neglect preferable.

2 The ending -hok^n, given by Dr. Michelson as a stem meaning "say," is common as a quotative. Text II, note 3.

3 nä^n-,?; īna^n-ei, hunt, go to hunt, probably containing -ei, causative; -hok^n, "quotative"; ha^{n}ta^{n}nī-, ha^{n}tī-, ha^{n}t-, purposive future, as in the preceding text; -ti, for -t^1, he, intransitive.

4 teī-, negative, teī-bä-, negative imperative; ta^{n}k-, nei-, not determined; ta^n-, when; na^n-, nah^a- (also independent, perhaps regularly loosely proclitic rather than prefixed), and; hä^n-, probably related to hä^{n}ix-, hä^{n}nä^n-, see note 29; a^{n}ha-w, stem, to see; -hok^n, "quotative"; -ti, -a^n-ti, ei-ti, 3rd pers.; -nä^n, not clear, but evidently pronominal, -nä occurring quite regularly as the subjective and objective element of the 2nd pers. plural.

5 ha^{n}tanī-, future; na^n-, and; hä^{n}nä-, "then"; tä^{n}bä-, just, only, first begin to; hä^{n}yaw-, if the translation obtained is literal, would mean "whenever" (independent, hä^n-tax^n, whenever, hä^n-you, what); itä^n-s, to come to; -ni, -niθi, -θi, modal-pronominal; -ti, see note 6.

6 These two words contain the 3rd pers. ending -(ei)-t^1, and are to all appearances verbs.

7 īha^{n}wu-, with pronominal prefix, a frequent form of the negative in verbs.

8 Cf. note 5.

9 hota^{n}nī- for ha^{n}ta^{n}nī-, cf. note 1; itou, stem.

10 tcitei, enter; cf. teīt-, teīθ-i-, in, entering.

11 These words all contain a locative suffix.

12 hä^n-θa^n-hok^n, he (A) said to him (B); hä^n-θei-hok^n, he (B) said to him (A). Cf. Michelson, Bur. Am. Ethn., Ann. Rep., XXVIII, 237, 1912. It appears that a similar distinction is made in other verbs in the transitive pronominal endings. The two contrasting forms are probably related to the two forms of the third person in Central Algonkin; but the writer is under the impression that, in Arapaho at least, the "suus-ejus" distinction has been far transcended, the two forms serving rather as a convenient and valuable means of expressing over considerable passages the ideas which in our legal documents are rendered by "the party of the first part" and "the party of the second part." If this view proves correct, the force of the paired Arahapo forms would be somewhat similar to the contrasting Yuki particles sa^n' and si', of which one indicates the continuance and the other a change of grammatical subject or agent in the sentences which they open.

13 Without the final -n in other occurrences in this text, as *ante*.

14 ta^n-, when; tcä^{n}θ-ei-, tcäθ-i-, off, away.

15 ina^n-, and; tcä^{n}θ-i-, away; īna^n-ei, go to hunt; -hoku, quotative.

16 tīc-, tīcīni-, when, after, with implication of completed action; hi-,?; -θa^n-, cf. hä^n-θa^n-hoku, note 12; -ti, he.

17 t-, tī-, tih^1-, ta^n-, tah^a-, when, after, to, because.

18 Compare the corresponding form in note 6.

19 na^n-, and; tcä^n-, back; ī-sä^n, go, come.

20 hä^{n}t-, hä^{n}t-a^n-, where; ī-sä^n, go, come.

21 hahä^{n}kä^n, crazy.

22 yä-neini-awä-t^1, the fourth, animate, yä-neini-awa-na', inanimate. The ending -nī is evidently the same as is found on the cardinal numbers from 11 to 19, and on words denoting measures of time.

23 tanä-s, pierce, make hole in. Cf. tä'-, tanä'-, tou-, tanou-, to stop, or by stopping; also the fourteenth word below in the text.

24 ta^n-, when, as; a^{n}ha-w, a^{n}ha-b, see; hŭhiθi-w- is evidently a form of the independent word hīhīθī'-i or hīθī'i (as below), probably for hīhīθ-ihi'.

25 θi-, iθi-, let me.

26 äsini-h, to anger; äsina-nä-t^1, anger; the same stem seems to be used to express the meanings of anger and hunger, which both imply stirring emotion; or has the similar sound of the English words led to confusion in translation? The ending -na^n is the regular intransitive of the 1st pers.

27 tcī-, positive or negative imperative; aⁿxaⁿ-wu, axa-wu, give to eat!

28 Objective of hisei.

29 aⁿtītci, plates, *ante;* -h-ei, causative; hänäⁿ-, häⁿnäⁿ-, correlative with häⁿix-, mentioned in the preceding text. The force of these two common prefixes is not clear. Informants left them untranslated or rendered them by "then." They appear to be relational to the discourse as a whole rather than syntactical or grammatical. For häⁿ- alone see note 4.

30 Compare Gros Ventre ha'äⁿty¹, lime, white earth; and haäninin, better ha'äninin, the Gros Ventre name for themselves, translated, perhaps in false etymology, as "lime-men." The myth refers to a time when the Arapaho at least knew pottery. For the ending -i-naⁿ compare bäcinaⁿ, a wooden one, just below, from bäc¹, wood.

31 ī-haⁿwu-, negative of verbs.

32 aⁿtītci, plates, as in note 29; -ta-n, -ta-na, to, for, of; either the initial n- or the final -naⁿ denotes the first person.

33 hī-, her; bīxūt¹, dress; wa'a, wa'aha, moccasin, plural -naⁿ.

34 īcī-bi, isi-bi, lie down.

35 -ihi'i, -ihi', the commonest suffix of adverbs.

36 Compare nähä', nuhu', this; hinä', that, visible; näuä-ni-naⁿ, I, it is I; nänä-häxkⁿ, he, it must be he.

37 naⁿ-, and; taⁿ-, when; haⁿt-, future intent, and aⁿwaⁿ, eat; or h-aⁿtaⁿ-, eat (cf. ata-wu, eat up for), and -wa, -bä, cause.

38 i-käⁿθei-n, cf. ka'äθei-n, cut open belly (ka'aⁿ-b, bite, kaⁿne-n, open, kaⁿu-s, cut off); -eit¹, he (B)—him (A).

39 nīs¹, two (counting), hä-nīs-ei, two, inanimate; -naⁿ, plural.

40 hanaxa'aha, young man; -hi'i, -hä', -hähi, diminutive; -aⁿ, for -aⁿ', -haⁿ, plural. For: hanaxa'ähihaⁿ'.

41 ite-n, take, catch.

42 Compare tcäseix, one, in counting.

43 ī-waⁿciei-w for waⁿcie-w, waⁿcie-b, take into water.

44 ī-θei-kū-θ for θei-ku-θ, put in; -äⁿ, he—him.

45 naⁿθī-,?; tcäⁿθi, for tcäθ-i-, away, usually a "prefix," here obviously the "stem," since it is followed directly by the pronominal ending.

46 tīc, or tīsi-, when, after, completed action.

47 teiaⁿ, child; -naⁿ, plural.

48 For: nähä' hinenⁿ¹.

49 This transitive stem seemingly is used without the usual connective consonant. Compare the endings of the two occurrences of the stem: -aⁿt¹ and eit¹, the A and B forms according to the table of pronominal endings, occur, here and elsewhere in the text, in subordinate verbs; -äⁿ, as in note 44, and notes 8 and 16 of Text II, is found on independent verbs.

50 Or xanou; also a prefix.

51 Transitive äⁿina-n. This form seems to be intransitive and without pronominal suffix.

52 taⁿ- once means that, once when.

53 tcīθ-i-, in, entering, to enter; aⁿha-b, aⁿha-w, to see. Perhaps best: he entering saw, he enter-saw. This word illustrates excellently the difficulty in distinguishing in Arapaho between verb stems with adverbial prefixes and binary compound verbs, as discussed above in the first part of the section dealing with verbs.

54 See note 38.

55 The expected ending -eθen¹, I—you, is lacking; n-ei- seems to be the part of the word meaning I.

56 bīwaⁿ-hu, to cry.

PART III

NOTES ON GROS VENTRE

PHONETICS

The sounds of Gros Ventre have been discussed in connection with those of Arapaho proper.   Certain sound correspondences between the two languages have been pointed out in Part I.

Vocalic changes, consonantal substitutions, increments, and reduplications or similar expansions, are frequent, but the laws by which they are governed are not often clear.

wos, bear; waotä^n--n-os, black bear.

hītäna^n(n)-ī-bī, buffalo cow.

nixa^{n}t-ou-iθä, white-man woman.

na^{n}ts^e, rabbit; na^{n}k-ā^{n}ts, ''white rabbit,'' jackrabbit; nawat-a^{n}ts, ''left-hand rabbit,'' cottontail rabbit.

na^{n}ts-ou-hītäna^n, white buffalo.

na^{n}k^u-θ-otei, ''white belly,'' donkey; wanot^e, some one's belly; na-na^{n}ty-ix-ty^i, he is white.

ha'a^n-ty^i, white clay, lime; ha'ā-n-inin, Gros Ventre; ha'ā-n-iθä, Gros Ventre woman.

b^i-teibyi, louse, ''some one's louse''; bei-teibyi, ''red louse,'' flea; θei-teibyi, ''flat louse,'' bedbug; baxa'a^n-teibyi, ''thunder louse,'' butterfly.

a^{n}wu, down; a^{n}wu-nihi'i, down along a stream; n-a^{n}w^i-na^{n}tyinei, ''lower-Assiniboines,'' Sioux.

kāka-ya^n, flat, it is flat; kāka-tyi, he is flat; kāk-ou-biθ, ''flat wood,'' cut lumber, planks.

bāθ-ani'i, ''large gopher,'' prairie-dog; bāθ-ā^{n}tsu, ''large mouse,'' rat; bäs-ou, bāθ-ei-(y)a^n, bänäθ-ei-(y)-a^n, large (inanimate), it is large, a large thing; bänäθ-ei-tyi, he is large, a large one; bās-initä^n, ''large person,'' a giant; häbäty-initä^n (häbä-ty^i-initä^n?), a large person.

baxa-a^n, red, inanimate; bei-x-ty^i, he is red, red (animate); bänä-ty^i, he is red; bā^{n}ä^n bis, red wood; bax-ou, ''red porcupine(?),'' badger; nix-bā-ä'ā-na^n, I was red headed; bänäbä-'tä-na^n, I have red ears; banä^{n}b(ä^n)-a^{n}tsö-na^n, I have red eyes.

COMPOSITION

Some body part stems when in composition are dissimilar to the independent stems of the same meaning; others are the same.

Distinct:

-ībä-, nose; be-ic^ä, nose.   Arapaho: -i-θä-, b-eic.

θä-n-ībä-ty^i, ''flat nose he is,'' pig

ta-n-ībä-ts, ''pierced nose they are,'' Nez Percé Indians

bä^{n}äs-öbä^n-na^n, ''large nose I am,'' I have a large nose

-ä'ä-, head; bī-tᵃ'ᵃⁿ (or bit-ᵃ'ᵃⁿ?), head. Arapaho: ä'ei-; ha-kuhäⁿ, head; bei-θe'ä, hair.

> bänäθ-ä'ä-naⁿ, I am large headed
> käka-ä'ä-nin, ''flat head men(?),'' Flat-head Indians

-täxä-, belly; wa-n-otᵉ, belly. Arapaho: wa-not.

> häⁿtyis-täxä-naⁿ, I am small-bellied

-aⁿtsö-, eye; be-söθ, eye. Arapaho: bä-cīsä.

> wanäⁿwaⁿθ-aⁿtsö-naⁿ, I have ugly eyes

Identical:

ityi-, mouth; be-tyī', mouth. Arapaho: bä-ti.

> wanäⁿθ-ityi-naⁿ, I am ugly mouthed

-ⁱtän-, ear; wa-n-otan, ear. Arapaho: wa-natana'.

> bänäbäθ-ⁱtän-(n)aⁿ, I have large ears

-aⁿtsötä-, tooth; bī-tsitⁱ, tooth. Arapaho: bei-tciθ.

> ninänⁱ-aⁿtsötä-naⁿ, I have pretty teeth

-öθana-, neck; wa-θana, neck. Arapaho: bä-sonaⁿ.

> bänäs-öθana-ni-naⁿ, I have a large neck

-tinä, mammae; be-ten, breast. Arapaho: bä-θen-etcⁱ, breast-water, milk.

> bänäbäs-tinä-naⁿ, I have large breasts

Several other nouns occur in two forms:

-okay-, house, in composition only; -yei, house, independent word with possessive pronoun; nīnᵃⁿ, house, independent word without possessive. Arapaho: -akac or -akay, -i-yei, nīnaⁿ.

> wux-n-okay-än, ''(?)-houses,'' the Minitari
> wasöin-hiyei-hi-ts, ''grass their houses,'' ''they have grass houses,'' a Shoshonean tribe

-äⁿwᵘ-, water, in composition only; netsⁱ, water. Arapaho: -aⁿwu, netcⁱ.

> bäⁿ-äⁿwᵘhaⁿθäⁿ-netsⁱ, red rain
> nananⁿk-äⁿwᵘ netsⁱ, white water
> tsök-äⁿwᵘ, clear water
> hou-n-äⁿwᵘ, muddy water
> waotäⁿ-n-äⁿwᵘ, black water
> waotäⁿ-notsⁱ, ''black water,'' coffee
> nixaⁿt-ou-netsⁱ, ''white man's water,'' whisky
> bete(n)-nitsⁱ, ''breast water,'' milk
> beθⁱ-nitsⁱ, ''wood-water,'' sap

VERBS

AFFIXES OF MODE AND TENSE

The tense and mode affixes observed are substantially the same as in Arapaho.

Prefixes

n-, nī-, naⁿ-, incomplete action, present; Arapaho: nī-
nihᶦ-, nīnihᶦ-, incomplete action, past; Arapaho: nihᶦ-
nih-īse-n-, completed action, past; perhaps: once continued action now completed; Arapaho: nih-īsi-
haⁿtaⁿ-, haⁿtaⁿni-, future, probably of intent; Arapaho: haⁿt-, haⁿt-ī-, haⁿtaⁿnī
nihᶦ-aⁿtaⁿ-, "was about to"; nihᶦ- and haⁿtaⁿ-
haⁿ-ē-, interrogative, present; Arapaho: kihᶦ-, kaⁿ-, kaⁿhei-, kaⁿhä-, kaⁿhu-
haⁿ-ex-, interrogative, past
haⁿ'aⁿtaⁿ-, interrogative, future
tsö-, tsu-, tsä-, tse-, negative; Arapaho: teī-, teih-
haⁿ-(n), optative, "let me"; Arapaho: hän-tī-, hän-tihᶦ
hax-, that, when, subordinating; Arapaho: taⁿ-, tahᵃ-
ihi-, if, past unreal supposition
nãⁿθei-, perhaps; Arapaho: naⁿxei-

A few etymological affixes have also been distinguished:

näye-x-tsö-, niyä-x-tsö-, try to; Arapaho: näye-
teäⁿ-sö-, begin to; Arapaho: teäsis-
naⁿwa-, näⁿbi-, make a motion to; Arapaho: nawu-, näbi-

Suffixes

-etyi, reflexive; Arapaho: -eti, -uti
-ēhi, -ōhu, agent; Arapaho: -ēhi, -ōhu
-n-äxku, added to personal ending, conditional; Arapaho: -h-äxkᵘ, n-äxkᵘ
-yaⁿ, ending of many adjectives in the absolute or inanimate form; Arapaho: -aⁿ, -yaⁿ

PRONOMINAL ENDINGS AND CONNECTIVES

The intransitive endings are:

	Gros Ventre	Arapaho
I	-naⁿ	-naⁿ
You	-nⁿn	-nᶦ
He	-tyᶦ	-tᶦ
We	-nin	-naⁿ
You	-näⁿ	-näⁿ
They	-ts(ᶦ)	-θi

The intransitive imperative is expressed by -ts; änity-i-ts, talk! This ending has not been observed in Arapaho.

The transitive conjugation is substantially the same as in Arapaho.

	Gros Ventre	Arapaho
I—you	-etin	-eθen[1]
I—him	-^{n}, -[1]	-a^n'
I—you (pl.)	-etina^n	-eθenä^n
I—them	-ou	-ou
I—it	-awa^n	-awa^n
you—him	-ots[1]	-a^{n}t[1]
he—me	-ein^{an}	-eina^n
he—you	-ein[1]	-ein[1]
he—him	-aty[1]	-a^{n}t[1]
they—you	-ein^{a}n([1])	-einani
they—him	-ots[1]	-a$^n\theta$i

The preceding consonant or connective also undergoes change much as in Arapaho.

Meaning	Verb	Me	You	Him	You	Them	It
see	a^{n}ha		b	kw[25]	b	w	t
strike	ta^n	b	b	w			
shoot	tcī	by	by	by			bit[26]
kick	täθa		n	n			
tell	n-ī		t[27]	t[27]		t[27]	
kill	naha			'			

The transitive imperative is -in; Arapaho, -in[i], un[i].

tci-by-in	shoot him!
nihi'-in	kill him!

The transitive endings occurring with the interrogative prefix ha^{n}ex- are evidently the same as the Arapaho personal suffixes used in the negative formed by -ī-ha^{n}wu-.

	Gros Ventre	Arapaho
I—you	-etä	-eθ
I—him	-ä^n	-a^n
you—him, them	-ä^n	-a^n, -a^{n}na'
he—me	-'	-e
he—him, them	-', -ä^n	-ä
they—me	-ei	-ei
they—him, them	-', -ä^n	-äna^n

One of the two personal elements seems to be expressed, the other understood.

The negative conjugation appears to be based on the use of the prefix tsö- (and its phonetic modifications), corresponding to Arapaho tcī-. The equivalent of the Arapaho negative in ī-ha^{n}wu- has not been observed.

ne-tsä-äsa^n, I am not swift
nä-tsä-ätcesöu-hi, I am not small
he-tsu-na^{n}ha-b-et[i], I do not see you

---

[25] Unparalleled in Arapaho.
[26] As in Arapaho.
[27] Corresponds to Arapaho s.

Nouns

The plural of nouns shows the same types as in Arapaho.
-n, -in, -an, corresponding to Arapaho -na^n, -i-na^n.

bear	wos(ö)	wosö'n
elk	(h)iwasö^n	(h)iwasöhi$n$
wildcat	beθa^{n}tyä	beθa^{n}tyän
crow	(h)ouu	(h)ou$n$
fly	nöubä^n	nöubän
feather	bīi	bīin
bone	hiθ^{an}	hiθan
tent	nin^{an}	nīnan
stone	(h)axa 'änä^{n}tyä^n	(h)axa 'änä^{n}tyän

-a^n, -ha^n, as in Arapaho.

mouse	ä^{n}tsu	ä^{n}tsuhih^{a}n
antelope	na^{n}sity	na^{n}sitya^n
rabbit	na^{n}ts^e	na^{n}ts'ha^n
gopher	(h)ani'i	(h)ani'iha^n
muskrat	īθos	īθosa^n
otter	nēi	nēih^{an}
squirrel	θaθa^{n}ya'ei	θaθa^{n}ya'eiha^n
cat, puss	wus	wusha^n
donkey	na^{n}k$^u\theta$otei	na^{n}k$^u\theta$oteihiha^n
bald eagle	na^{n}k^{u}tiyēhi	na^{n}k^{u}tiyēhi^{an}
turtle	bä 'änou	bä 'änouha^n
fish	na^{n}w^u	na^{n}wuh^{an}
butterfly	baxa 'a^n-teibyi	baxa 'a-teibyihiha^n[28]
river	nītsä	nītsaha^n

Lengthening of the final, often surd or inaudible, vowel to -ī, -ū, or a phonetic equivalent, as in Arapaho.

deer	bihi'i	bihi'ihi
beaver	(h)äbes	(h)äbesöi
skunk	θou	θoue
cattle	wä^{n}kety^i	wä^{n}ketyī
mountain sheep	(h)ot$^{(e)}$	(h)otēi
wooden house	bätyiθou	bätyiθou'u
ear	wanatan	wanatanou
water	nets^i, nots	notsä^n
louse	b^{i}teibyi	b^{i}teiwuh[28]

Words for "domestic animal," or compounded with it, take -ibī, Arapaho -äbi.

dog	(h)ot^e	(h)otibī
horse, "elk-dog"	hiwas'hä$^n\theta$	hiwas'hä$^n\theta$ebī
dragon-fly, "insect dog"	bīθa^{n}hä$^n\theta$	bīθa^{n}hä$^n\theta$ibī

A few words change final -s or -ts to -t.

tooth	bītsits	bītsit
horn	nīnis	nīnit
parfleche bag	houwanos	houwanot

---

[28] Apparently different plurals on the same stem.

Animateness or inanimateness of nouns is indicated in the conjoined verb, adjective, or numeral; or, as they should collectively be called, the verb. The "animate" gender, however, includes many names of lifeless things. Such are: sun, moon, stars, thunder, wagon, mowing-machine, which travel; and snow, stone, tree, log, cedar, pine, pipe, and money, which do not move. Inanimate are the nouns for sky or clouds, lightning, rainbow, rain, water, river, spring, earth, iron, willow, sage, grass, mountain, gun, bow, arrow, and wind, several of which denote moving objects.

A locative is formed by a vocalic suffix, as at times in Arapaho.

earth	bīta'āw^n	bīta'āwū
stone	(h)axa'änä^{n}tyä^n	(h)axa'änä^{n}tyēi
parfleche bags	houwanot	houwanote
bed	(h)ä^{n}w^u'	(h)ä^{n}bä'

The types of possessive pronominal prefixes are those occurring in Arapaho. The third person frequently shows a vocalic suffix increment.

Word	Father	Mother	Son	Grandmother
vocative	nīθä^n	na'ä^n	neihe'	nīp
my	nīθina^n	neina^n	eihe'	eip
your	īθina^n	eina^n	īha'aha^n	inīwaha
his	inīθina^n	īnan^a		
our (incl.)	īθinan			
our (excl.)	äniθinan$^i n$			
your	īθinanina^n			

Word	Grandchild	Mother's brother	Hair	Mouth
vocative	nīsŏ	nis'hä^n		
my	nīsä	nis'	nänīt^a^{n}	netyi'
your	īsä	äs'	änīt^a^{n}	etyi'
his	inīsaha^n	isa'^{a}^{n}	inīt^a^{n}	ityi'
somebody's			bīt^a^{n}	betyi'

It is probable that an h-, which is fainter in Gros Ventre than in Arapaho, occurs before all the above words written as commencing with a vowel.

PRONOUNS

As in Arapaho, the so-called "pronoun" is a verbal sentence.

ni-nä	it is it, that is it
ni-nä-ni-na^n	"I," literally, it is I
nih-nä-ni-na^n	it was I
ha^{n}ta^n-nä-ni-na^n	it will be I
ni-nä-ni-ts	"they," it is they

NUMERALS

	Counting	Cardinal	Ordinal
1	tyåθei	äh-nīθi-ty¹ (an.)	ni-nīt-awä^n-ty¹
		äh-nīθ-ᵉ (inan.)	
2	nīθä	äh-nīsi-ts (an.)	ni-nīsa-uwä^n-ty¹
		äh-nīθ-ēi (inan.)	
3	nåθä	äh-nīxi-ts (an.)	ni-näsa-uwä^n-ty¹
		äh-näθ-ī (inan.)	
4	yän¹	äh-yäni-ts (an.)	ye-nåna-uwä^n-ty¹
		äh-yän-ei (inan.)	
5	yätan¹	äh-yätani-ts (an.)[20]	ye-nätana-uwä^n-ty¹
6	neityä^{n}tos		ni-neitya^{n}tos-awä^n-ty¹
7	nīθä^{n}tos		
8	nåθä^{n}tos		
9	änhäbetä^{n}tos		
10	betä^{n}tos	äh-betä^{n}tsi-ts (an.)	båtä^{n}tos-awä^n-ty¹

The above ordinals are animate. The inanimate forms lack the animate intransitive ending -ty^i. The form for "second" was obtained without the prefixed reduplication. "First" is nītawū. The difference of consonant in the animate cardinals for "one" and "two" follows that in Arapaho.

Eleven to 19 are formed from 1 to 9 by -īn, -ȫin, Arapaho -ini: tyåθēin, nīsȫin, nåsȫin, yänīn, yätanīn, neityä^{n}tosȫin, nīθä^{n}tosȫin, nåθä^{n}tosȫin, änhäbetä^{n}tosȫin or änhänīθȫu. Here the θ of "two" and "three" reverts to its Arapaho form, s. Twenty to 100 are made by -ȫu; Arapaho, -a^n', -a', -u': nīθȫu, nåθȫu, yänȫu, yätanou, neityä^{n}taθou, nīθä^{n}taθou, nåθä^{n}taθou, änhäbetä^{n}taθou, betä^{n}taθou. Here s becomes θ. Twenty-two is nīθȫu nīsȫin, 39 änhäyänȫu, 200 nīθä betä^{n}taθou, 1000 bås betä^{n}taθou, "great hundred."

The only appearance of a "classifier" noted is -an-, corresponding to Arapaho -ä^{n}nä, a collective.

tya^n'ä^{n}yä^{n}tei biθ yätan-an-ei, "heaps wood five," five piles of sticks

TEXT IV—TANGLED HAIR

ini'n — A man
hōuxnīθä^{n}tcībä''ä^n — was living alone.
ä^n'tasnä^{n}ka'nī — In the morning
hōu'xa'atsō'u — he went hunting,

hītō'uäni — in the evening
wa^{n}tyīnänä^n'nīia^{n}tyē'ity^i — he returned.
nohuūtc^{i}hä'ntinän — "When I am away,
nohuū'θä^{n}ts — when comes

ini'tä^n — a person,
tsäb^{i}hē'i — do not
tsō'tits^{i}nē'hin — invite him!"
wä^{n}tyī'tä^{n}tyi — he told her
ini'n^a — his wife.
ta'tä^n — "Even

hänä'yeisȫn — if he is about to
tsō'tyä^{n}ts — enter,
tsō'tyä^{n}ts — enter
tsäb'hi'īsiin — do not let him."
a^{n}hi'ta^{n}wū' — And indeed

ä^n't'asōj^{i}hä^n'tē'i — when he was away
i'n-ini'n — this man,
hōuu'ta^{n}wū — surely
nōunentä^{n}tc'ihini — some one came.

---

[20] Or: hä^n-yätani-ts, animate; hä^n-yätan-ei, inanimate.

i'ninīn   naxkāⁿ'kaⁿ   hītsö'watcătcini   āⁿh   no'hu   ini'täⁿ
His wife   just   would not say anything.   And   that   person

kāⁿkaⁿ'   hōūxnāⁿäⁿθāⁿ'tⁱ   hinī'n'aⁿ   haⁿhītsö'watyātyin
just   walked about.   His wife   would not say anything.

hi'niθän   hōū'xtānī   i'θawū   tsö'tsödjäⁿ   haⁿhu'ityinä-
He made as if to   in   enter,   but he did

ītsöwatyī-īstsö'djäⁿ   nah'noū'uθä'nts   hi'n-inin   hōū'xnäⁿtcitanä
not enter.   Returned   this man,   asked her:

häⁿäxtsö-nōune'nitäⁿt   nī'watyītäⁿt   hinī'n   wa'ē'idyⁱyäⁿts
"Has some one come?"   he said to her   his wife.   "Indeed he did!"

niwatcī'teityⁱ   hih^a'āⁿ'   nī'watcītaⁿ   hanāⁿ'dyäⁿ   ta'tāⁿ
she said to him.   "Is that so?"   he said to her.   "Now   even

hänä'yeisö   hiθawū'   tixi'ī'   tsötyäⁿtsⁱ   tsötyäⁿts   tsä'bh^e'isi'n
if he is about to   in   enter,   enter   do not let him!"

wäⁿtyī'taⁿtyi   inī'n   naxtā'θⁱ   hō'uxats'ōu   nu'hu-inen
he said to her   his wife.   And again   went hunting   that man.

haxkouta'nixtyⁱ   houxtcī'   nōune'nitäⁿtē'hinin   nu'hu   inī'n
When he was away long,   again   some one came   that   man.

wäⁿtyīnä'xnī'ī'   tayanī'   ti'īsö'   tsötyänits   nu'hu   ini'tän
He was about to   but did not   enter,   that   person

nuhuū'   īnōunenitäⁿtē'itan   hōū'xkäⁿkanītäkō'utyīn   hitidjē'naⁿ
who   came.   Then he flapped   the door.

waⁿtyīnehi'ī'tsaⁿnīne'ixtyⁱ   tsödjäⁿts   waⁿtyītäⁿ'tyⁱ   āⁿh'ine'n
She began to restrain herself no longer.   "Enter!"   she said to him.   And a man

ōuxtsö'djänī   waⁿtyīnēhī'ī'   byītsiwäⁿnaⁿ   hö'hūsöⁿ'
it was who entered.   She began to   cook for him.   When she had

byītsi'waⁿna   waⁿtyīnehī'ī'   haθa'waⁿtyⁱ   āⁿhīyō'u-wäⁿtyī'nits
cooked,   she went to   give him food.   And he said:

ītsünänī''iθōu   näⁿtyī'tsötaⁿ   waⁿtyī'teityⁱ   waⁿtyīnehi'ī'
"That is not the kind   I use as plates,"   he said to her.   She went to

ä'nätetyin   āⁿtyī'tshāⁿ'tyi   āⁿ'htaⁿθ   ītsönänī'θou   näⁿtyītsö'tan
change   his plate.   And again,   "That is not the kind   I use as plates,"

waⁿtyī'teityⁱ   ni'watcī-ka'sö   ānatyī'tsaha'aⁿ   āⁿh   hōū'uxnī'θ^ä
he said to her.   Constantly she changed   his plates   and   the same

nītē'idjⁱ   waⁿtyīne'hi'ī   bihī   hatyī'tsahaⁿ   ī'nan
he said.   Then she began   all   to use her plates,   every kind.

waⁿtyīnäⁿ'nī'ī   ityhō'uwin   aⁿtyī'tshäⁿtyi   waⁿtyīnä''nī'ī'
Then she began   not to know   what to use as a plate.   Then she began

notyänäⁿtaⁿ   otnäⁿdji'ts^ahäⁿtyi   waⁿtyīnē'hī'ī   nät'a'hnī'ī
to think   what to use as a plate.   Then she went and   drew off

äxnī'θetyin   hīw^aa'xa'   waⁿtyīnä'n   aⁿtyītshaⁿtyⁱ   wū'uu
one of   her moccasins.   And she went and   used it as a plate.   "Ha,

tanä'nⁱnäⁿ   waⁿtyītē'ityⁱ
that is very near,"   he said to her.

www.ingramcontent.com/pod-product-compliance
Lightning Source LLC
Chambersburg PA
CBHW070344090426
42733CB00009B/1284